KIDS

LOVE

TENNESSEE

3rd Edition

Your Family Travel Guide to Exploring Kid-Friendly Tennessee 500 Fun Stops & Unique Spots

Michele Darrall Zavatsky

Dedicated to the Families of Tennessee

© Copyright 2013, Kids Love Publications

For the latest major updates corresponding to the pages in this book visit our website:

www.KidsLoveTravel.com

- **REMEMBER:** *Museum exhibits change frequently. Check the site's website before you visit to note any changes. Also, HOURS and ADMISSIONS are subject to change at the owner's discretion. Note: FAMILY ADMI____N RATES generally have restrictions. If you are tight on time or r___ the attraction's website or call before you visit.*

- **INTERNET PRECAUTION:** *All websites mentioned in KID_ WISCONSIN have been checked for appropriate content. Howe___, due to the fast-changing nature of the Internet, we strongly urge parents to preview any recommended sites and to always supervise their children when on-line.*

- **EDUCATORS:** *There are suggestions for finding FREE lessons plans embedded in many listings as helpful notes for educators.*

-

-

TABLE OF CONTENTS

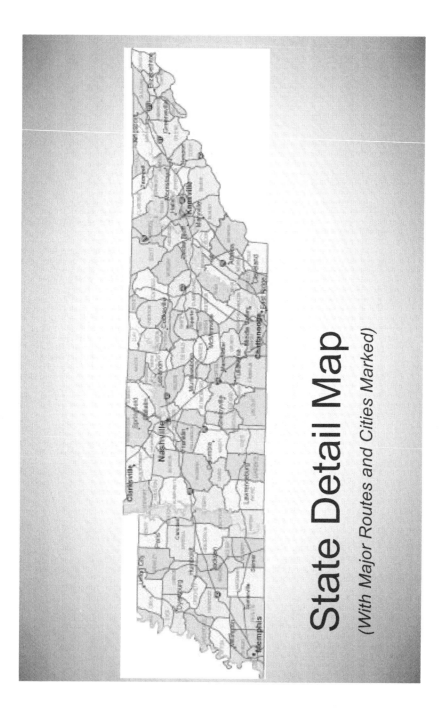

State Detail Map

(With Major Routes and Cities Marked)

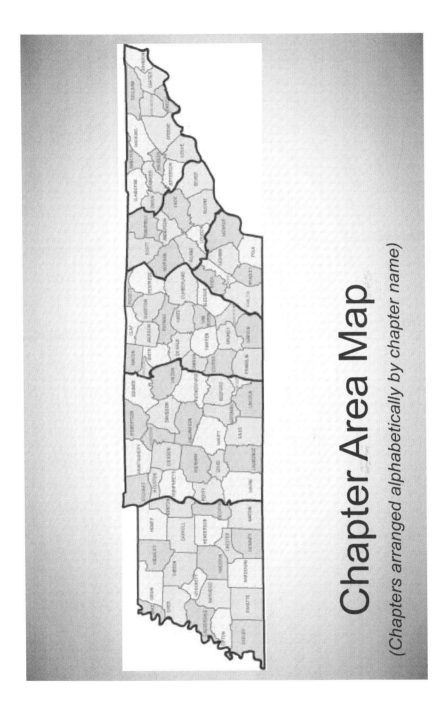

Chapter Area Map

(Chapters arranged alphabetically by chapter name)

HOW TO USE THIS BOOK
(a few hints to make your adventures run smoothly:)

BEFORE YOU LEAVE:

* Each chapter represents a two hour radius area of the state or a Day Trip. The listings are by City and then alphabetical by name, numeric by zip code. Each listing has tons of important details (pricing, hours, website, etc.) and a review noting the most engaging aspects of the place. Our popular Activity Index in back is helpful if you want to focus on a particular type of attraction (i.e. History, Tours, Outdoor Exploring, Animals & Farms, etc.).

* Begin by assigning each family member a different colored highlighter (for example: Daniel gets blue, Jenny gets pink, Mommy gets yellow and Daddy gets green). At your leisure, begin to read each review and put a highlighter "check" mark next to the sites that most interest each family member or highlight the features you most want to see. Now, when you go to plan a quick trip - or a long van ride - you can easily choose different stops in one day to please everyone.

* Know directions and parking. Use a GPS system or print off directions from websites.

* Most attractions are closed major holidays unless noted.

* When children are in tow, it is better to make your lodging reservations ahead of time. Every time we've tried to "wing it", we've always ended up at a place that was overpriced, in a unsafe area, or not super clean. We've never been satisfied when we didn't make a reservation ahead of time.

* If you have a large family, or are traveling with extended family or friends, most places offer group discounts. Check out the company's website for details.

* For the latest critical updates corresponding to the pages in this book, visit our website: www.kidslovetravel.com. Click on Updates.

ON THE ROAD:

* Consider the child's age before you stop at an exit. Some attractions and restaurants, even hotels, are too formal for young ones or not enough adventure for teens.

* Estimate the duration of the trip and how many stops you can afford to make. From our experience, it is best to stop every two hours to stretch your legs or eat/ snack or maybe visit an inexpensive attraction.

* In between meals, we offer the family snacks like: pretzels, whole grain chips, nuts, water bottles, bite-size (dark) chocolates, grapes and apples. None of these are messy and all are healthy.

* Bring along travel books and games for "quiet time" in the van. (see tested travel products on www.kidslovetravel.com) As an added bonus, these "enriching" games also stimulate conversation - you may get to know your family better and create memorable life lessons.

* Plan picnics along the way. Many Historical sites and State Parks are scattered along the highway. Allow time for a rest stop or a scenic byway to take advantage of these free picnic facilities.

WHEN YOU GET HOME:

* Make a family "treasure chest". Decorate a big box or use an old popcorn tin. Store memorabilia from a fun outing, journals, pictures, brochures and souvenirs. Once a year, look through the "treasure chest" and reminisce."

WAYS TO SAVE MONEY:

* Memberships - many children's museums, science centers, zoos and aquariums are members of associations that provide FREE or Discounted reciprocity to other such museums across the country. AAA Auto Club cards offer discounts to many of the activities and hotels in this book. If grandparents are along for the ride, they can use their AARP card and get discounts. Be sure to carry your member cards with you as proof to receive the discounts.

* Supermarket Customer Cards - national and local supermarkets often offer good discounted tickets to major attractions in the area.

* Internet Hotel Reservations - if you're traveling with kids, don't take the risk of being spontaneous with lodging. Make reservations ahead of time. We don't use non-refundable, deep discount hotel "scouting" websites (ex. Hotwire) unless we're traveling on business - just adults. You can't cancel your reservation, or change them, and you can't be guaranteed the type of room you want (ex. non-smoking, two beds). Instead, stick with a national hotel chain you trust and join their rewards program (ex. Choice Privileges) to accumulate points towards FREE night stays.

* State Travel Centers - as you enter a new state, their welcome centers offer many current promotions.

* Hotel Lobbies - often have a display of discount coupons to area shops and restaurants. When you check in, ask the clerk for discount pizza coupons they may have at the front desk.

* Attraction Online Coupons - check the websites listed with each review for possible printable coupons or discounted online tickets good towards the attraction.

Check out these businesses / services in your area for tour ideas:

AIRPORTS

All children love to visit the airport! Why not take a tour and understand all the jobs it takes to run an airport? Tour the terminal, baggage claim, gates and security / currency exchange. Maybe you'll even get to board a plane.

ANIMAL SHELTERS

Great for the would-be pet owner. Not only will you see many cats and dogs available for adoption, but a guide will show you the clinic and explain the needs of a pet. Be prepared to have the children "fall in love" with one of the animals while they are there!

BANKS

Take a "behind the scenes" look at automated teller machines, bank vaults and drive-thru window chutes. You may want to take this tour and then open a savings account for your child.

CITY HALLS

Halls of Fame, City Council Chambers & Meeting Room, Mayor's Office and famous statues.

ELECTRIC COMPANY / POWER PLANTS

Modern science has created many ways to generate electricity today, but what really goes on with the "flip of a switch". Because coal can be dirty, wear old, comfortable clothes. Coal furnaces heat water, which produces steam, that propels turbines, that drives generators, that make electricity.

FIRE STATIONS

Many Open Houses in October, Fire Prevention Month. Take a look into the life of the firefighters servicing your area and try on their gear. See where they hang out, sleep and eat. Hop aboard a real-life fire engine truck and learn fire safety too.

NEWSPAPERS

You'll be amazed at all the new technology. See monster printers and robotics. See samples in the layout department and maybe try to put together your own page. After seeing a newspaper made, most companies give you a free copy (dated that day) as your souvenir. National Newspaper Week is in October.

PETCO

Various stores. Contact each store manager to see if they participate. The Fur, Feathers & Fins™ program allows children to learn about the characteristics and habitats of fish, reptiles, birds, and small animals. At your local Petco, lessons in science, math and geography come to life through this hands-on field trip. As students develop a respect for animals, they will also develop a greater sense of responsibility.

PIZZA HUT & PAPA JOHN'S

Participating locations. Telephone the store manager. Best days are Monday, Tuesday and Wednesday mid-afternoon. Minimum of 10 people. Small charge per person. All children love pizza – especially when they can create their own! As the children tour the kitchen, they learn how to make a pizza, bake it, and then eat it. The admission charge generally includes lots of creatively made pizzas, beverage and coloring book.

KRISPY KREME DONUTS

Participating locations. Get an "inside look" and learn the techniques that make these donuts some of our favorites! Watch the dough being made in "giant" mixers, being formed into donuts and taking a "trip" through the fryer. Seeing them being iced and topped with colorful sprinkles is always a favorite with the kids. Contact your local store manager. They prefer Monday or Tuesday. Free.

SUPERMARKETS

Kids are fascinated to go behind the scenes of the same store where Mom and Dad shop. Usually you will see them grind meat, walk into large freezer rooms, watch cakes and bread bake and receive free samples along the way. Maybe you'll get to pet a live lobster.

TV / RADIO STATIONS

Studios, newsrooms, Fox kids clubs. Why do weathermen never wear blue/green clothes on TV? What makes a "DJ's" voice sound so deep and smooth?

WATER TREATMENT PLANTS

A giant science experiment! You can watch seven stages of water treatment. The favorite is usually the wall of bright buttons flashing as workers monitor the different processes.

U.S. MAIN POST OFFICES

Did you know Ben Franklin was the first Postmaster General? Most interesting is the high-speed automated mail processing equipment. Learn how to address envelopes so they will be sent quicker (there are secrets). To make your tour more interesting, have your children write a letter to themselves and address it with colorful markers. Mail it earlier that day and they will stay interested trying to locate their letter in all the high-speed machinery.

General State Agency & Recreational Information

Call *(or visit websites)* for the services of interest. Request to be added to their mailing lists.

Tennessee Department of Environment/Conservation, Bureau of Parks/Recreation, Nashville. (423) 532-0001 or (800) 421-6683.

Tennessee's Civil War Heritage Trail: A Path Divided. Tennessee Historical Commission, Nashville. (615) 532-1550 or **www.state.tn.us/environment/hist/**

Pick Tennessee Products **www.picktnproducts.org**.

Whitewater Rafting/Kayaking **www.chattanoogafun.com**

Tennessee Department of Tourist Development, Nashville. **www.tnvacation.com** or (800) GO2-TENN.

Tennessee State Parks, Nashville. (888) TN-Parks or **www.tnstateparks.com**

M - Clarksville Convention & Visitors Bureau, Clarksville. **www.clarksville.tn.us** or (800) 530-2487.

NE - Johnson City Convention & Visitors Bureau, Johnson City. **www.johnsoncitychamber.com** or (423) 461-8002.

M- Nashville Convention & Visitors Bureau, Nashville. **www.nashvillecvb.com**

M - Sumner County Convention & Visitors Bureau, Gallatin. **www.sumnercountytourism.com** or (888) 301-7866.

M - Rutherford County Convention & Visitors Bureau, Murfreesboro. (800) 716-7560 or **www.rutherfordchamber.org**.

M - Wilson County Convention & Visitors Bureau, Lebanon. **www.wilsoncountycvb.com** or (800) 789-1327.

ME - Gatlinburg Dept of Tourism, Gatlinburg. (800) 568-4748 or **www.gatlinburg.com**

ME - Knoxville Tourism & Sports Corporation, Knoxville. **www.knoxtsc.com** or (800) 727-8045.

ME - Pigeon Forge Dept of Tourism, Pigeon Forge. **www.mypigeonforge.com** or (800) 251-9100.

SE - Chattanooga Area CVB. **www.chattanoogafun.com**. (800) 322-3344.

SE - Smoky Mountain Convention & Visitors Bureau, Townsend. **www.smokymountains.org** or (865) 448-6134.

W - Memphis Convention & Visitors Bureau, Memphis. **www.memphistravel.com** or (901) 543-5300.

W - West Region Department of Tourism, Jackson. (731) 426-0888 or **www.tnvacation.com**

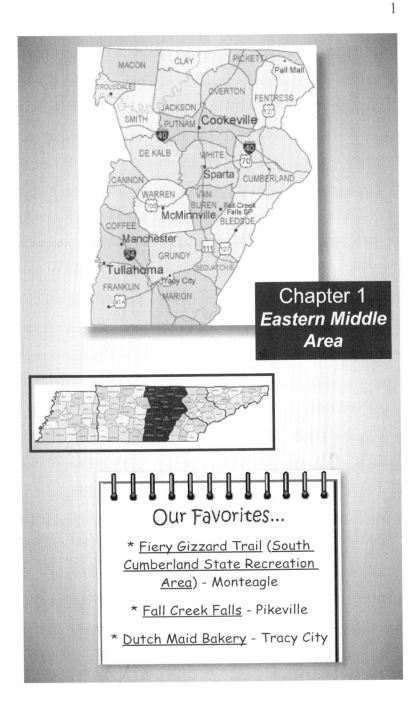

Chapter 1
Eastern Middle Area

Our Favorites...

* <u>Fiery Gizzard Trail</u> (<u>South Cumberland State Recreation Area</u>) - Monteagle

* <u>Fall Creek Falls</u> - Pikeville

* <u>Dutch Maid Bakery</u> - Tracy City

FALLS MILL

Belvidere - 134 Falls Mill Road (1 mile north of U.S. 64 at Old Salem) 37306. Phone: (931) 469-7161. www.fallsmill.com Hours: Monday-Saturday 9:00am-4:00pm, Sunday 12:30-4:00pm except closed Wednesdays and Thanksgiving, Christmas and New Years, and most of January. Admission: $1.00-$3.00.

Built as a cotton and woolen factory in 1873, the mill was later converted to a cotton gin, then a wood-working shop before its present use as a grist mill. Visitors begin with an introductory history of the mill and then take a self-guided tour of the buildings and scenic grounds. The millstones, printing press, and the ever-popular dog-powered butter churn are on the first floor. The country store and weaving room are on the second floor. Stone-ground cornmeal, grits, and flour may be purchased at the mill and through mail order. Bring lunch and picnic by the cascading waterfalls.

CORDELL HULL BIRTHPLACE & MUSEUM STATE PARK

Byrdstown - 1300 Cordell Hull Memorial Drive (1.5 miles off Hwy 111 on SR 325) 38549. Phone: (931) 864-3247. www.cordellhullmuseum.com Hours: Daily 9:00am-4:00 or 5:00pm. Notes: The hike to the overlook is 3/4 mile (1.5 miles round-trip), and the hike to the cave entrance is an additional ½ mile (2.5 miles round-trip). Meandering through the mixed deciduous forest, the hiker may be able to view a variety of plant and animal life. Spring wildflowers in late March - early May are exceptional. The view of the cave is most impressive, the entrance measures 100 feet wide and 50 feet tall. Visitors are welcome to explore the beginning of the cave but are required to obtain a permit from the park office to venture past the cave entrance.

The site consists of Hull's original log cabin birthplace, an activities center and a museum housing documents and artifacts. The collection includes his Nobel Peace Prize that is on display. President Roosevelt praised Secretary Hull as "the one person in all the world who has done the most to make this great plan for peace an effective fact." The 1945 Nobel Prize for Peace was given to Hull in recognition of his work in the Western Hemispheres, for his international trade agreements, and for his efforts in establishing the United Nations.

CUMBERLAND MOUNTAIN STATE PARK

Crossville - 24 Office Drive (I-40 exit 317, Hwy 127, 9 miles south of town) 38555. www.tennessee.gov/environment/parks/CumberlandMtn/index.shtml Phone: *(931) 484-6138 or (800) 250-8618 cabins. Hours: 7:00am-10:00pm.* Miscellaneous: *Concert in the Park summertime series.*

Centered on Cumberland Mountain (elev. 2,000 feet), it is America's largest forested plateau. The Homestead Museum, located one mile from the park, depicts the Cumberland Homestead Community of the 1930s. Rustic cabins are nestled in the woods at Cumberland Mountain State Park and have fully equipped kitchens, cable TV, fireplaces (except single cabins), linens, picnic tables and grills. The restaurant is open for lunch and dinner. The park's pride, catfish is served on Fridays. The park offers several miles of moderate trails around the lake, creek and in the woods. Other activities: camping, golfing, swimming, fishing and boating.

CUMBERLAND COUNTY PLAYHOUSE

Crossville - 221 Tennessee Avenue 38557. www.ccplayhouse.com Phone: (931) 484-5000.

With two indoor stages and one outdoor theatre, the Cumberland County Playhouse is one of the premier Southern pro theaters. Considered "Tennessee's Family Theater", they perform shows like High School Musical and Scrooge and family music concerts. Tickets typically range $11.00-$23.00.

OZONE FALLS

Crossville - (I-40 exit 329, follow US 70 east) 38557. Phone: (931) 484-6138. www. tennessee.gov/environment/na/natareas/ozone/

A "hidden" waterfall which is accessible to almost everyone, Ozone Falls lies just a couple of miles from I-40 and it is a 100+ foot waterfall with a nice basin and pool at the base. A steep trail located 70 yards west of the parking area will lead you to the base of the falls and allows you to walk behind the falls.

DID YOU KNOW? Ozone Falls was selected for filming scenes for the movie "Jungle Book."

COKE OVENS PARK

Dunlap - 114 Walnut Street, downtown 37327. Phone: (423) 949-2156. www. cokeovens.com

The walking tour around the Coke Ovens Park offers the visitor an opportunity to spend some time walking through the quiet woods discovering the ruins of a once great industrial complex. The more strenuous Incline Hike includes climbing the 3900 foot incline to the top of the bluffs to explore the area where coal was once mined. Stop by the museum first to borrow a hand carved walking stick. Open free of charge daylight hours.

BATTLE OF HARTSVILLE DRIVING CIVIL WAR TOUR

Hartsville - 240 Broadway (Chamber office) 37074. Phone: (615) 374-9243 (C of C). http://www.civilwar.org/civil-war-discovery-trail/sites/battle-of-hartsville-driving-tour.html. Hours: Sunrise to sunset.

Called "the most successfully executed cavalry raid of the War Between the States," it was from this battle that Col. John Hunt Morgan received his commission to brigadier general. Driving tour includes buildings used as hospitals, sites where Morgan rushed 1,834 prisoners after the 75-minute battle, river crossings, rendezvous points, homes and a cemetery. Open daily. Self-guided tour includes 17 stops related to Gen. John Hunt Morgan and the Battle of Hartsville. Brochure and map available at the chamber office.

STANDING STONE STATE PARK

Hilham - 1674 Standing Stone Park Hwy (I-40 exit 288, Hwy 111N to Hwy 52W to Hwy 136) 38568. Phone: (931) 823-6347 or (800) 713-5157 cabins. www.tennessee. gov/environment/parks/StandingStone/index.shtml Hours: Day use park closes at sunset.

The rustic park is noted for its outstanding scenery, spring wildflowers, fossils and other natural diversity. The park takes its name from the "Standing Stone," an eight-foot tall rock standing upright on a sandstone ledge, which was supposedly used as a boundary line between two separate Indian nations. The park is known for its annual *National Rolley Hole Marble Competition* each September. Standing Stone State Park has an Olympic-size pool with one low dive and a kiddie pool. The pool is located within walking distance of cabins and camping via a paved foot trail. Also, located next to the pool is the Recreation Hall, tennis courts, volleyball and basketball courts. Ten miles of hiking trails wind through the wilds where hikers can observe diversity in plant and animal life from the trails as they trek across swinging bridges. Standing Stone is equipped with four types of cabins: Rustic, Timberlodge, Modern and Overton Lodge (group lodge). Other activities: camping, fishing, and boating.

PICKETT STATE PARK

Jamestown - 4605 Pickett Park Highway (Hwy 154, northeast of town) 38556. www. tennessee.gov/environment/parks/Pickett/index.shtml   Phone: (931) 879-5821 or (877) 260-0010 cabins. Hours: Office: 8:00am-4:30pm. Park: 7:30am-dark.

Situated in a remote area of the Cumberland Mountains, the 17,372-acre Pickett State Park and Forest possess a combination of scenic, botanical and geological wonders found nowhere else in Tennessee. Of particular interest are the uncommon rock formations, natural bridges, numerous caves and remains of ancient Indian occupation. Pickett features five chalets, five rustic stone cottages and five wooden cottages ideally suited for vacations. Each is completely equipped for housekeeping. Other Activities: Camping, boating, fishing, swimming and hiking/horseback trails.

OLD STONE FORT STATE ARCHAEOLOGICAL PARK

Manchester - 732 Stone Fort Drive (I-24 turn southwest at the Highway 53, Exit 110 and follow the signs) 37855. Phone: (931) 723-5073. www.tennessee.gov/ environment/parks/OldStoneFort/index.shtml   Hours: Park: Daily 8:00am-sunset. Museum: 8:00am-4:30pm.

An earth and stone enclosure built as a sacred site by prehistoric Indians about 2,000 years ago. It consists of mounds and walls that combine with cliffs and rivers to form an enclosure measuring 1-1/4 miles around. The 50-acre hilltop enclosure moundsite is believed to have served as a central ceremonial gathering place for some 500 years. The Visitor Center and exhibit hall complex includes exhibits relating to the history, archaeology, and legends surrounding the Old Stone Fort and its builders, the Woodland Indians. Other Activities: camping, hiking and fishing.

CUMBERLAND CAVERNS

McMinnville - 1437 Cumberland Caverns Road (7 miles southeast of town on Hwy 8 or Hwy 55, from US 70 or I-24) 37110. Phone: (931) 668-4396. www. cumberlandcaverns.com Hours: Daily 9:00am-6:00pm (May-October). Spelunking and group tours rest of year by reservation. Admission: $18.00 adult, $10.00 child (6-12). Online coupons.

Tennessee's largest cave is so big they have an underground ballroom complete with chandelier and organ music for group meals. Most all the rooms on tour are large and some of the formations include shapes described as the Twin Trolls, the Three Chessmen or Moby Dick. The tour includes a look at an 1812 saltpeter mine, pools and waterfalls. An original underground pageant of light and sound, "God of the Mountain", is shown on every tour.

SOUTH CUMBERLAND STATE RECREATION AREA

Monteagle - Rte. 1, US 41 (3 miles from I-24 between Monteagle and Tracy City) 37356. Phone: (931) 924-2980 or 924-2956. www.tennessee.gov/environment/ parks/SouthCumberland/index.shtml Hours: Sunrise to sunset. Visitors Center open 8:00am-4:30pm.

FIERY GIZZARD TRAIL, LITTLE GIZZARD CREEK SMALL WILD AREA - 2.2 mile west of Foster Falls. Vistas of the Cumberland. Hike down into Laurel Branch gorge. Primitive camping. **FOSTER FALLS SMALL WILD AREA** (423-942-5759) - 60 feet waterfall plunges into a deep pool. Mountain laurel, azaleas and hemlocks grow above the falls, along the

sandstone overlook and in the gorge below. Picnic, camping and hiking. **CARTER STATE NATURAL AREA** - 140 acres with **LOST COVE CAVE** - impressive cave mouth (100ft. Wide, 80 ft. high) with cave stream and a cold drafting air. It is necessary to climb up and down over large rocks and wade thru a stream in order to traverse the remainder of the cove. The Great Stone Door, a 100-foot-deep crevice at the crest of the plateau, guards the western access to the trail system.

Off to explore...

For updates & travel games visit: **www.KidsLoveTravel.com**

SGT. ALVIN C. YORK STATE HISTORIC AREA

Pall Mall - (7 miles north of Jamestown on SR 127) 38577. Phone: (931) 879-3657. www.tennessee.gov/environment/parks/SgtYork/index.shtml Hours: Open year-round daylight hours for park. Museum Home open daily 9:00am-5:00pm. (closes at 4:00pm in winter) Admission: FREE. Notes: Andrew York is the son of Alvin C. York and is a Park Ranger at the homesite. If notified in advance, interpretive programs can be scheduled.

The historic area is a memorial to the man General Pershing called the "greatest soldier of the World War" and the places Alvin knew and loved all his life are here: his family home and farm, the rock ledge where he married his beloved "Miss Gracie"; the church he helped to build, and the post office/general store he built and operated. In the area are scenic views of Wolf River and a gristmill. The York homesite museum includes a collection of wartime and personal mementos, including historical photographs, family portraits and personal items.

FALL CREEK FALLS STATE PARK RESORT

Pikeville - Route 3 (entered from Hwy 111 or Hwy 30) 37367. Phone: (423) 881-5298 (866) 836-3297 reservations. www.tennessee.gov/environment/parks/FallCreekFalls/index.shtml Hours: Open 24 hours, roads to Falls close at dark.

Fall Creek Falls is the highest waterfall east of the Rocky Mountains, plunging 256 feet into a shaded pool at the base of its gorge. The park's other falls, (Piney, Cane Creek, and Cane Creek Cascades), though smaller, are just as impressive. Some are waterfalls, cascades, sparkling streams, or gorges. The park offers hiking trails, bicycle trails (a three-mile long paved bicycle path leads from the inn to the falls), horseback riding, swimming pools (one at the Inn, one near campgrounds), canoeing, paddle boats and golf plus an inn/restaurant (great views, all rooms waterfront w/ good Southern cuisine

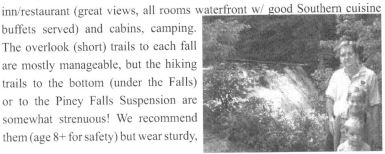

buffets served) and cabins, camping. The overlook (short) trails to each fall are mostly manageable, but the hiking trails to the bottom (under the Falls) or to the Piney Falls Suspension are somewhat strenuous! We recommend them (age 8+ for safety) but wear sturdy,

rugged shoes and maybe bring a flashlight. There are many steep paths made of layered rock. What an adventure, though! Be sure to stop at the tunnel of cold air at Fall Creek Falls. Stop by the Nature Center to chat with rangers and look thru displays. The Village Green has shops and recreation areas. You'll find many seasonal, daily family activities at the Nature Center or Village Green. The kids might get to meet their first salamander or baby snake on the trail!

High atop the suspension bridge...no bouncing please...

ROCK ISLAND STATE PARK

Rock Island - *82 Beach Road (Rte. 287) 38581. Phone: (931) 686-2471 or (800) 713-6065 cabins.* *www.tennessee.gov/environment/parks/RockIsland/index.shtml Hours: Daily 7:30am-10:00pm.*

The scenic beauty of this wooded park is dominated by the Great Falls of the Caney Fork River - an imposing limestone gorge (called a gulf in southern culture). It provides scenic overlooks, waterfalls and deep pools for fishing, rock-hopping and exploring. Rock Island's cascading Great Falls forms a spectacular backdrop for a natural beach, located on the headwaters of Center Hill Lake. Picnic areas, boat launch, camping and cabins available. The park's Blue Hole is good for fishing.

EDGAR EVINS STATE PARK

Silver Point - *1630 Edgar Evins State Park Road (I-40 at exit 268 at State Hwy. 96 and Center Hill Lake) 38582. Phone: (931) 858-2114 or (800) 250-8619.* *www. tennessee.gov/environment/parks/EdgarEvins/index.shtml Hours: Daily 6:00am-10:30pm.*

Located north of Smithville on the forested hillsides of Center Hill Reservoir, the park mostly attracts water enthusiasts. The park has cabins, campsite, boat launch ramps, marina, pool for cabin guests, lake swimming, hiking, and playgrounds. A popular fall cruise extends 50 miles upstream to Rock

Island State Park. For the hiker, a scenic two-mile trail, beginning at the park visitor center, meanders around the edge of the lake. The marina restaurant specializes in fried catfish.

BURGESS FALLS STATE PARK

Sparta - 4000 Burgess Falls Drive (SR 155, north of town) 38583. www.tennessee. gov/environment/parks/BurgessFalls/index.shtml Phone: (931) 432-5312. Hours: 8:00am until 30 minutes before sundown when gates close. Park is closed when the river is high or when there is snow on the roads and/or trails.

A stream-side nature trail winds beside Falling Water River to the plunging Burgess Falls. The 1-mile Ridge Top Trail is very scenic with views down the main canyon of the Falling Water River. Trails are moderate in difficulty. All trails are foot trails. Bikes, horses, etc. are not permitted. Park visitors can visit the large Native Butterfly Garden located adjacent to the upper parking lot. Also fishing and hiking offered.

VIRGIN FALLS STATE NATURAL AREA

Sparta - (Hwy 70, follow signs to Scott Gulf Road) 38583. Phone: (931) 836-3552 (local C of C). www.state.tn.us/environment/na/natareas/virgin/

Formed by an underground stream that emerges from a cave, these falls drop over a 110 foot cliff and disappear into a cave at the bottom. The natural area is operated as a Bowater Pocket Wilderness Area and has 8 miles of hiking trails and backcountry camping. Virgin Falls is located within the greater Scott's Gulf region and adjacent to the BRIDGESTONE / FIRESTONE CENTENNIAL WILDERNESS (Eastland Rd). The 10,000 acre gift from the company has hiking trails to Cancy Fork River and bluffs overlooking the gorge.

DUTCH MAID BAKERY & MUSEUM

Tracy City - 111 Main Street (I-24 west to US 41north at Jasper, head into town) 37387. Phone: (931) 592-3171. www.thedutchmaid.com Hours: Daily 7:00am-mid afternoon (CST). Employees bake on Tuesdays, Thursdays and Saturdays. Closed Thanksgiving and Christmas. Admission: FREE Notes: The café is open for breakfast and lunch beginning at 7:00am most mornings. Or, take you baked goodies down the road to Foster Falls for a snack with a view!

Tennessee's oldest family operated bakery, established in 1902 by Swiss immigrants, is now under new ownership. They still use old recipes and make much the same breads and pastries. Still, too, they offer tours if you call ahead. Old World recipe breads and famous "applesauce" fruitcakes are baked year-round.

Most of the Dutch Maid Bakery's equipment dates back to the 1920s, and the recipes are from the 1880s. The old Bakery is actually a functioning museum. The primary mixers date from 1929 and 1945, the oven 1923, and the old bread slicer/bagger from 1916. When new parts are required, they have to be made. Salt Rising bread prep requires 22-24 hours from starter to sponge, mix, mold, proof, bake, cool, dry, slice and bag. On your short, casual tour, you'll learn how they measure only by weight, how they don't bake by time, but by color, and even get a chance to walk in the "rising room". Many people travel to Tracy City to taste the salt-rising bread. Remember, "Brot" is German for bread. Thank goodness this old favorite survives!

TIMS FORD STATE PARK

Winchester - 570 Tims Ford Drive (Hwy 130 or Hwy 64) 37390. Phone: (931) 962-1183or (800) 471-5295 cabins. ***www.tennessee.gov/environment/parks/TimsFord/index.shtml*** *Hours: Recreation Center (games and pool) open Tuesday through Sunday 10:00am-6:00pm (summer); open on week-ends only in the Spring and Fall.*

Tims Ford State Park, located on the Tims Ford Reservoir in the rolling hills of southern middle Tennessee, is an outstanding recreational area and fishing paradise. The lake offers recreational facilities for camping, swimming, fishing, boating, bicycle and hiking trails and water-skiing. The park has almost 5 miles of paved trails that allow the hiker and cyclist to explore the natural surroundings of Tims Ford Lake. Stay in one of the rustic cabins or stop by the marina for boating launches or eateries. Every other Saturday night, they welcome "Pickin and Grinnin" entertainment to come visit and perform.

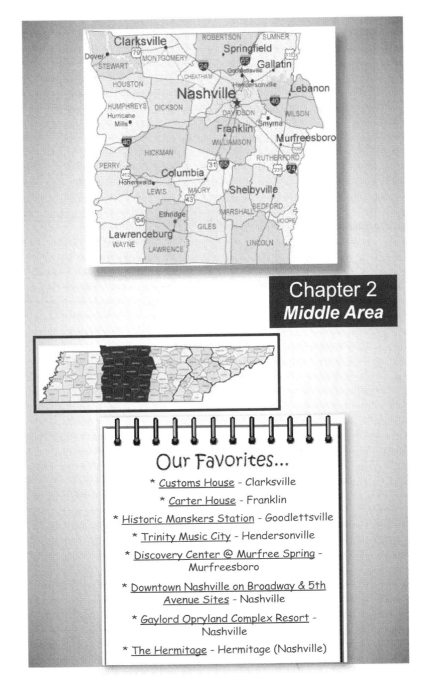

Chapter 2
Middle Area

Our Favorites...

* <u>Customs House</u> - Clarksville

* <u>Carter House</u> - Franklin

* <u>Historic Manskers Station</u> - Goodlettsville

* <u>Trinity Music City</u> - Hendersonville

* <u>Discovery Center @ Murfree Spring</u> - Murfreesboro

* <u>Downtown Nashville on Broadway & 5th Avenue Sites</u> - Nashville

* <u>Gaylord Opryland Complex Resort</u> - Nashville

* <u>The Hermitage</u> - Hermitage (Nashville)

PORT ROYAL STATE PARK

*Adams - 3300 Old Clarksville Hwy (off Hwy. 76, five miles east of I-24, Exit 11)
37010. Phone: (931) 358-9696. www.tennessee.gov/environment/parks/PortRoyal/
index.shtml Hours: 8:00am-sundown.*

The site of one of the state's earliest communities, the park is a place of
quiet beauty featuring a hiking trail, picnicking, canoeing and fishing. It has a
covered bridge spanning the Red River. Port Royal is designated as an official
site on the Trail of Tears National Historic Trail. MUSEUM: Exhibits display
artifacts, tools, and weapons from aboriginal peoples (Cherokee on their way
on the Trail of Tears) through frontier life and the Civil War period to present
day tobacco farming. An exhibit also details the history of the Port Royal
Covered Bridge.

MONTGOMERY BELL STATE RESORT PARK

*Burns - 1020 Jackson Hill Rd. (Take Highway 70 West to White Bluff) 37029. www.
tennessee.gov/environment/parks/MontgomeryBell/index.shtml Phone: (615) 797-
9052 or (615) 797-3101. Hours: Daily 6:00am-10:00pm.*

The treasure was iron ore, and it lured men by the hundreds to this area
of Middle Tennessee. This is the site of the first Cumberland Presbyterian
Church. They also offer an arcade, ball courts, golf course, campsites, modern
cabins, lake swimming, fishing, hiking, and paddleboat and rowboat rentals.
Nearby, at the Narrows of the Harpeth park, are canoeing and an Indian
ceremonial art center. The Inn and restaurant feature modern lodging and
dining. Amenities include indoor year-round pool, jacuzzi, and outdoor pool
(seasonal), exercise room and laundry facilities. Every room has a view of the
lake. Ranger programs offered in Cultural Heritage and Discovering Nature.

BLEDSOE'S FORT HISTORIC PARK

*Castalian Springs - State Hwy 25 (SR 25 & SR 49) 37031. Phone: (615) 452-5463.
http://www.bledsoeslick.com/fort.htm Hours: Daily daylight to dusk. Admission:
FREE Note: Re-Enactors (4th weekend each month April - December).*

The self-guided walking tour of Bledsoe Fort Historical Park is a one mile
walk through the shaded hills retracing the pioneer footprints along the Avery
Trace, the first road leading from eastern Tennessee into middle Tennessee.
The tour continues past the 1890s Parker Cabin, the Hugh Rogan house, a

200 year old stone cottage from the Indian War period, the pioneer cemetery including the markers of brothers Isaac and Anthony Bledsoe, and the Cavern of Skulls. The tour is interpreted by signs providing historical information relating to the sites.

CRAGFONT

Castalian Springs - 200 Cragfont Road (off Hwy 25) 37031. Phone: (615) 452-7070. www.state.tn.us/environment/hist/stateown/cragfont.shtml Hours: Tuesday-Saturday 10:00am-5:00pm, Sunday 1:00-5:00pm (Mid-April thru October). Admission: $5.00 adult, $4.00 senior (55+), $3.00 child (6-12).

When completed in 1802, it was the finest mansion house on the Tennessee frontier. Built by General James Winchester - a frontiersman, politician, soldier and one of the founders of Memphis. A visit to Cragfont is a step into the past combining cultural and architectural history. Named Cragfont because it stood on a rocky bluff with a spring at its base, the house is furnished with Federal antiques, some of which are original to the Winchester family. The basement holds an authentic weaving room. Summertime brings Day Camps and Pioneer Days involving crafts, games, storytellers, and daily refreshments (camp fee).

WYNNEWOOD

Castalian Springs - 210 Old Hwy 25 37031. Phone: (615) 452-5463. www.state.tn.us/environment/hist/stateown/wynnwood.shtml Hours: Wednesday-Sunday 10:00am-4:00pm (mid-April-October). Closed all holidays. Admission: $5.00 adult, $4 senior (55+), $3 child (6-12), $1.50 teens.

This two-story tall and 142-foot long large log structure (1828) served as a stagecoach inn and later as a mineral springs resort. By the 1840s the Wynnes had built a row of cottages on the lawn east of the inn and set up a race course in the bottom near Lick Creek. Most guests were attracted by the medicinal qualities of the mineral waters but one frequent visitor, Andrew Jackson, liked the race course best. He usually brought a favorite thoroughbred to run against one of Wynne's horses when he visited.

HENRY HORTON STATE PARK RESORT

Chapel Hill - 4358 Nashville Highway (I-65 to exit 46 east on Hwy 412 to 431S, turn right, then left on Hwy 99 to Hwy 31A) 37034. Phone: (931) 364-2222 or (800) 250-8612. www.state.tn.us/environment/parks/HenryHorton/index.shtml Hours: Public area gate closes at 10:00pm.

The park is located on the former estate of the late Henry H. Horton (36th governor of Tennessee). The shores of the historic Duck River provide hours of recreational enjoyment. The Resort Inn with restaurant (Southern cuisine at popular prices) is open daily with continental breakfast provided for inn/cabin guests. The seasonal swimming pool is open summers. Furnished cabin rentals are available, too.

CUSTOMS HOUSE MUSEUM & CULTURAL CENTER

Clarksville - 200 South Second Street (downtown at the corner of Second St. & Madison St) 37040. www.customshousemuseum.org. Phone: (931) 648-5780. Hours: Tuesday-Saturday 10:00am-5:00pm, Sunday 1:00-5:00pm. Admission: $7.00 adult, $5.00 senior (65+), $5.00 college students, $3.00 student (age 6-18). FREE on 2nd Saturdays.

Built in 1898 as a US Post Office and Customs House for trade, this site is now a regional history museum. Memory Lane/Main Street has many actual artifacts with a great walk-in log cabin. The Explorer's Floor is a special area for the entire family to solve puzzles and play games. Learn in fantasy in Aunt Alice's Attic, the Kroger Jr. grocery store, optical illusions and a Bubble Room. What is a Fantasmagraph? Make your own Zoetrope. Model trains run every Sunday afternoon. Otherwise, there are push buttons to start different trains in motion. "Neat!" was the kids' reaction.

CLARKSVILLE SPEEDWAY

Clarksville - 1600 Needmore Road 37041. www.clarksvillespeedway.com Phone: (931) 645-2523. Hours: Saturday nights (April-November). Admission: $12-$25.00.

For updates & travel games visit: **www.KidsLoveTravel.com**

1/8 mile Drag Races for street cars and motorcycles. 1/4 mile high bank clay oval track for mini, street, prostreet, UMP openwheel & late model cars. Go-cart race track for all ages. Fenced park area for children.

CUMBERLAND RIVERWALK & "AS THE RIVER FLOWS" EXHIBIT

Clarksville - McGregor Park, Riverside Drive   37041. Phone: (931) 645-7476. Hours: Daylight hours for park. Daily 8:00am-5:00pm (Center). Extended hours (April-October) until 8:00pm. Admission: FREE

The riverfront promenade includes an amphitheater, overlooks, a playground, picnic areas, a boating ramp, etc. The RiverCenter has a permanent exhibit featuring a chronological display with mural map showing the settlement of the town (1780-1784) and 12 display panels showing the history of the Cumberland River from 15,000 BC to present day. What crop did they send along the river (called Black Patch)? Most families like to walk the Riverwalk & picnic on nice days, enjoying the modern amenities the river offers.

DUNBAR CAVE STATE PARK

Clarksville - 401 Old Dunbar Cave Road 37041. Phone: (931) 648-5526. www.state. tn.us/environment/parks/DunbarCave/index.shtml   Hours: Daily 8:00am-sunset. Visitors Center 8:00am-4:30pm.

This 110-acre park has a cave and surrounding mineral springs (once a resort in the early 1900s). In the 1930s and 40s, the huge cave served as a naturally air-conditioned venue for Big Bands and was once owned by country music legend, Roy Acuff. Picnic areas, hiking and fishing are popular and occasional guided cave tours along with a historical slide show. There are three trails on the natural area that range from a leisurely walk to a fairly strenuous hike. All trails begin and end at the visitors' center.

L & N TRAIN STATION

Clarksville - Commerce & 10th Streets 37041. Phone: (931) 553-2486.   Hours: Tuesday, Thursday & Saturday 9:00am-1:00pm. Admission: $1.00.

Built in 1890, the L & N Train Station was the scene for the Monkees' hit, Last Train to Clarksville. Once one of the busiest locations in Clarksville with soldiers and civilians arriving and departing daily, the facility is now open for public viewing for short visits.

HISTORIC COLLINSVILLE

Clarksville (Southside) - 4711 Weakley Road (SR 13S to Rte. 48S, east of Southside Rd, follow signs) 37171. www.historiccollinsville.com Phone: (931) 648-9141. Hours: Thursday - Sunday 1:00-5:00pm (mid-May to mid-October). Admission: $4.00 general (age 5+), $5.00-$10.00 special events. Note: Picnic areas and walking trails. Seasonal events like old-fashioned jubilees and Pioneer Days Open House and food each quarter.

A self-guided tour of a living-history museum featuring 16 restored log homes and outbuildings on 40 acres. The structures date from 1830 to 1870 with authentic furnishings. Indians once traveled this land, soldiers of the North and South once met here, and, cotton and sheep were raised by the early

 settlers and then transported down the Cumberland River. Stop by the Judge's home to see a Black Hawk Corn Sheller invented by Mr. Patch of Clarksville. Kids will gravitate to the Wildwood School and Church structure. See a Teacher's portable Library and try some lessons. In the Dogtrot House, look for an early baby walker and a bench that's also a cradle and table. A new Wildlife center displays historic animals of Tennessee and the world. See a mountain lion, elk, river otters and beaver in surroundings similar to the 1800s. Living history weekends really bring the village to life.

JAMES K POLK HOME

Columbia - 301-305 W. Seventh Street (I-65 exit 46, US 412 to US 31 south. One block west of US 31) 38401. www.jameskpolk.com Phone: (931) 388-2354. Hours: Monday-Saturday 9:00am-4:00pm, Sunday 1:00-5:00pm. Open until 5:00pm (April-October). Admission: $7.00 adult, $6 senior, $4 child (6-college age). Family $20. Educators: Lesson Plans - www.jameskpolk.com/education.asp and excellent links for biographies on James and Sarah Polk.

The James K. Polk Ancestral Home is the only surviving residence of the eleventh U.S. President (excluding the White House). Samuel Polk, a prosperous farmer and surveyor, built the brick house in 1816 while his oldest son James was attending the University of North Carolina. When the future President graduated in 1818, he returned to Tennessee and stayed with his parents until his marriage in 1824. While living in his family's Columbia home, James practiced law and began his political career by successfully running for the State Legislature. Today, the Home displays original items from James K. Polk's years in Tennessee and Washington, D.C. including furniture, paintings, and White House china. Polk's Sisters Homes and detached kitchen building are part of the tour (including intro video). Visitors to the kitchen see period cooking implements and household accessories. Demonstrations of early 19th century crafts and chores presented occasionally.

RENAISSANCE CENTER

Dickson - 855 Hwy 46S 37055. www.rcenter2.org/default.asp Phone: (615) 446-4450. Hours: Monday-Saturday 9:00am-9:00pm.

Multi-faceted center with a planetarium & laser light shows, educational theater, science theater and hands-on classes. Take a journey back in time to the Michael Faraday Theatre, a re-creation of the famous laboratory at the Royal Institution of Great Britain in London. Depicting life in the 1830s, you'll find a London street scene complete with gas lamps, cobblestone paving and characters in period costumes. In the Faraday lab, students will experience real life chemistry and physics demonstrations designed to spark interest in the sciences. Training/shows in 3D multi-media is their specialty.

CROSS CREEKS NATIONAL WILDLIFE REFUGE

Dover - Route 1, Box 556 (3 miles east of town off Hwy 49) 37058. Phone: (615) 232-7477. http://gorp.away.com/gorp/resource/us_nwr/tn_cross.htm Hours: Refuge: Monday-Friday 7:00am-5:00pm, Saturday 9:00am-5:00pm (March-October). Visitors Center open year round.

Recreational opportunities on the refuge include public fishing, a limited hunting season, wildlife observation, photography, nature study, boating, and mushroom, berry and grape picking. Bicycling and horseback riding are also permitted on established roads during open periods. During the winter months, a foot trail and nature drive are available and the visitors center always offers wildlife exhibits and audio-visual programs.

FORT DONELSON NATIONAL MILITARY PARK

Dover - (I-24 north, then US 79 west - off Hwy 79) 37058. Phone: (931) 232-5706. www.nps.gov/fodo/ Hours: Daily 8:00am-4:30pm. Closed Christmas. Dover Hotel only open Noon-4:00pm in the summer. Admission: FREE . Educators: Lesson PLans on forts, weapons of the Civil War here: www.nps.gov/fodo/forteachers/lessonplans.htm

Fort Donelson interprets a crucial Civil War battle in which General U.S. Grant first gained fame. This is the site of the first major Union victory during the War. Accessible by a six-mile self-guided tour, you can see the earthen fort, river batteries, outer earthworks, the Dover Hotel (Surrender House) and the National Cemetery. Use the brochure as a guide and consider an optional audio tour. Attend park programs and presentations. Hike the park trails. Stand at the cannon emplacements on the Cumberland River Bluff and imagine the bombardment of gunboats below. Find out why the Federals threw away their coats and blankets when a snowstorm was coming.

LAND BETWEEN THE LAKES NATIONAL RECREATION AREA

Dover - (north of US 79 between Dover & the Tennessee River) 37058. Phone: (270) 924-2000 or (270) 924-2020. www.lbl.org Hours: Central Time. Specific hours vary depending on facility. Admission: FREE, except for specific sites with fees. Canoe/Kayak rentals: $10/hour.

Rediscover the simple pleasures of playing in the outdoors. Located in Western Kentucky and Tennessee, LBL offers 170,000 acres of wildlife, history, and outdoor recreation opportunities, wrapped by 300 miles of undeveloped shoreline. In Tennessee, there are opportunities to boat, fish, camp and hike or bike trails. Also, near the Kentucky border, **THE HOMEPLACE** serves as a living history farm of 1850. The farm re-creates daily activities of a typical rural family living near the river. Interpreters are dressed in period clothing and talk to guests while doing chores. The complex is formed of 16 buildings (many original), an interpretive center with exhibits/video, and many seasonal festivals. (Daily, April-October; closed Monday and Tuesday, November & March. Hours: 10:00am-5:00pm. Admission: $3-$5).

CARNTON PLANTATION

*Franklin - 1345 Carnton Lane (I-65 S exit 65, turn right, go to Mack Hatcher Pkwy,
left, turn right on Hwy 431) 37064. www.carnton.org Phone: (615) 794-0903. Hours:
Monday - Saturday 9:00am-5:00pm, Sunday Noon-5:00pm. Last tour one hour before
closing. Admission: $15.00 adult, $12.00 senior (65+), $6.00 child (6-12).*

Late in the afternoon on November 30, 1864, the plantation was at the center
of one of the largest and deadliest battles of the War Between the States. Over
20,000 members of the Confederate Army of Tennessee repeatedly charged
the entrenched Union troops in a battle to take Franklin. The McGovack
plantation house soon came into service as a hospital and when the house
was filled, the dead and wounded were tended to in the surrounding yard.
Numerous blood stains are still visible, especially on the porch.

CARTER HOUSE & FRANKLIN CIVIL WAR MUSEUM

*Franklin - 1140 Columbia Avenue (I-65 exit 65, Hwy 96 west) 37064.
Phone: (615) 791-1861. www.battleoffranklintrust.org/carterhouse_history.
htm Hours: Monday-Saturday 9:00am-5:00pm, Sunday Noon-5:00pm. *NOTE
during Daylight Savings Time site closes at 4:00pm. Closed Sundays during
month of January and some holidays.
Admission: $15.00 adult, $12.00
senior (65+), $8.00 child (6-12).
Notes: Military Summer Camps, Girls
1800s Summer Camp. Anniversary of
Battle of Franklin. On November 30 -
remember the 1864 Battle of Franklin
with ceremonies, a two-mile walk to
The Carter House, lectures, and living
history programs.*

See actual bullet holes
and blood stains...

During the November 1864 Battle of Franklin, it was used as a Federal
Command Post by General Jacob D. Cox. During the battle, the Carter family
hid in the cellar, avoiding the crossfire from the Union and Confederate forces
that heavily damaged the house and surrounding buildings. You actually wa'
down into the cellar/family room to see where they fearfully hid. One of
Carter boys, however, Captain Tod Carter, was killed during the battle, a

with over 2,000 Federal and 6,000 Confederate forces. Evidence of the battle is still noticeable today, as innumerable bullet holes still scar the house and other structures. Feel the bullet hole in the porch and hear the story about the soldier it nearly hit. Then go inside and see the blood stains in the corner. Why is the spindle in the upper staircase upside down? Your guided tour includes a video presentation, the house and the Franklin Civil War Museum.

BLEDSOE CREEK STATE PARK

Gallatin - 400 Ziegler's Fort Road (Hwy. 25 East at the intersection of 31-E and 25 East) 37066. Phone: (615) 452-3706. Hours: 7:00am-sunset. www.tennessee.gov/ environment/parks/BledsoeCreek/index.shtml

Situated on the Bledsoe Creek embankment, the park provides hiking trails and boating, skiing and fishing on Old Hickory Lake. There are approximately 6 miles of hiking trails, 1 mile of which is paved and accessible to persons with a disability. Many historical sites are nearby.

HISTORIC MANSKER'S STATION FRONTIER LIFE CENTER

Goodlettsville - 705 Caldwell Lane, Moss Wright Park (I-65 to exit 97, Goodlettsville/ Longhollow Pike, east) 37072. Phone: (615) 859-3678. http://manskers. historicalifestyles.com/manskersmain.html Hours: Monday-Friday 9:00am-4:30pm (early March-1st wkend in December). Admission: $5.00 adult, $4.00 senior (62+), $3.00 student. Includes Bowen Plantation tour. Note: The first weekend in May the fort site comes alive with the 18th Century Colonial Fair.

An authentic reconstruction of the 1779 frontier forted station typical of Kasper Mansker's first fort. Masker's Fort allows you to experience the lifestyle of early settlers in the 18th century. The Life Center tour includes a video (starts with a screaming Indian) to set the mood - could you survive? Through "living history" demonstrations (mostly in first person), you can touch the hand-hewn timbers, hear the steady click of the spinning wheel, see the blacksmith work, and smell the smoke of the cook fires. Help make

"Don't see any enemy yet...", says Daniel.

a fire (borrow a tinderbox) or pretend your family is staying in one of the family cabins. The **BOWEN PLANTATION HOUSE** is the area's earliest residence and region's oldest brick structure. Help make shortbread (yummy, try some) or beaten biscuits (kids can beat the dough 500 times!) or pretend you're having tea in the parlor.

MUSIC CITY RACEWAY

Goodlettsville - 3302 Ivy Point Road (track: Music City Raceway) 37072. Phone: (615) 264-0375. www.musiccityraceway.com

Long-time NHRA championship drag racing with their season running March-November on Tuesday, Friday and Saturday nights. Admission varies but children 12 and under are FREE.

OLD HICKORY LAKE VISITOR CENTER

Hendersonville - Rockland Road, 5 Power Plant Road (I-65N exit 96, Rte. 386E, right on Conference Dr, left on 31E to Rockland Rec Area) 37075. www.lrn.usace.army. mil/Locations/Lakes/OldHickoryLake.aspx Phone:(615) 822-4846. Hours:Most days, 10am-4pm.

Old Hickory Lake Visitor Center offers an interactive history of the lake and the navigational lock and dam system, operated by the US Army Corps of Engineers. Museum-style displays, playground, beach (Rte. 2) and picnic sites are also available.

ROCK CASTLE

Hendersonville - 139 Rock Castle Lane (south of Gallatin Road, Rte. 31 on Indian Lake Road, turn right) 37075. Phone: (615) 824-0502. www.historicrockcastle.com. Hours: Tuesday-Saturday 10am-5pm (Feb-Dec), Sundays 1-5pm (April-November) Admission: $7.00 adult, $6.00 senior, $5.00 child (6-12). Educators: excellent TN History curriculum: www.historicrockcastle.com/getdoc/4b6ce94b-e34b-4218-bb07-301b5c34b0e3/EDU12_4thGradeCurriculum.aspx.

General Daniel and Sarah Smith's 1794 home is built of limestone (first rock structure in Tennessee) and furnished with period antiques and walnut woodwork. The Family Bible, private letters, and Daniel Smith's library of over two hundred books, are in the collection here. The general acted as surveyor for this frontier, produced the state's first map and is credited with naming the state of Tennessee. Summer Kid Day Camps.

TRINITY MUSIC CITY USA

Hendersonville - One Music Village Blvd. (I65N to SR 386 exit, then to exit 8, take 2 rights) 37075. Phone: (615) 826-9191. www.tbn.org Hours: Monday-Thursday 11:00am-6:00pm, Friday-Saturday until 7:00pm. Summer holidays & Sundays 1:00-5:00pm. Closed Thanksgiving, Christmas & New Years. Tours: Tuesday-Sunday at 3pm. Admission: FREE Note: Mention to the gift shop staff that you read about this site in KIDS LOVE TENNESSEE, and receive a "HAPPY PACK" FREE fun pack. Participate in exciting revival services at TMC Church on Sundays at 2:00pm. TBN presents live "Praise The Lord" broadcasts Friday nights at 7:00pm.

Start with a grounds tour or the Virtual Reality Theatre, but, be sure to do both! In the theatre, you'll first see a short intro video about the complex and Conway Twitty's origins here (before it became Trinity). Then, walk down the recreated streets of Jerusalem to the Virtual Reality Theatre where you'll view a 1 hour motion picture production of "The Revolutionary" (walk the streets with Jesus) or "The Emissary" (exciting events from the book of Acts). At times, you'll hear sound from all directions and even feel your seats rumble. It's very engaging!

Tours include the original estate of Conway Twitty of country music fame (love all the royal blue velvet).

Then, walk through a recording studio used by many famous Christian artists. See the large mixing boards and separate rooms for vocals and each instrument played. Now, check out the WPGD TV studios and theatre. See the various sets and stages used for regular programming like "Praise the Lord." Look out for the boom cameras lurking about. What fun to see a motion picture, a recording studio and a TV station…all for FREE!

LEWIS COUNTY MUSEUM OF NATURAL & LOCAL HISTORY

Hohenwald - 108 East Main Street 38462. Phone: (931) 796-1550 www. lewiscountymuseum.com Hours: Tuesday-Saturday 10:00am-4:00pm. Admission: $2.00-$5.00 per person (students to adults). Educators: Lesson plans under Educators icon.

There are over 120 specimens of rare and exotic animal trophy mounts at the Lewis County Museum of Natural and Local History. One of the largest collections of wild animal mounts in the Western Hemisphere. You can admire tiny dik-diks and giant elands, the smallest and largest of the antelope family. You can see an elephant's tail used as a fly swatter, and you can walk through a doorway framed with a pair of seven feet long ivory tusks. You can wander down aisles and gaze upon hartebeest, gazelle, oryx, nyala, gnu, bushbusk, kudu, the elusive bongo, and water and cape buffalo.

The museum also contains displays on Lewis County's history beginning with early Indian artifacts and Meriwether Lewis' untimely death on the Natchez Trace in 1809. You can enter a log cabin replica and see how early country folk lived. Other displays recall the Swiss and German settlements of the 1890s, iron ore and phosphate mining ventures, Civil War relics, and 125 bird and snake eggs from around the world.

NATCHEZ TRACE PARKWAY HISTORIC SITES

Hohenwald - (stretching from SW Nashville to the TN/AL border and further into MS) 38462. Phone: (800) 305-7417 Information, (931) 796-7264 Farmstead. **www.nps.gov/ natr/** *Hours: Trail open daily during daylight hours. Educators: Lesson Plans for all ages -* **www.nps.gov/natr/forteachers/index.htm**

The 444-mile Natchez Trace Parkway commemorates an ancient trail that connected southern portions of the Mississippi River to salt licks in today's central Tennessee. Over the centuries, the Choctaw, Chickasaw and other American Indians have left their mark on the Trace. Today, visitors can experience this All-American Road through hiking, biking, horseback riding and camping.

BLACKBURN FARMSTEAD & PIONEER MUSEUM - US Hwy 412, Mile Marker 391. Open most weekends April-November. Circa 1810 log buildings. The first Lewis County Court met in this historic house until the first courthouse was built. The grand jury is said to have convened in the log corn crib still standing behind the house. Both buildings are listed on the National Register of Historic Places. Various artifacts from the pioneer days and Native American artifacts found nearby are on display.

MERIWETHER LEWIS NATIONAL MONUMENT - Pkwy and Hwy 20. Site of the mysterious death and grave of American explorer Meriwether Lewis, one of the leaders of the Lewis & Clark Expedition along the Missouri River. The surrounding park contains a display on Lewis. Also hiking trails, picnic areas and a campground. FREE.

BAKER'S BLUFF - near Shady Grove (931) 729-5774. Scenic view overlooking the Duck River and farmlands.

THE GORDON HOUSE - near Shady Grove built around 1817 by Capt. John Gordon, a prominent early settler (also acclaimed as a fearless spy).

JACKSON FALLS - Shady Grove historic rest stop with large spring and waterfalls that made for a good camping site for troops (even Andrew Jackson, for whom the falls were named).

LORETTA LYNN'S RANCH MUSEUM &
CAMPGROUND

Hurricane Mills - 44 Hurricane Mills Road (I-40 exit 143, Hwy 13 North) 37078. Phone: (931) 296-1840. www.lorettalynn.com Hours: Daily 9:00am-5:00pm.   Admission: Individual museums $12.50 or packages: $20 Plantation Home & Museum. $25 Home, Museum, Coal Mine, Butcher Holler Home. Kids 10 years and under are FREE.

The ranch offers tours of Loretta's plantation home and Coal Miner's Daughter Museum, as well as horseback riding, swimming and canoeing. Visiting this complex, you'll see a complete history of her life, including displays honoring her family, home life, ranch life and musical career.

Walk through her tour bus and see the 1977 Cadillac she loved to write hit songs in while driving on tour. See some of her original song sheets on notebook paper or her first homemade dress to perform in.

Glimpse inside detailed replicas of her first Nashville home with original furnishings and the little one-room schoolhouse she attended in the hills of Kentucky. She has even scattered hand-written notes in many displays putting the artifact descriptions in "her own words".

Loretta Lynn's Family Campground features Boone Hill Cabins and Stagecoach Hill Log Cabins, plus tent and RV camping sites. Westerntown has shops and snacks.

DAVID CROCKETT STATE PARK

Lawrenceburg - 1400 West Gaines (west of the city on US 64) 38464. www.tennessee. gov/environment/parks/DavidCrockettSP/index.shtml Phone: (931) 762-9408. Hours: Daily 7:00am-Dark (park). Museum: Daily 10:00am-5:00pm (summers) and weekends only the rest of the year.

In 1817, the infamous Davy Crockett moved to Lawrence County and served as a justice of the peace, a colonel of the militia, and as state representative. Along the banks of Shoal Creek, he established a diversified industry consisting of a powdermill, a gristmill and a distillery. You can stop at the environmental classroom overlook shelter and view the area where Crocketts' industrial operations were located on Shoal Creek below Crockett Falls. Financial difficulties from a flood in 1821 caused Crockett to move to West Tennessee where he was elected to Congress. Crockett died at the Alamo Mission while aiding the Texans in their fight for independence from Mexico. The park museum exhibits depict the life and times of Crockett as a pioneer, soldier, politician and industrialist.

A park naturalist and recreation director are on duty throughout the summer months. Both provide a variety of planned activities and programs including guided tours, organized games, arts and crafts, historical demonstrations and presentations, campfires, movies, slide shows, hayrides and the *Tennessee Valley Jamboree* every summer Friday night. The restaurant overlooks 40-acre scenic Lake Lindsey and features home-style cooking served up buffet style. Other activities: camping, fishing, boating, biking & hiking. An Olympic-sized swimming pool with a bathhouse and concession stand open summers.

FIDDLERS GROVE HISTORIC VILLAGE

Lebanon - 945 Baddour Pkwy, James E. Ward Agricultural Center (I-40 east to the 239B exit) 37087. www.fiddlersgrove.org Phone: (615) 443-2626. Hours: Daily 10:00am-3:00pm (May-October) Admission: Guided tours, $5.00/person. Walking tours: $4/person.

Village of more than 40 structures, original and replicated, with local historical significance. Witness what life was like in the 1800s for a resident of Wilson County. Sit in a chair in the schoolhouse, peak in the sheriff's office and old jail. See Sam Houston's house or a slave family's first home. Self guided and guided tours available.

LEBANON MUSEUM AND HISTORY CENTER

Lebanon - 200 Castle Heights Avenue N. (lower entrance of the City of Lebanon Administration Building) (off I-40, US 231N, left on Main St., right into Castle Heights) 37087. Phone: (615) 443-2839. Hours: Monday-Friday 8:00am-4:00pm. FREE.

Walk through the history of Lebanon from prehistoric to modern times. Audio descriptions by famous residents introduce visitors to the periods on display and take advantage of the touch-screen computers for your own research. Start with fossils from town - can you guess what the bones come from? Learn about slaves during and after the war. Look for kids items like the  Tank Bank. General Patton trained maneuvers here. You can arrange a tour of Sellars Mound from this site. As you round the square, on your way to the museum, take note of the 1800 Neddy Jacobs log cabin.

CEDARS OF LEBANON STATE PARK

Lebanon - 328 Cedar Forest Road (6 miles south of I-40 on U.S. Highway 231/SR 10) 37090. Phone: (615) 443-2769 or (800) 713-5180 cabins. www.tennessee.gov/ environment/parks/Cedars/index.shtml Hours: Summer 8:00am-10:00pm, Winter 8:00am-8:00pm.

Cedars of Lebanon State Park is named for the dense cedar forest that existed in the Biblical lands of Lebanon. 831 acres are open to the public with a variety of recreational activities such as hiking, an Olympic-plus size swimming pool, playground, horseshoe pits, softball field, volleyball courts, and tennis courts. Cedars of Lebanon has nine modern, two-bedroom cabins that can sleep up to six people. Eight miles of hiking trails meander through the "cedar" forests and glades - each trail is easy and fairly short. In April, look for over 20 native wildflowers, which can be seen in the cedar glades during the annual wildflower tours.

NASHVILLE SUPERSPEEDWAY

Lebanon - 4874-F McCrary Road 37090. www.nashvillesuperspeedway.com Phone: (615) 726-1818.

The 1.33- mile "D" oval hosts major NASCAR and Indy events. A special alcohol & tobacco free grandstand area is perfect for making race day a real family outing. Events sell out early, so be prepared.

MOUSETAIL LANDING STATE PARK

Linden - Rte. 3, box 280B (I-40 west to exit 143, Hwy 13S for 9 miles. Right on Hwy 438 for 25 miles) 37096. Phone: (731) 847-0841. www.tennessee.gov/environment/ parks/MousetailLanding/index.shtml Hours: Park, 7:00am-10:00pm. Office/Center, 8:00am-4:30pm.

Located on the east banks of the Tennessee River, the park office serves as a museum/interpretive center. Exhibits include a snake skin, stuffed beaver, owl, hawk, turkey, duck and a goose. There is an Indian artifact collection and other area artifacts. The scenic Buffalo River flows nearby, providing opportunity for family canoe float trips. A swimming beach and a small stream at the entrance of the park are enjoyable for small children and adults to wade in with its cold, clear water. Also picnic areas, playgrounds, fishing and boating.

LYNNVILLE RAILROAD MUSEUM

Lynnville - 1722 Main Street (I-65 exit 27, Rte. 129 or Rte. 31N, turn right on Rte. 129) 38472. Phone: (931) 527-3700. www.lynnville.org/railroadmuseum.htm Hours: Tuesday-Saturday 10:00am-4:00pm, Sunday 1:00-4:00pm. Admission: $1.00-$2.50.

Inside, a telegrapher sits at his post, keying a message to the station down the line. The conductor stands at the window, watch in hand, mindful of his schedule. An operating HO scale model railroad depicts Lynnville as it was in the 1930s.

Enjoy the comforts of a vintage passenger coach, in the original seats, and watch a video on present day operating steam & diesel tourist railroads. The Milky Way Farms Museum, contained in a vintage passenger coach of a restored steam locomotive, details some memories of the candy giant and his enormous farm nearby. Sit in the engineer's seat, grab the levers, blow the whistle and clang the bell.

Stop by the restored Lynnville Pharmacy, Soda Pop Junction, built in 1860, and order a soft drink from the circa 1940 soda fountain. A small admission is charged.

CANNONSBURGH VILLAGE

Murfreesboro - 312 South Front Street (I-24 exit 78B, turn right on Broad St.) 37130.
www.facebook.com/pages/Friends-of-Cannonsburgh-Village/119762194776434
Phone: (615) 890-0355.   Hours: Tuesday-Saturday 10:00am-5:00pm, Sunday 1:00-
5:00pm (May-November).

Since Murfreesboro's original name was Cannonsburgh, it seems appropriate

that this collection of buildings in downtown Murfreesboro should again pay tribute to Minos Cannon, a prominent early settler. Particularly notable, is the 1,500 gallon red cedar bucket which was made in Murfreesboro in 1887, where it represents the industrial past of the area. There's also a one-room schoolhouse, chapel, gristmill, blacksmith and doctor's office (back when they made house calls). The most interesting buildings are the old Leeman house (check out the Newspaper insulation/ wallpaper) and the General Store (look for the original cash register). Best to visit during seasonal festivals when there is activity in the village.

See the world's largest cedar bucket...over 1,500 gallons!

DISCOVERY CENTER AT MURFREE SPRING

Murfreesboro - 502 Southeast Broad Street (I-24 exit 81B) 37130. Phone: (615) 890-
2300. www.explorethedc.org Hours: Monday-Saturday 10:00am-5:00pm. Sunday
1:00-5:00pm. Closed major holidays. Admission: $6.00 general (ages 2+).

The facility has 15 permanent, indoor exhibit areas plus 20 acres of outdoor wetland habitat (our favorite area) and Nature Play water and sand tables amid activities to climb, slide, balance and leap frog. Accessible by boardwalks, the habitat has interpretive signs with weekly guided walks and studies. Look for the giant carp and large beaver dams. Inside, play with simple machines, fly an airplane or climb on a real fire truck, visit a train station or farmers market, or relive history. Tiny Town (age 5 & under w/ care-givers) includes a Tiny Town Kroger, Home Depot, a country cottage for family role play, postal center, and music store. Neat, unique exhibits included Creation Station nutrition workshop area, Super Slide, and Simple Machines (move the heavy bowling ball with teamwork and simple gizmos). We really appreciated the moderate size inside (not overwhelming) yet having the ability to let the kids expend energy outside while sneaking in some lessons on seasons and nature.

STONES RIVER NATIONAL BATTLEFIELD/ FORTRESS ROSECRANS

Murfreesboro - 3501 Old Nashville Hwy. (Hwy 41/70 north to Thompson Lane) 37133. Phone: (615) 893-9501. www.nps.gov/stri/ Hours: Daily 8:00am-5:00pm. Closed Christmas. Admission: FREE Notes: From late May through mid-November ranger walks and talks are presented daily. On summer, and occasional spring and fall weekends, living history programs are presented. A spur connector to the Greenway System bike/hike trail is open during daylight hours. Educators: Lesson Plans with stories, quizzes, archeology, recipes, and games - www.nps.gov/ stri/forteachers/curriculummaterials.htm.

A fierce battle took place at Stones River between December 31, 1862 and January 2, 1863. General Bragg's Confederates withdrew after the battle, allowing General Rosecrans and the Union army to control middle Tennessee. This was the bloodiest Civil War battle in the state. Portions of Fortress Rosecrans, a large earthen Union fort constructed after the battle, still stand. A Visitor center contains a small museum and very detailed video program about the battle. The battlefield may be toured by car or foot along a loop tour road. Best for students interested in battle strategies.

NASHVILLE SPORTS TEAMS

Nashville -

NASHVILLE PREDATORS HOCKEY - Gaylord Entertainment Center. www.nashvillepredators.com. Hard-hitting, fast-action NHL Hockey with their regular season running October-April. Evening games begin at 7:00pm, home afternoon games begin at 2:00pm.

NASHVILLE SOUNDS BASEBALL - Greer Stadium. A pro team operating as a AAA affiliate of the Milwaukee Brewers and a member of the Pacific Coast League. 72 games played early April-early September. www. nashvillesounds.com. Admission: $6.00-$10.00.

DOWNTOWN NASHVILLE ON BROADWAY

Nashville - 37201. Phone: (615) 256-2805.

Some sites of interest include:

HATCH SHOW PRINT: The Hatch Brothers started in 1870 and still

continues to use the same techniques employed in the 15th century. Hatch has always been a leading poster printer for circuses and best known for posters of Grand Ole Opry stars. Visit the shop, watch them prepare a typical poster and, if you like what you've seen, pick out your own piece of Hatch Show tradition.

TENNESSEE FOX TROT CAROUSEL: (end of Broadway @ Riverfront Park), $2.00/ride, weather permitting. This whimsical carousel was designed so that each sculpture represents someone or something of local fame. For example, Chet Atkins, President Andrew Jackson, Davy Crockett or Olympian Wilma Rudolph.

ERNEST TUBBS RECORD SHOP: famous posters and pictures of many who performed here and were discovered (ex. Loretta Lynn, Alan Jackson).

COUNTRY MUSIC CLUBS: many open in the daytime and early evenings where you can hear acts and grab a bite to eat.

We recommend every visit to Nashville include a walk down **BROADWAY STREET**, downtown. The amusing characters you'll see is enough entertainment in itself! Our kids love spending time looking and stopping *(daytime)* in places like Tootsies or Wildhorse for a snack and beverage. You never know who might be singing their way to stardome that day…just waiting to be discovered…it's magical on Broadway.

PARTHENON, THE

Nashville - 2600 West End Avenue (Centennial Park) 37201. Phone: (615) 862-8431. www.parthenon.org Hours: Tuesday-Saturday 9:00am-4:30pm (year-round). Sundays 12:30-4:30pm (April-September only).

Completely gold-plated in 2002, the grey-eyed goddess Athena Parthenos stands 42 feet tall in the Parthenon. The goddess' floor-length robe, helmet, shield, spear and the statue perched in her hand are dressed with gold touches. The process of applying little sheets of gold leaf paper (after Athena was iced down) is interesting to learn. This is the tallest indoor sculpture in the Western world.

ADVENTURE SCIENCE CENTER

Nashville - 800 Fort Negley Blvd. (I-40 exit 210C or I-65 exit 81, follow signs toward stadium) 37203. www.adventuresci.com Phone: (615) 862-5160. Hours: Daily 10:00am-5:00pm. Closed on Thanksgiving, Christmas Day. Admission: $13.00 adult, $11.00 child (2-12). Planetarium and Special exhibits, extra $4.00-$6.00. Note: Planetarium shows throughout the day.

7 levels of fun!

Climb the Adventure Tower - all seven levels! Power an elevator by bicycling, lift a car off the ground using a fulcrum, then climb through the roof inside the Adventure Tower's giant glass pyramid. Spend a day in the life of your

body in BodyQuest. Design parachutes and launch air rockets. Space Chase has a solar walk, wall, table and even a spaceship. In Mission Possible, enable a disabled person in a wheelchair by trying to use a wheelchair yourself to do simple tasks. Be a construction worker building a city. Stand inside the body of a giant guitar, pluck the strings and FEEL the vibration. Where else but Music City, USA, could you do this and get the best view of town...all, in one tower?

COUNTRY MUSIC HALL OF FAME AND MUSEUM

Nashville - 222 5th Avenue S (I-65 exit 209B, Broadway) 37203. Phone: (615) 416-2096 or (800) 852-6437. www.countrymusichalloffame.com Hours: Daily 9:00am-5:00pm. Closed Thanksgiving, Christmas and New Years. General Admission: $22.00 adult; $20.00 senior (60+), $14.00 youth (6-17). Add Studio B - $12.00-$15.00 more. Note: Grill - southern style lunch menu. Music Store, Demonstration Gallery and live performances most days.

Hear and see how country music has evolved. Once inside, an enormous

Minnie Pearl Fish...

two-story Wall of Gold Records is cased so that you can listen to the words and tunes that have earned these recording artists' fame. See rare costumes (Dale Evans & Roy Rogers original boots), instruments (Elvis' gold piano or Mother Maybelle Carter's Gibson guitar) and artifacts (like Elvis' solid gold Cadillac or Minnie Pearl's straw hat (w/ price tag of $1.98). Kids love the cowboy convertible. Nearby, sit down and laugh a spell watching old Hee Haw shows. Through video, you hear Garth Brooks talk about George Jones or Tim McGraw talk about life on the road. Favorite country songs are played everywhere. With touch-screen computer stations, visitors can design costumes, ask songwriters and stars programmed questions, learn country dancing, select and view a video clip, visit a star's web site or choose their own country music classics to listen to.

Jenny...singing into the microphone that made so many people famous...

RCA'S STUDIO B - the museum has returned the interior and exterior to their look during the glory days when Chet Atkins ran the studio. The oldest recording studio in Nashville, it helped form the "Nashville Sound" in the 1960s. Some of the famous hits recorded: Elvis' "It's Now or Never" and "Are You Lonesome Tonight?"; Roy Orbison's "Only the Lonely", the Everly Brothers "All I Have to Do is Dream" and Dolly Parton's "Jolene". You actually see, touch and hear the instruments and microphones used by the stars! The studio tour includes a detailed commentary of Music Row sites you pass en route.

FRIST CENTER FOR THE VISUAL ARTS

Nashville - 919 Broadway (I-40W or I-65N exit 209B, turn right on Demonbreun Street, traveling toward downtown) 37203. Phone: (615) 244-3340. ***www.fristcenter.org*** *Hours: Monday-Saturday 10:00am-5:30pm, Thursday & Friday until 9:00pm, Sunday 1:00-5:30pm. Closed major winter holidays. Admission: $10 adult, $7.00senior (65+) and Military; $7.00 college students. Children FREE (18 & under).*

The old downtown post office was converted into this art deco of rotating exhibits from around the world. The fun for kids is located in the second-floor ArtQuest Gallery, featuring 30 art stations where visitors can design their own exhibit, make art or play with visual concepts after they've been inspired by the works currently on exhibit...and, items in everyday life and culture. Then, they can take their artwork home. (best for students 4th grade and up, who have been exposed to some artistic concepts).

TENNESSEE SPORTS HALL OF FAME

Nashville - 501 Broadway, Gaylord Entertainment Center main level 37203. Phone: (615) 242-4750 or (888) 846-8384. ***www.TSHF.net*** *Hours: Tuesday-Saturday 10:00am-5:00pm. Admission: $2.00-$3.00 (age 4+).*

This site focuses on everything from team to extreme sports with a continuous video stream of Tennessee sports images. After a brief introductory video in one of two theaters, students are encouraged to explore and experience the museum on their own using our student activity booklet filled with learning activities and facts.

The Museum also features interactive games such as a virtual reality, one-on-one basketball game, a strength training apparatus used by Olympic swimmers, college football and basketball exhibits, NASCAR video games, two 30-seat theaters with sports videos, and more.

TENNESSEE AGRICULTURAL MUSEUM

Nashville - Ellington Agricultural Center (I-65: Take Exit #78-A east on Harding Place) 37204. http://tnagmuseum.org/about.html Phone: (615) 837-5197. Hours: Weekdays 9:00am-4:00pm except state holidays. Admission: FREE. Educators: Study guides & games - http://tnagmuseum.org/materials.html

The museum has an extensive collection of home and farm artifacts from the 19th and early 20th centuries along with rural Tennessee prints and folk art sculptures. Textiles, a woodworking collection, buggies, wagons and large items like the McCormick reaper and Jumbo steam engine are exhibited in a renovated plantation barn. Log cabins, a small farm house, kitchen/herb garden, perennial garden and nature trail are also part of the museum tour.

BELLE MEADE PLANTATION

Nashville - 110 Leake Avenue, 37205. Phone: (615) 356-0501 or (800) 270-3991. www.bellemeadeplantation.com Hours: Monday-Saturday 9:00am-5:00pm, Sunday 11:00am-5:00pm. (Closed Thanksgiving, Christmas, and New Year's). Admission: $16.00 adult, $14.00 senior (65+), $10.00 student (13-18), $8.00 child (6-12). Note: On-site restaurant. The cabin now features rotating Living History activities including storytelling, Voices of the South, vignettes, period dance, 19th century demonstrations of blacksmithing, gardening, food preparation and preservation and more during weekends and special events.

Did you know Seabiscuit, Secretariat, Funny Cide, Smarty Jones, Giacomo and Barbarro?

They are just some of the great Thoroughbreds that trace their bloodlines back to Belle Meade Plantation!

This "Queen of Tennessee Plantations", 1853 Greek Revival mansion was once a major thoroughbred stud farm and nursery. Tours are given by lavishly costumed interpreters around the grounds, log cabin, huge Carriage House and especially the mansion. During the Battle of Nashville, Union and rebel forces skirmished in the front yard, and the mansion's massive stone columns were riddled with bullets, the evidence still visible today. Check out the family portraits in the foyer…they're horses, not people.

CHEEKWOOD BOTANICAL GARDEN & MUSEUM OF ART

Nashville - 1200 Forrest Park Drive (Harding Place to Belle Meade Blvd to Page Road to Forrest Park Dr) 37205. ***www.cheekwood.org*** *Phone: (615) 356-8000. Hours: Tuesday-Saturday 9:30am-4:30pm, Sunday 11:00am -4:30pm. Admission: $12.00 adult, $10.00 senior (65+), $5.00 youth (6-17) and college, plus military discounts. Note: Take a lunch break at The Pineapple Room Restaurant! Enjoy southern food in a bistro atmosphere. Or you can enjoy a picnic lunch on the grounds. Seasonal events are best for kids: Scarecrows, Pumpkin Patch, Summer Family Night Out or Trains.*

The estate, turned art museum and botanical gardens, has interactive learning centers, the Wildflower Garden's pond full of frogs, and the 16-foot rabbit made out of balls of wire on the Woodland Sculpture Trail.

NASHVILLE CHILDREN'S THEATRE

Nashville - 724 Second Avenue South 37210. ***www.nct-dragonsite.org*** *Phone: (615) 254-9103. Hours: Monday-Friday 10:00am and 11:30am. Select Saturday and Sunday 2:30pm. Admission: $7-$14 for preview shows & homeschool days. A bit more for regular shows.*

A non-profit, long-standing pro theatre that brings magical productions of award-winning children's literature and folk tales each season (ex. Three Little Pigs, Treasure Island). Performed at different theatres throughout town (ex. Hill Theatre).

TENNESSEE CENTRAL RAILWAY MUSEUM

Nashville - 220 Willow Street 37210. ***www.tcry.org*** *Phone: (615) 244-9001. Hours: Tuesday, Thursday, Saturday 9:00am-3:00pm (Museum). Admission: Varies with each type of excursion. Best to visit website for details. Generally $21.00-$32.00 per person.*

Tour the museum full of timetables, locks, switch keys, menus, bells, headlights, cabooses, camp cars, passenger cars and locomotives on display. Excursion Train Rides visit Watertown or Lebanon for a stop and a chance to visit shops and enjoy a meal. Trips include re-enactments of a train robbery or fairyland with Mother Goose style characters or a Civil War re-enactment with Morgan's Raiders. All of the cars are climate-controlled and every seat provides a great view of the countryside. Seating from coach to first class with a dining car, dome car and gift shop car.

NASHVILLE ZOO AT GRASSMERE

Nashville - 3777 Nolensville Road (I-24 exit 56 or I-65 exit 78, follow signs) 37211. Phone: (615) 833-1534. www.nashvillezoo.org Hours: Daily 9:00am-6:00pm (mid March to mid-October), 9:00-4:00pm (rest of year). Closed major winter holidays. Admission: $15.00 adult, $13.00 senior (65+), $10.00 child (2-12). (a little cheaper fall/winter). Parking $5.00. Train and carousel rides extra.

Visitors get up close to the animals at Critter Encounters (monkeys, lemurs, goats, sheep and baby camels). While it's early yet, head over to the Nashville Zoo in the morning when the temperature is just right and the animals are alert and feeding. Along with the newer spaces: Bamboo Trail and the Meerkat exhibit, you will probably want to catch the Elephant Habitat. It

...giant walk-in snake's mouth!

includes several viewing points, as well as wading pools for the pachyderms and tall trees for shade. Also open is the Lorikeet Habitat. Guests enter this habitat near the new elephant area and walk a winding path lined with beautiful landscaping as up to 50 lorikeets move freely inside the meshed habitat. They're very friendly and love to be feed treats. Some exhibits that have been there a while are still our favorites. Unseen New World still has many reptiles that are humongous! ...the largest turtles, salamanders and snakes we've ever seen. Maybe you like to spend a good amount

of time at the Jungle Gym. Tall treetop towers, a walk-in snakes' mouth, lots of bridges and climb, climb, climb to your little heart's content. Our favorite animal in the zoo is still the Siamang Gibbons. Their huge throat sac inflates and they make loud calls while they swing. What hams! You can also tour the historic home and working farm to experience life in the 19th century...with animals. Cool off at the Terrace rain room or under shadowing vines.

For updates & travel games visit: **www.KidsLoveTravel.com**

COOTER'S PLACE NASHVILLE

Nashville - 2613 McGavock Pike (Opryland exit off Briley Parkway) 37214. Phone: (615) 872-8358. www.cootersplace.com Hours: Opens 9am. Closes at 8pm or 6pm (sundays) Admission: FREE

If you love "the Dukes of Hazzard", you will love a visit to Cooter's Garage... operated by none other than ol' "Cooter" himself. Ben Jones, who played the Duke Boys sidekick, is your host. It features pictures, props, costumes, and memorabilia from the television show. Look for The General Lee, Dukes of Hazard toys or watch old shows. Cast members visit frequently and Cooter will be in Nashville almost every week and hosts the DukeFest in Nashville in June.

GAYLORD OPRYLAND RESORT

Nashville - 2800 Opryland Drive (I-40 to Briley Pkwy, exit 12) 37214. Phone: (615) 889-1000 or (877) 234-OPRY reservations. www.gaylordopryland.com

The kids enter the lobby and never stop the "oohs and aahs". They couldn't believe everywhere we walked was under one roof! Pretty cool to go on a long nature trail (Garden Conservatory) and never leave the building. It's always a comfortable 72 degrees under the glass atriums that encompass acres and acres of lush indoor gardens, winding pathways, and sparkling waterfalls.

Step aboard one of the Delta River Flatboats ($5.00/person, age 5+, depart every 15-20 minutes) and take a scenic cruise down a winding indoor river where you'll pass gardens and majestic waterfalls. The tour includes interesting little-known facts about the Hotel, and if you're lucky you may catch a glimpse of Danny, the eighty-pound catfish. Look for laser-light and fountain shows, too.

A boat ride <u>inside</u> a hotel...
Now that's different!

Choose from several restaurants including a grand Antebellum-style restaurant, Old Hickory Steakhouse, any of island eateries (Pizza, barbeque, grill, deli, ice cream, etc.), or Cascades Atrium.

There are four outdoor swimming pools and a fitness center on the premises.

Kids Station is a drop-in childcare "resort within a resort," where kids ages three to twelve years old can stay for an hour or play for a day. Your children will be entertained as they explore the 2,500-square-foot Kids Station where they can happily do crafts, perform or watch videos.

Rooms rates: Guestrooms (average $135-$211 per night) & numerous suites higher. Family packages filled with activities included start at ~$200.

GENERAL JACKSON SHOWBOAT

Nashville - 2812 Opryland Drive (I-40 exit Briley Pkwy to exit 12, Opryland, follow signs) 37214. Phone: (615) 871-6100. **www. generaljackson.com** *Hours: Cruises depart daily late February - mid November. Midday Cruise is 2 1/2 hours departing at Noon. Meal cruises board at 11:30am. Admission: Midday $37-$59.00 per person (age 4+). Without a meal option, less expensive ($28-$42) midday party cruises occasionally available spring-fall (good weather seasons). Additional food is available for purchase. Note: Holiday Cruises and Evening Cruises for special "dinner & dancing" style fine cruising.*

Great show... great food...great fun!

Styled in the grand tradition of the paddlewheel riverboats that cruised the great Southern waterways in the 1800s, the General Jackson was named after the first steamboat to operate on the Cumberland River in 1817. We recommend the midday cruise for families. This casual, country-themed cruise includes a delicious lunch buffet (chicken & pulled pork BBQ w/ fixins) and a show, featuring famous local entertainers (full of laughs and great songs). Children's activities are scheduled on midday cruises from May- mid September. General admission tickets include outer deck seating (with snacks and beverages served inside), live band entertainment and a kids tour. Children can take a walking tour of the boat with Miss Sarah and hear tall tales about life on the river. Plus, each child will receive a custom coloring page. Historical points of interest you'll hear about are locks, dams, riverfront parks, navigational lights and a cave. Well worth the time while in Nashville!

GRAND OLE OPRY

*Nashville - 2804 Opryland Drive (Briley Pkwy to exit 11, Opry Mills Drive) 37214. Phone: (615) 871-OPRY. **www.opry.com** Hours: Friday 7:30pm, Saturday 6:30pm and 9:30pm. Tuesday 7:00pm (Memorial Day-mid December only). Winter shows @ Ryman Auditorium. Generally 2 1/2 hours. Admission: $35-$57 adult, $25-$57 child (ages 4-11), under 3 FREE if sit on lap.*

Whether you attend a Grand Ole Opry show, a live episode of USA Network's Nashville Star, a huge concert or  a small party, you'll find that star treatment and southern hospitality are the norm. From Nashville to all points within reach, the Opry has been broadcast live over WSM AM 650 since 1925 (world's longest-running live radio show). Aspiring performers will share the stage with legends in country, bluegrass, and comedy. One of the Opry's priceless qualities continues to be the uniqueness of each show-guests never know who might strike up a rare duet or who might stop by for a surprise appearance! We saw famous stars like Whispering Bill Anderson, T. Bubba (comic), Little Jimmy Dickens and Steve Wariner ("Holes in the Floor of Heaven" fame). You'll see a two hour program full of 6-8 artists...mostly singing old-time, knee-slapping country. Special memory note – cameras are allowed!

MUSIC VALLEY WAX MUSEUM

Nashville - 2515 McGavock Pike (near Opryland Complex) 37214. Phone: (615) 883-3612. Hours: Daily 9:00am-9:00pm (summer), closes at 5:00pm rest of year. Closed Thanksgiving and Christmas. Admission: $3-$5.00.

The Wax Museum features more than 50 wax figures of old-time country music's stars. Many look like the famous folks and they are dressed in original costumes, in original surroundings. Look for the "Sidewalk of the Stars" where 250+ entertainers have placed their footprints, handprints and signatures in concrete.

NASHVILLE TROLLEY TOURS

Nashville - Second Avenue & Broadway (tickets at Gray Line Visitor Center) 37214. Phone: (615) 248-4437. http://graylinetn.com/music-city-trolley-hop/ Admission: $20.00 adult, $10.00 child (4-11)

Nashville's first and only Hop-on, Hop-off Trolley service is a treat for anyone! Check out all the major attractions of Historic Downtown; see the Stars' favorite hangouts and world famous Music Row; learn about the history and present day happenings of Music City as you stay on and ride along...or get off and explore on your own.

One hour downtown and Music Row narrated tour aboard an old-fashioned trolley. Tour departs from the Hard Rock Visitors Booth on 2nd Avenue. The tour includes a drive by sightseeing tour of Historic Downtown, Ryman Auditorium, State Capitol, the Parthenon, Vanderbilt Museum, Country Music Hall of Fame, Fort Nashborough, Bicentennial Mall, and Music Row.

RAINFOREST CAFÉ EDUCATIONAL TOURS

Nashville - Opry Mills 37214. www.rainforestcafe.com Phone: (615) 514-3000.

The theme restaurant and wildlife preserve is filled with live and mechanical animals: ongoing rainstorms (even thunder and lightning); a talking rainforest tree; giant "walk-thru" aquarium; and hand-sculpted "cave like" rock everywhere. Preschoolers love the fish tank but may be uneasy with the motorized large gorillas and elephants. Did you know they give Educational Group Tours? What a light-hearted way to introduce your kids to the animals, plants and environs of the rainforest. The Adventure uncovers why elephants have big ears and why the Café's residents collect pennies for charity. What is your favorite fish in the coral reef? Include a group lunch afterwards in your plans (for around $10.00 per person). Nibble on Jurassic Tidbits or Paradise Pizza plus drink and dessert.

TEXAS TROUBADOUR THEATRE

Nashville - 2416 Music Valley Drive (Opryland area) 37214. Phone: (615) 885-0028. www.thenashvilleking.com or http://etrecordshop.com Hours: Vary with show. Nashville King shows are Mondays & Thursdays at 7pm (March-October). Admission: FREE for Jamboree and Cowboy church. Fee for special shows.

The Ernest Tubb Midnight Jamboree, a live country music radio broadcast every Saturday night from the theatre on WSM AM, has followed the Grand Ole Opry for many years. Nashville Cowboy Church is here. The Music Valley Jubilee, a spectacular 2 hour musical and special Tribute shows (ex. Elvis) are here, too.

"*A Tribute To The King*" is a family-friendly, two hour show. This "Elvis" has all the right moves and sound. It starts out calm...but by the end, "there's a whole lotta shakin' goin' on!". You might steal a kiss from "Elvis", girls!

WAVE COUNTRY

Nashville - 2320 Two Rivers Parkway (near Opryland) 37214. Phone: (615) 885-1052. www.nashville.gov/Parks-and-Recreation/Water-Activities/Wave-Country.aspx Hours: Daily 10:00am-5:00pm (Memorial Day weekend thru the first day of school). Weekends only after school starts thru Labor Day. Admission: $12.00 adult, $10.00 child (3-12), FREE for children 2 and under. Wave Runner Special: Kids admitted for half price after 3:00 PM, Monday - Thursday.

The area's only wave-action swimming pool where you can ride the waves, or just let them lap at your feet. There are floats available for you to rent, and there are calm, "non-wave" periods as well. Or, have fun on the three water slides in the park, a children's playground, or sand volleyball pits. Extensive fast-food concessions available.

NASHVILLE SYMPHONY ORCHESTRA

Nashville - Jackson Hall, TN Performing Arts Center 37215. Phone: (615) 783-1200 office or (615) 783-1212 tickets. www.nashvillesymphony.org   Admission: $14.00-$23.00 general for Pied Piper concerts.

The Symphony features a full schedule of classical, pops and special events concerts. Happy Holidays Concerts are brimming with holiday favorites, sing-alongs, and a visit from jolly Old Saint Nick. This interactive celebration is a wonderful way for your family to kick-off the holiday season (Thanksgiving weekend). Pied Piper concerts are shorter, more interactive concerts designed for children ages 3-8. Families are encouraged to join activities that relate to the concert beginning at 10:15am, before each performance. Kids can check out their own website: **www.nsokids.org** for fun interactives about symphonies.

RYMAN AUDITORIUM

Nashville - 116 Fifth Avenue North (downtown) (I-40 to Broadway east, towards downtown and Cumberland River, left on 5th Ave) 37219. Phone: (615) 889-3060 tickets or (615) 458-8700 general. **www.ryman.com** *Hours: Daily 9:00am-4:00pm. Closed New Years, Thanksgiving and Christmas. Admission: $13.00 adult, $6.50 child (4-11). Guided tours: 17.00 adult, $10.50 child. Evening performance rates vary.*

The Ryman Auditorium, a former home of the Grand Ole Opry (1943-1974),

offers self-guided tours that showcase the legendary stars who have graced her stage, from country's biggest names to Mae West, Rudolf Valentino, and W.C. Fields. Have a seat in the original pews as you watch "If These Walls Could Talk", a short film featuring the people and events that have made the Ryman famous. Step onto the actual stage and get your picture taken holding the microphone and strumming a guitar. Then stroll past hallways of old photos and posters and videos.

Daniel & Jenny "perform" at the legendary Ryman...

On the guided tour, the Ryman has also opened up its backstage to the public. Patrons are allowed to take a guided tour through the dressing rooms dedicated to the stars of the Ryman's rich musical past, including Minnie Pearl and Johnny and June Carter Cash. In the evening, you can return to the performance hall for one of many shows and concerts scheduled year-round.

RADNOR LAKE STATE NATURAL AREA

Nashville - 1160 Otter Creek Road (6 miles southwest of downtown) 37220. **www. tennessee.gov/environment/parks/RadnorLake/index.shtml** *Phone: (615) 373-3467.*

Radnor Lake is a wildlife sanctuary which provides outstanding scenic beauty

For updates & travel games visit: **www.KidsLoveTravel.com**

and nature observation. Popular among bird watchers and photographers, the park has hiking trails ranging from easy to strenuous, an interpretive program (special hikes and canoe floats), and a museum and visitors center (generally open 9:00am-5:00pm).

TRAVELLERS REST HISTORIC HOME

Nashville - 636 Farrell Parkway (I-65 exit 78B, Harding Place West to US31S, follow signs) 37220. www.travellersrestplantation.org Phone: (615) 832-8197. Hours: Monday-Saturday 10:00am-4:00pm, Sunday 1:00-4:00pm, except Thanksgiving, Christmas Day, and New Years Day. Admission: $12.00 adult, $9.00 senior (65+), $5.00 child (7-11). Note: Celebrate John Overton's birthday (reduced admission) on April 9th. Trades Festival-skilled artisan demos & hands-on history (late Sept. wkend)

Discover "One Thousand Years of Tennessee History" at an 18th century historic home where docents share stories on the 50 minute tour. The site's history begins with its first inhabitants, pre-historic Native Americans. Then, the exhibits take you through the early national period, the Antebellum  period and the tragedy of the Civil War. The slaves cared for the kids almost completely. Why was sugar locked up at night? Who were some of the travelers through this house? Tours can have a lifestyle focus or a war battle focus.

The Travellers Rest Tracewalking trail has seven different stops with interpretive wayside exhibits that survey significant events in the site's, and the city's, historic past. A new observation deck overlooking Radnor Yard examines early railroad history in Nashville and explores the events at Peach Orchard Hill on the second day of the Battle of Nashville. The hill was part of the Overton Plantation. Other interpretive exhibits look at the Arabian horse farm at Travellers Rest in the 1930s and 40s, the new herb garden, the use of smokehouses in pre-industrialized America, and the Native American Mississippian civilization that once lived throughout middle Tennessee, and used the site as a village and burial ground from 1100 A.D. to 1450 A.D.

CHAFFIN'S BARN DINNER THEATRE

Nashville - 8204 Highway 100 37221. Phone: (615) 646-9977 or (800) 282-BARN. *www.dinnertheatre.com* *Admission: $40.00-$60.00 adult, $25.00 -$30.00 child.*

Musicals, comedies and mysteries combine Nashville talent with great Broadway style plays. Pre-parties and camps for kids before new shows (mostly summertime). The Main and Backstage theatres perform Thursday through Saturday evenings with occasional Sunday Matinees and Thursday Senior Matinees. Buffet is served before the evening shows.

TENNESSEE TITANS FOOTBALL

Nashville - Baptist Sports Park, 460 Great Circle Road (Home Field: The Coliseum) 37228. Phone: (615) 565-4000. *www.titansonline.com*

NFL pro team plays at the Coliseum located on the east bank of the Cumberland River, downtown. Hey kids, if you're a Titans fan and 14 years old or younger, you'll have a blast as a member of the Titans Kids Club. An official membership card lets you into a Special Titans Day at The Coliseum for members only (and your parent(s)/guardian) where you can enjoy Titans games lunch, and a chance to interact with Titans players.

BICENTENNIAL CAPITOL MALL STATE PARK

Nashville - 598 James Robertson Parkway (Located at the foot of the State Capitol between James Roberson Parkway, Jefferson Street, 6th and 7th Avenues) 37243. *www.tennessee.gov/environment/parks/Bicentennial/index.shtml Phone: (615) 741-5800. Hours: Daylight hours.*

Opened in 1996 to celebrate Tennessee's 200th birthday, the park pays tribute to the history, architecture and geography of the state. It compliments the tour of the state Capitol building. Tour Tennessee's History via a 200-foot granite map of the state. See 31 fountains designating major rivers. Marble columns divide the history of the state into decades. The park also has a Wall of History, WWII Memorial, Court of Three Stars and Walk of Counties. Picnic tables, restrooms and vending machines are located under the railroad trestle. A visitor center/gift shop is also located under the trestle.

TENNESSEE STATE CAPITOL

Nashville - (Charlotte Avenue between 6th & 7th Avenues) 37243. Phone: (615) 741-0830. www.bonps.org/tour/capitol.htm Hours: Monday-Friday 9:00am-4:00pm Admission: FREE.

The Tennessee State Capitol stands today, much as it did in 1859. The grounds of the State Capitol contain statues honoring Sam Davis, Sgt. Alvin York, and Presidents Andrew Jackson and Andrew Johnson. The tombs of President and Mrs. James K. Polk are also located on the Capitol grounds.

TENNESSEE STATE MUSEUM

Nashville - 505 Deaderick, Polk Cultural Center (Fifth Avenue, between Union & Deaderick) 37243. Phone: (615) 741-2692. www.tnmuseum.org Hours: Tuesday-Saturday 10:00am-5:00pm, Sunday 1:00-5:00pm. Closed all major holidays. Admission: FREE.

Here you'll find the historical highlights of Tennessee from different periods of time. Trace the prehistoric Woodland Indians to Daniel Boone's & Davy Crockett's time, Civil War weapons and 18th and 19th century dioramas with stories. Look for Andrew Jackson's top hat, Andrew Johnson's piano, James Polk's walking cane, Daniel Boone's musket, Davy Crockett's powder horn, or Sam Davis' torn boot (cut by soldiers to try to find enemy papers). There are reproductions of an early 19th century grist mill and authentic settings of an 18th century print shop, frontier cabin, Antebellum parlor, and Victorian painting gallery. In addition, there are exhibits about African-American soldiers in the Civil War, a free black family living in Knoxville before and after that war, and the women's suffrage movement.

The MILITARY MUSEUM is located in the War Memorial Building across the street. Exhibits cover America's overseas conflicts, beginning with the Spanish-American War and ending with World War II in 1945. On display, Sgt. Alvin York's uniform.

LONG HUNTER STATE PARK

Nashville (Hermitage) - 2910 Hobson Pike (Hwy 71, I-40 exit 226A) 37076. www.
tennessee.gov/environment/parks/LongHunter/index.shtml Phone: (615) 885-2422.
Hours: 7:00am to sunset. Admission: $3.00 per vehicle, per day.

Situated on J. Percy Priest Lake, the park features boating, sailing, fishing, hiking, picnicking, camping, swimming and wildlife observation. There are several hiking trails at Long Hunter designed to provide pleasant walking experiences for all. Among the more popular is the Lake Trail around Couchville Lake. The Lake Trail is hard surfaced and barrier free and is a self-guided nature trail. The visitors center offers exhibits and information on the park's unique flora and fauna (due to the unique cedar glade environment).

NASHVILLE SHORES OUTDOOR WATER PARK

Nashville (Hermitage) - 4001 Bell Road (Take I-40 East from Nashville to Old
Hickory Boulevard (Exit 221B) and go South. Turn Right on Bell Road) 37076. Phone:
(615) 889-7050. www.nashvilleshores.com Hours: Summertime, usually 10:00am-
7:00pm. Admission: $20.00-$25.00 (age 3+). General Admission is half-off after
3:00 pm every day. Treetop Adventure runs another $25-$50 per person.

The park features the seven largest waterslides in Tennessee, as well as giant pools, beaches and mini-golf. At over three stories tall and 180 feet long, The Hippo is the world's largest freestyle slide. Navigate the challenging obstacle course, cruise the lake with your friends, or relax on the banks of the brand new Kayak Cove. Rafts and body slides, some open, some enclosed.

A new Treetop Adventure Park (zipline/ropes course) is open to add to your outdoor fun. The Treetop Adventure Park is an aerial adventure course set in the beautiful woods of Nashville Shores featuring suspended bridges, 10 zip lines, cargo nets, ladders, Tarzan jumps, and other thrilling elements. Parker Sandbox ... complete with revolutionary irrigation system to produce wet sand ... allows for some of the best sand castle building around. Cabin, pontoon, parasailing and jet ski rentals also.

THE HERMITAGE, HOME OF PRESIDENT ANDREW JACKSON

Nashville (Hermitage) - 4580 Rachel's Lane (I-40 exit 221 onto Old Hickory Blvd.) 37076. Phone: (615) 889-2941. www.thehermitage.com Hours: Daily 9:00am-4:30pm. Extended hours April thru mid-October. Closed Thanksgiving, Christmas, and third week in January. Admission: $19.00 adult, $16.00 senior (62+), $14.00 students (13-18), $9.00 child (6-12). Note: Special events throughout the year: Battle of New Orleans, Andrew Jackson's Bday (March), Fall Fest and Summers: Sundays Live - costumed interpreters focus on Jackson's early life, the women of the Hermitage, friends of Jackson's such as Sam Houston and Ralph E.W. Earl, Jackson's military career, and music of the 19th century.

Sure looks like a President's house...

President... General... "Old Hickory"... Hero. He so dominated his era that it is now known as the "Age of Jackson" - the transition from untamed wilderness to international power.

Here is the place Jackson and his beloved wife, Rachel, called home for over 40 years and where he returned in 1837 after two turbulent terms as president. Historically costumed interpreters guide you through the 30-minute mansion tour, recounting objects and tales of his family life (original furniture, sword, glasses, Bible, etc.). On the first floor are the master bedrooms (even the room where he died). In the library, what are the huge books on the floor? On the remainder of the plantation cabins, gain insight into the daily lives of slaves working the property (growing cotton, raising livestock). Over the years, archaeologists have uncovered secrets of the plantation's past. What did they find? Toys?

The Visitors Center Museum features changing exhibits about Jackson's life and career (w/15-minute film presentation) and you can walk to the gardens where Andrew and Rachel Jackson are buried.

JOHNSONVILLE STATE HISTORIC PARK

New Johnsonville - Route 1, Box 374 (off US 70) 37134. Phone: (931) 535-2789. www.tennessee.gov/environment/parks/Johnsonville/index.shtml Hours: *Daily 8:00am-sundown. Each November they have a garrison reenactment wkend.*

This 600-acre park on the eastern side of Kentucky Lake overlooks the site of the Battle of Johnsonville. Cavalry forces under Lt. Gen. Nathan Bedford Forrest sank four Federal gunboats downstream and destroyed a Union Army supply depot at Johnsonville.

Four of the original rifle pits are beautifully preserved. Two large forts in the park are open to visitors. A six mile hiking trail leads the visitors throughout the park area. Hikers will pass by the historical portions of Johnsonville and the Union encampment including well-preserved redoubts, rifle pits, cemeteries, railroad turn-around, and home locations. Interpretive tours are available and the on-site museum exhibits the history of the battle. Fishing and hiking are available.

SAM DAVIS TRAIL

Pulaski - 100 South Second Street 38478. Phone: (931) 363-3789.

Self-guided tour provides cassettes and brochure to follow stops at sites related to Sam Davis, Boy Hero of the Confederacy, who was captured by the Union army and executed as a spy. Sites include a monument, museum, cemetery and statue on the town square. Brochures available at the Chamber of Commerce Monday-Friday FREE admission.

SAM DAVIS HOME

Smyrna - 1399 Sam Davis Road (I-24 exit 66B, Rte. 102N, follow signs) 37167. Phone: (615) 459-2341. www.samdavishome.org Hours: *Monday-Saturday 10:00am-4:00pm, Sunday 1:00-4:00pm. Extended summer hours. Admission: $8.50 adult, $6.50 senior, $3.00 child (6-12). Take off a few dollars per person for just the Museum. Note: Start with the video and then guided tour at the new Visitors Center and museum. Educators: Pre-and-post Activities: www.samdavishome.org/education. php#EDU_ACTIVITIES.*

Sam Davis was a 21-year-old Confederate Army courier soldier who was hanged as a spy when he refused to identify an informant after being captured by Union forces in 1863. His boyhood house museum situated on 168 acres is dedicated to the Confederate hero.

Visit the state-of-the-art museum and view "Sam Davis: His Life, Legend, and Legacy" video. Then, tour the 1850s historic home and original outbuildings (overseer's office, kitchen, smokehouse, and privy). Afterwards, you may tour the cemetery and slave quarters at your leisure.

His last words, now famous, were "If I had a thousand lives to live, I'd give them all rather than betray a friend". Read the last letter that Sam sent to his mother. Why was he really not a spy, just a courier for spies? See Sam's boyhood bedroom - look for the original laptop desk. Ask about Hush Puppies in the kitchen.

RIPPAVILLA PLANTATION

Spring Hill - 5700 Main Street (on Hwy. 31, one quarter of a mile south of the Saturn Parkway exit off I-65) 38402. www.rippavilla.org Phone: (931) 486-9037. Hours: Monday-Saturday 9:30am-4:30pm, Sunday 1:00-4:30pm. Reduced hours in the winter. Admission: $10.00 adult, $8.00 senior (62+), $5.00 child (6-16). Additional small fee for TN Farm LIfe Museum and the Corn Maze (fall). Guided Battlefield tours are additional fee offered at 10:30am on 2nd and 4th Thursday of the month. Battle of Spring Hill late November. Vintage Marketplace 1st wkend in December.

The restored 1855 plantation home and gardens offer a guided tour. Around Rippavilla, the grounds contain several Historic structures from the past and an excellent view of a portion of the Battle of Spring Hill fought on November 29, 1864. Just behind the Plantation house is an original Freedman's Bureau school. Further back on the property, you'll find several foundations for slave cabins and one slave residence.

This land is where, on the morning of November 30th, 1864, General John Bell Hood met with his Generals to have breakfast before the army of Tennessee marched north to engage in the battle of Franklin. The kids might be interested in the Farm Life Museum on the property to see farming machinery and artifacts from the late 19th and early 20th century.

SUGGESTED LODGING AND DINING

EMBASSY SUITES AIRPORT. **Nashville**. 10 Century Boulevard, 37214. **http://embassysuites3.hilton.com/en/hotels/tennessee/embassy-suites-nashville-airport-BNANAES/index.html** Begin your overnight stay at the Embassy Suites Nashville Airport Hotel (just southeast of town, 615-871-0033). Ride the complimentary shuttle to and from the airport, relax in the light, open atrium and unwind with complimentary snacks and beverages at the nightly Evening Reception*. Included with your reservation is a deluxe, hot, made-to-order full breakfast with loads of very fresh breakfast items available – complimentary to guests each morning. You can even take an early swim in their large, clean indoor pool. Every room here is a suite with plenty of room to spread out.

WILDHORSE SALOON. **Nashville**. 120 Second Avenue North (I-40 Broadway exit east, left on Second). Phone: (615) 902-8200 or **www.wildhorsesaloon.com**. The Wildhorse is Nashville's premiere country music dance & dining club. The Wildhorse opens daily at 11:00am, serves a full menu until midnight, and offers live entertainment beginning at 7:00pm. Often, stars or, "soon-to-be" stars perform (check their website for show schedules) while you enjoy dessert. After a satisfying meal, step onto the dance floor and work it off! Free dance lessons are offered daily (7:00-9:00pm weekdays, 2:00-9:00pm weekends). That's why anyone who visits the Wildhorse can't help but join in the dancing. Entrees range from around $16.00 ($4.00+/kids menu). We recommend the steak!

COUNTRY INN & SUITES. **Clarksville**. I-24, exit 4 (931-645-1400 or **www.countryinns.com/clarksvilletn**). Indoor/outdoor pool, full deluxe hot continental breakfast, frig & micro in every room. Rates start around $90.

Chapter 3
Middle East Area

Our Favorites...

* *Christus Gardens* - Gatlinburg
* *Ober Gatlinburg* - Gatlinburg
* *Ripley's Aquarium* - Gatlinburg
* *Knoxville Zoo* - Knoxville
* *James White Fort* - Knoxville
* *Women's Basketball Hall of Fame* - Knoxville
* *Museum of Appalachia & Norris Dam Area* - Norris
* *American Museum of Science & Energy* - Oak Ridge
* *Dollywood Attractions* - Pigeon Forge
* *Cades Cove* - Townsend

COVE LAKE STATE PARK

Caryville - 110 Cove Lake Lane (Hwy 25W) 37714. Phone: (423) 566-9701. **www.**
tennessee.gov/environment/parks/CoveLake/index.shtml *Hours:* *Daily* *8:00am-*
sunset.

Situated in a mountain valley setting on the eastern edge of the Cumberland
Mountains, there are scenic nature trails and bike trails leading through the
open grasslands and woodlands. In the winter, several hundred Canadian
Geese make this lakeshore their feeding ground. Nearby is the Devil's Race
Trace whose steep pinnacle rock affords a panoramic view. There is a 3.5
mile paved hiking trail that is also used for biking. Other activities: camping,
swimming, recreation center, boating and fishing.

RIVER RIDGE FARMS ON THE CLINCH RIVER

Clinton - 220 Mike Miller Lane 37716. **www.riverridgefarmtn.com** *Phone: (865)*
457-6774.

KITE FLYING DAYS - Free Kite Flying in hay field on top of River Ridge.
Picnic tables available for (bring your own) lunch or snack. Bring Your Own
Kite. 12:00-6:00pm each day. Wagon rides available for a small fee. See
their home page for dates.

NOSTALGIA DAYS - Special rates for grandparents who bring their
grandchildren. $4.00/person for a 20 minute ride. 12:00-6:00pm each day.
Picnic tables available for (bring your own) lunch or snack.

SPRING FLOWER TOUR - Come along for the spring farm tour through
several wildflower habitats, upland oak forests, meadow, moist river bluff.
They provide a horse drawn wagon ride to the river. (wagon holds 8 people
but the group may be of any size). The 2-hour ride takes you across the ridge
with a view of the Cumberlands and the Clinch River Valley down to the river
and along its banks. Cost: $90.00. The 4-hour ride with lunch or afternoon
snack covers the same area but allows time for the snack and for a stroll along
the river and bluff. Cost: $150.00 plus cost for a sandwich, chips, cookie and
fruit, soft drink or bottled water for each passenger.

AUTUMN COLOR TOUR - along the same route as the spring flower tour
with a wagon ride to the river. (2 hours (minimum) or 4 hours with lunch or
afternoon snack. Cost is the same as the Spring Flower Tour)

COUNTRY ROAD TOUR - a wagon ride up river road from the farm to Miller Island with an optional stop at the Sunlight Gardens wildflower nursery. (4 hours with lunch or afternoon snack. Cost: $150.00 plus cost for a sandwich, chips, cookie or fruit, soft drink or bottled water for each passenger.)

A WALK IN THE WOODS

*Gatlinburg - 4413 Scenic Drive East 37738. Phone: (865) 436-8283. **www. awalkinthewoods.com** Admission: $31.00-$44.00 per person (includes snacks). 20% discount for children (under 18) and 10% for seniors. Group discount 5+ people.*

Come for A Walk in the Woods and explore meadows sparkling with wildflowers...the majesty of old-growth trees....the beauty of a waterfall. Or stand on top of a mountain, surrounded by a floating mist.

Erik and Vesna Plakanis have hiked hundreds of miles through these mountains and they'll lead you to some of their favorite hidden spots. When you take a walk with them, you'll hear Cherokee lore and Appalachian tall tales. You'll also find out what people of this area did for food and medicine before the invention of the grocery store and pharmacy. You might even get to sample a tasty mountain treat. Every walk is geared towards enjoying the journey at a pleasant pace.

CHRIST IN THE SMOKIES MUSEUM & GARDENS

*Gatlinburg - 510 River Road (one block from the center of town, behind the aquarium) 37738. Phone: (865) 436-5155. **http:// christinthesmokies.com/index.html** Hours: Daily 9:00am-5:00pm. Last tour 45 minutes before closing. Closed Christmas Day. Admission: $12 adult, $5 child (6-12). Discount coupon on website.*

The Greatest Story Ever Told. You will have the experience of walking through a Biblical world of 2000 years ago, seeing life-size, life-like representations of important scenes from the life of Jesus Christ.

Every scene has figures and costumes with tremendous detail and includes short narratives. Look at the "Carrara Face" sculpture - not only the eyes but the entire face seems to follow your every movement (remember your parents saying... "The Lord is always watching")! The Biblical Coin Collection includes the Shekel of Tyre, possibly a part of Judas' Thirty Pieces of Silver, and "widow's mite" and "tribute penny." Looking for spiritual refreshment away from the hub-bub of the busy tourist town?...this is the place.

COOTER'S PLACE GATLINBURG

Gatlinburg - 542 Parkway (light #5) 37738. www.cootersplace.com Phone: (865) 430-9909. Hours: Most days during daylight hours. Admission: FREE. Go-Karts & Mini-Golf extra fee.

If you love "the Dukes of Hazzard", you will love a visit to Cooter's Garage... operated by none other than ol' "Cooter" himself. Ben Jones, who played the Duke Boys sidekick, is your host. It features pictures, props, costumes, and memorabilia from the television show. Look for The General Lee, Cooter's Tow Truck, Daisy's Jeep and Rosco's Police Car. On some weekend evenings, they convert the garage into a theatre, and present the "Hazzard County Hoedown," a foot stomping, hand clapping show with the best in bluegrass and classic country music. Cast members visit frequently and Cooter is in Gatlinburg almost every week.

GATLINBURG SKYLIFT

Gatlinburg - 765 Parkway (traffic light #7) 37738. Phone: (865) 436-4307. www. gatlinburgskylift.com Hours: Daily 9:00am-9:00pm. Extended hours (June-October). Admission: $14.00 adult, $10.50 child (3-11). Note: Gift shop, snack bar. Digital photos taken at the top for a fee.

Sky lift up Crockett Mountain for a scenic view of the Smokies.

GREAT SMOKY MOUNTAINS NATIONAL PARK

Gatlinburg - US 441, Newfound Gap Road (I-40 to US 66 to US 441S to park headquarters) 37738. www.nps.gov/grsm/index.htm Phone: (865) 436-1200. Hours: Daily 24/7. Visitors Centers generally 8am-5pm. Admission: FREE. Note: Molasses making and other pioneer activities are part of the park schedule each day. Educators: really interesting lesson plans on wildlife and mountain life: www.nps.gov/grsm/ forteachers/classrooms/curriculummaterials.htm

SUGARLANDS VISITOR CENTER - located near the park's main, northern entrance. Park film shown in  a state-of-the-art theater. Natural history exhibits include mounted specimens of park animals in re-creations of their habitats and reproductions of journals kept by the first park naturalists. Ranger talks and slide shows daily (spring & fall).

ALUM CAVE BLUFFS - The 100 foot high Bluffs have been used to mine saltpeter and alum used in making gunpowder, medicines and munitions manufacturing. Day hikers begin at Newfound Gap Road near CHIMNEY TOPS pinnacles Overlook (strenuous). The trail goes 5 1/2 miles one-way and goes through Arch Rock.

CHEROKEE ORCHARD ROAD AND ROARING FORK MOTOR NATURE TRAIL - Along these roads and trails are collections of historic sites including the remains of the Ogle Homestead, log cabins and a cemetery. Closed roads in winter. No large vehicle access.

CLINGMANS DOME - Highest spot in the Smokies with forest and an observation platform rising above the evergreens. Drive to Clingmans Dome Road southwest off Newfound Gap. Reaching the platform requires a steep, half-mile walk from the parking lot. Closed in winter.

CADES COVE - see separate listing

OCONALUFTEE VISITOR CENTER - located near the main southern entrance of the park. The adjacent Mountain Farm Museum contains a fascinating collection of log structures including a farmhouse, barn, smokehouse, applehouse, corn cribs and others. Demonstrations of farm life are conducted seasonally. Mingus Mill nearby.

GUINNESS WORLD OF RECORDS MUSEUM

Gatlinburg - 631 Parkway (between traffic light #6 & #7) 37738. Phone: (865) 430-7800. www.attractions-gatlinburg.com/guiness.html Hours: Daily 10:00am-9:00pm Admission: $12.99 adult, $7.99 child (3-11).

See hundreds of exhibits from the best-selling Guinness Book of World Records. Featured are memorabilia of famous record-holders: Elvis, Beatles and the Batmobile. Displays of the World's oldest man, the tallest man, or who receives the most fan mail? Look for and hop on the longest motorcycle. Also, Animal shows, Interactive record games and many areas to sit and watch Guinness News Network shows and specials. Very interesting place.

Riding the World's
Longest Motorcycle...

OBER GATLINBURG

Gatlinburg - 1001 Parkway (stoplight #9) 37738. Phone: (865) 436-5423. www. obergatlinburg.com Hours: Tramway runs Daily mid-morning to mid-evening, depending on season. Amusements open at 10:00am, close around 6:00-9:00pm.

Points of interest include:

AERIAL TRAMWAY - Enjoy spectacular views of downtown, the mountains and the Black Bear Habitat year-round from aboard a 120 passenger Aerial Tramway. Departs regularly from downtown Gatlinburg to Ober Gatlinburg Ski Resort & Amusement Park. $12.00 adult, $9.50 child (7-11). Admission good all that day and the next. You can also drive up the hill.

ALPINE SLIDE - Your ride combines a Scenic Chairlift ride up the mountain

with a fun-filled weaving, wandering dipping descent on one of two 1800' tracks through woods and ski trails. You can control your own speed with a braking device on each sled. Accelerate or slow down as you ride down the mountain through curves, straight-aways and hairpin turns into the valley. No special skills or clothing are needed.

$7.00 per person. (Ages 6 and under are free but must ride with ticketed adult age 18 or older). This ride is unique and the best ride in the park!

WILDLIFE ENCOUNTER - educational look at furry neighbors including yearlings. There's a curator on hand to answer any questions you might have. $5-7.00 per person (age 7+).

WATER RIDES (without getting too wet!) - Lightnin' Raft Ride: Come as you are - No swimwear necessary to enjoy Ober's Lightnin' Raft Ride and covered Shoot-the-Chute Water Rides. These "dry-ride" water rides have a 40 foot vertical drop. Blue Cyclone Rapids: Get a good grip on the handles of your air-inflated bob sled as you plunge from over 60 feet high into a dark hole pushing "white water" waves as you race down a fully-enclosed fiberglass chute. $5.00-$7.00 per person.

SKI TRAILS - offers 8 ski trails serviced by two quad and one double chairlift which keeps you out of lift lines and on the slopes.

SCENIC CHAIRLIFT - for $7.00 per person, The Scenic Chairlift offers one of the most awe-inspiring views of the Great Smokies. On top, your photo is taken and available to you for a small charge.

OTHER FUN - Trampoline Thing, Bungee Run (not drop), Arcade, Go Karts, Indoor Ice Skating, Kiddie Land play fort, Miniature Golf ($2.50 per person), Velcro Wall Jump. Restaurant.

RIPLEY'S AQUARIUM OF THE SMOKIES

Gatlinburg - 88 River Road (traffic light #5) 37738. Phone: (888) 240-1358. www. ripleysaquariumofthesmokies.com Hours: Daily 9:00am-9:00pm. Open later on weekends and summers. Admission: $25-27 adult, $15-$16 child (6-11), $7-$8 preschooler (2-5).

A world-class aquarium with over 1.4 million gallons of water. Travel through the world's longest underwater tunnel and see the World's greatest shark exhibit. Over 10,000 exotic sea creatures, thrilling hourly dive shows, and their touch pools allow you to touch stingrays & horseshoe crabs.

This must-see attraction is the place to see schools of fish, mean piranha, an unbelievable frogfish (don't they look like coral?), or baby-with-daddy seahorses. Walk by the top of the shark tube, then go under the tube thru the world's longest shark tube. It will "freak you out" when the first giant

Jenny...off for a deep
sea dive...

RIPLEY'S AQUARIUM (continued)

sawfish, shark or sting ray sneaks over your head! This is just amazing!

Tropical Rain Forest, Coral Reef (meet loads of reef fish like Dory and Nemo), Discovery Center, Gallery of the Seas, and Touch-a-Bay Ray.

Ooh! Aah! All over this place! Love the "mood" music they play, too!

Be sure to catch a dive show at any one of the massive tanks at this wonderful aquarium (our favorite anywhere!).

RIPLEY'S BELIEVE IT OR NOT MUSEUM

Gatlinburg - 800 Parkway (traffic light #7) 37738. Phone: (865) 436-5096. **www. ripleys.com** *Hours: Daily 9:00am-9:00pm. Open later summers. Admission: $16.99 adult (12+), $9.99 child (6-11).*

During his career, Ripley visited 198 countries, traveling a distance of 19 complete trips around the world. He began collecting unusual artifacts featured in his unique newspaper "Believe It or Not!". Meet the Giraffe-necked woman from Burmal, see a genuine shrunken head or the real Fiji Mermaid. Rolling your tongue in the trick mirror is probably the best exhibit. Seeing really is believing, or not? A little scary and bizarre for younger kids.

RIPLEY'S MOVING THEATER

Gatlinburg - (traffic light #8 on parkway) 37738. Phone: (865) 436-9763. Hours: Daily 10am-9pm. Note: Must be 43" tall to ride. This is a worthwhile stop for any families with strong backs and stomachs! Admission: $7.99-$13.99.

Feel the rain, the wind, and the snow when you visit the Ripley's Moving Theater! See two 3D movies on our giant screen. Bump, dip, and turn with seats that move in eight different directions and experience the 6 channel digital surround sound audio…truly makes you feel like you're in the show. Both movies included in one low price.

For updates & travel games visit: **www.KidsLoveTravel.com**

SPACE NEEDLE

Gatlinburg - 115 Historic Nature Trail-Airport Road (traffic light #8) 37738. Phone: (865) 436-4629. www.gatlinburgspaceneedle.com Hours: Monday-Thursday, 10:00am-10:00pm, Friday, Saturday, and Sunday, 9:00am-12 midnight. Admission: $4-$8.50 per person (age 5+).

Ride the Glass Elevator over 400 feet above the Pigeon River and step out to breathtaking 360 degree views of the Smokies by day or Gatlinburg lights by night. Don't forget your camera. Free admission to Family Arcade.

STAR CARS MUSEUM

Gatlinburg - 914 Parkway (near traffic light #8) 37738. Phone: (865) 430-7900. www.starcarstn.com Hours: Daily 9:00am-10:00pm Admission: $12.99 adult, $6.99 child (6-12). Online discount pricing.

From the Ghostbuster's ambulance, to the Beverly Hillbilly's Jalopy (look for Granny in the rocking chair), George Barris has created tons of famous Hollywood vehicles. See the Love Bug display, Jurassic Park, the talking Knight Rider car, Flintstones car and the original Batman studio and prop car. Recent additions have been the Back to the Future Time Machine, Days of Thunder Mello Yello race car and The Beach Boys' 1955 Thunderbird. Three theaters show movie footage about the cars and Barris' extreme career. Even learn the trick to how ghost cars operate. Great visuals and many favorite photo-ops.

WILD BEAR FALLS WATERPARK

Gatlinburg - *(Located in Westgate Smoky Mountain Resort) 37738. Phone: (865) 430-4800. www.wgsmokymountains.com/index.htm Hours: Daily 10:00am-11:00pm. Admission: with overnight package starts at $115.*

On the foothills of the Smoky Mountains, this waterpark is one of the biggest in the South. It certainly seems that way, with 60,000 square feet of watery fun. Between the 900-foot lazy river to the pair of slides (one body, one tube) the park also features an entry level pool for toddlers and an interactive waterplay area. Wild Bear Falls is an indoor waterpark for Westgate resort guests, but only when it wants to be. The greenhouse roof is retractable opening up when the climate is nice outside.

WORLD OF ILLUSIONS

Gatlinburg - *(Located on the Parkway in Gatlinburg, next to Reagan Terrace Mall in the heart of the Downtown Shopping District) 37738. Phone: (865) 436- 9701. www.attractions-gatlinburg.com/world_of_illusions.html Hours: Daily 10:00am-11:00pm. Admission: $6.99 adult, $4.99 child (6-11).*

Make your friends DISAPPEAR and reappear at your command. Stop a tornado with the wave of your hand. See Merlin the Wizard levitate right before your eyes or join Ali Baba's Genie who is trapped inside a glass bottle. The kids will try to figure out the endless collection of grand illusions, mystifying magic and interactive exhibits.

INDIAN MOUNTAIN STATE PARK

Jellico - *Indian Mountain Road (I-75 exit 160, go north on U.S. Hwy. 25 to State Hwy. 297, make a right on London and a left on Dairy Street) 37762. www.tennessee.gov/ environment/parks/IndianMtn/index.shtml Phone: (423) 784-7958. Hours: Daily 7:00am-sunset.*

Located at the base of the Cumberland Mountains, this park is popular with campers. Park visitors can enjoy fishing at the two small lakes, picnicking, camping, and two walking trails (one paved and one unpaved). The park has a 80' x 42' swimming pool that is open from Memorial Day through late summer.

FORT SOUTHWEST POINT

*Kingston - (near Hwy. 58, overlooking junction of TN, Clinch, and Emory Rivers)
37763. Phone: (865) 376-3641. www.southwestpoint.com Hours: Tuesday-Saturday
10am-4pm (April-September). Admission: FREE, donations accepted. Note: Best to
visit during family weekend activities & reenactments like the Early American Trade
Fair in June.*

Fort Southwest Point is the only fort in Tennessee being reconstructed on its original foundation. The completed sections of the fort include a barracks, a blockhouse and 250 feet of palisade walls. A separate building houses the welcome center and museum. The fort is owned, operated, and maintained by the City of Kingston. The fort was constructed in 1797 and remained a working fort through 1811 when it was deemed that soldiers were no longer needed. At its peak there were over 625 soldiers stationed here.

WATTS BAR LAKE AREA

Kingston - (Hwy 58) 37763. Phone: (865) 376-4201.

Watts Bar Lake provides 783 miles of shoreline for fishing, boating, swimming, camping, hiking, and skiing. There are numerous boat docks and launching ramps throughout Roane County. Watts Bar Lake's many coves and islands, with natural sand beaches, make it an ideal lake for all water sports. Bird watchers will enjoy spotting eagles, herons, egrets, woodpeckers and others along the reservoir. For breathtaking views on the valley, lake and mountains, hike through the Mount Roosevelt State Forest running thru the area (Rockwood).

EAST TENNESSEE HISTORY CENTER

*Knoxville - 601 South Gay Street (corner of Gay & Clinch Avenue, downtown) 37901.
www.easttnhistory.org Phone: (865) 215-8824. Hours: Monday-Friday 9:00am-
4:00pm, Saturday 10am-4:00pm, Sunday 1:00-5:00pm. Admission: FREE.*

A visit to the Center will bring you face to face with the region's history makers. Here you will find larger than life figures, such as David (Davy) Crockett, Nancy Ward, and Sgt. Alvin C. York. Visitors enter in the year 1750 and follow the road to statehood in 1796 in a streetscape exhibit featuring a recreated drugstore and restored streetcar.

The signature exhibit, Voices of the Land, covers narratives of many important characters. The legacy of the Cherokee Indians' "Trail of Tears" is illustrated, as well as an overcoat made by President Andrew Johnson, an East Tennessee tailor by trade.

The Children's area is called Davy's Attic with a small log cabin full of clothing like Davy Crockett wore, books and puppets. The Museum also has "hold-it" boxes stationed everywhere. The boxes contain items that children can pick up and examine that relate to the period. Find out why a Governor's battle was called the "War of the Roses" or why Oak Ridge is called the "Secret City".

KNOXVILLE SYMPHONY ORCHESTRA

Knoxville - 406 Union Avenue (most concerts @ Tennessee Theatre or Civic Auditorium) 37901. Phone: (865) 291-3310 tickets or (865) 523-1178 office. www. knoxvillesymphony.com

Artists, mascots and superstars join the Maestro and the musicians for Pops, Youth Orchestra, Family and Holiday concerts. The Family Concert pre-show has a fun "Instrument Petting Zoo" where kids touch and play real orchestra instruments and learn why and how they produce different sounds.

BLOUNT MANSION

Knoxville - 200 West Hill Avenue (downtown, corner of Gay St & Hill Ave, near Volunteer Landing) 37902. Phone: (865) 525-2375. www.blountmansion.org Hours: Tuesday-Saturday 9:30am-5:00pm, Sunday 1:00-5:00pm (early March - mid December). Closed major holidays. Admission: $6-$7.00 adult, $5 child (6-17). Educators: Constitution and Daily Living Lesson Plans: www.blountmansion. org/education/education.html

This National Historic Landmark is the 1792 home of Territorial Governor William Blount (and signer of the US Constitution), the first and only governor of the Territory Southwest of the River Ohio. It is also the birthplace of Tennessee statehood in 1796. The frontier capital still stands on the original site.

For updates & travel games visit: **www.KidsLoveTravel.com**

Known by the Cherokee Indians as "the house with many eyes," Blount Mansion watched American history parade through its rooms and on the streets outside.

Start with a short introduction video that focuses on his diplomacy with the Cherokee. Hear about the many changes to the house. Look for the elegant original Blount shoe buckles and the children's toys. See the room where the state Constitution was signed. Interesting details shared throughout the tour about Blount family life, too.

KNOXVILLE TROLLEY

Knoxville - (several downtonw locations for pickup, look for signs) 37902. Phone: (800) 727-8045. www.knoxville.org. Hours Monday-Friday 7am-6pm.

Knoxville Trolley Lines, a downtown trolley service, provides a convenienct way to see all the attractions in the downtown area. The trolley service also connects to the City's regular bus service (KAT) for trips outside of the downtown area, including malls, parks and other attractions.

In addition, a Late Line Trolley operates every 15 minutes on Friday and Saturday nights (8pm-2am) with service to Knoxville's historic Old City, the Knoxville Convention Center and other entertainment spots. Go online for a trolley map. Maps are also available at the downtown Visitors Center.

STAR OF KNOXVILLE, TENNESSEE RIVERBOAT COMPANY

Knoxville - 300 Neyland Drive (Volunteer Landing) 37902. Phone: (865) 525-7827 or (800) 509-BOAT. http://tnriverboat.com

The authentic, Mississippi-style paddlewheel boat offers a view of Knoxville from the water on a brunch, luncheon, dinner (includes food & entertainment) or sightseeing cruise ($12-$16 per person, departs 3:00pm, Thursday-Sunday, summers). Their staff is very friendly and their food is wonderful! The lunch tour is great if you want to combine a fair price ($18.00-$29.00) for yummy buffet food along with a nice historic commentary of the sites/events along the river. Join the sightseeing cruise for a look at original historic sights along the beautiful Tennessee River. During the history commentary, the Captain will show points of interest along the river. The Star of Knoxville is fully air-conditioned and heated.

...crossing the river trestle

THREE RIVERS RAMBLER

Knoxville - Neyland Drive (Volunteer Landing between Calhouns & the boathouse) 37902. **www.threeriversrambler.com** *Phone: (865) 524-9411. Hours: Saturday & Sunday 1:00pm and 4:00pm, peak weekends also 10am (April-October). Railgate tours on football game days. Christmas Express trains run long weekends (Thanksgiving thru Christmastime). Admission: $26.50 adult, $25.50 senior (55+), $15.50 child (3-12), $7.50 toddler. Pullman luxury car $19.95 (all ages). Special trains run higher.*

This vintage steam engine train takes guests on a 90-minute excursion to the Forks of the River and back, through some historic and scenic countrysides. On the trip back, stop for a while on the trestle bridge to feel like the train is flying in mid-air. Learn a little of the history of the town and famous folks who helped build it. An open air rail car is available to ride and each car is supplied with a uniformed conductor who explains the sites and is available for questions. At the Asbury Quarry, the train makes a brief stop where the locomotive is switched to return back to the depot. If it's very hot (90 F.+)... pay the extra for the air-conditioned luxury car.

EAST TENNESSEE DISCOVERY CENTER

Knoxville - 516 N. Beaman St. at Chilhowee Park (I-40 exit 392, follow signs) 37914. Phone: (865) 594-1494. **www.etdiscovery.org** *Hours: Monday-Friday 9:00am-5:00pm, Saturday 10:00am-5:00pm. Admission: $4.00-$5.00 (age 3+).*

Hands-on science exhibits, Planetarium, Kidspace area for younger kids, Lego Lab, Simple Machines and Energy experiments, and live arthropod, marine and reptile exhibits. Current living "creatures" include Madagascar giant hissing cockroaches, a honey bee colony, a scorpion, tarantula, black widow spider, millipedes, a leopard gecko and a ball python. Enter the Discovery Space shuttle and explore the universe through interactive control panel switches, spacecraft dioramas, question and answer lightboxes, and a shuttle "monitor" from which you can view space-related videos. Then step into the "Moon Room", where you can imagine what it would be like on the moon.

KNOXVILLE ZOO

Knoxville - 3500 Knoxville Zoo Drive (I-40, near Rutledge Pike exit #392) 37914. Phone: (865) 637-5331. **www.knoxville-zoo.org** *Hours: Daily 10:00am-4:30pm every day except Christmas. Spring & Fall weekend hours extended. Summer hours extended every day. Admission: $19.95 adult, $16.95 senior (65+) and child (2-12).*

...all kinds of animals live here!

Winter fees are half price. Parking $5.00 Note: Camel rides for $5.00. Safari Splash (seasonal) water play is included in admission.

Mamie, Jana, Ellie and Tonka would like you to visit them in their new African Elephant Preserve (barn, pools, mud hole and man-made trees). Another set of animals love visitors at Black Bear Falls. The exhibit has been recreated from an actual setting in the Smoky Mountains and brings visitors as close as they should get to a black bear. A 40-foot long tunnel designed as a huge hollow log provides up close "cubby" views of the black bears. Chimp Ridge is a 1.5 acre, open-air exhibit housing chimpanzees...with two full viewing areas to allow children to observe the animals. The Meerkats exhibit includes the ever-present "lookout" meerkat on duty. The zoo also features many other natural environments including Prairie Dog Pass (kids can crawl under and get a "Prairie Dog view" of the world), Pridelands, Penguin Rock and Tortoise Territory. Love the nature trails!

The KIDS COVE is like life in Cades Cove in the Smokies during the 1800s. There are theatrical cabins, vegie gardens, animals and play spaces where kids interact with animals and role-play as farmers and zookeepers. Ride the Fuzzy-go-Round, play in the water, get close to beavers and birds, sit in a giant bird's nest, practice milking a cow, climb a giant spider web, slide through a waterfall or go eye-to-eye with goats. A newer feature is the Lego Play Lodge. You can even buy what you build!

JAMES WHITE FORT

Knoxville - 205 East Hill Avenue (Volunteer Landing area) 37915. www.jameswhitesfort.com Phone: (865) 525-6514. Hours: Monday-Friday 10:00am-4:00pm (December-March), Monday-Saturday 9:30am-4:30pm (April-November). Closed during UT home games. Admission: $4.00 adult, $2.00 child (6-12).

Located on a bluff above the Tennessee River near downtown, the fort was built in 1786 by General James White, Knoxville's founder. General White brought his wife and children across the mountains from North Carolina to claim land given to him for his service in the American Revolution. Originally it consisted of his home, three cabins and the stockade wall used to protect the little community from Indian attacks and the threat of wild animals. What would the pioneers eat? They often used bread bowls instead of plates. How would you cook? What are your chores? The guides here really ask questions and engage the kids in what pioneer life was like.

KNOXVILLE ICE BEARS

Knoxville - 500 Howard Baker, Jr Drive (games played at Knoxville Coliseum) 37915. Phone: (865) 521-9991. www.knoxvilleicebears.com

Between October and March, the Ice Bears play 29 home games (part of the SPHL - Southern Pro Hockey League). $7.00-$20.00 per ticket.

VOLUNTEER LANDING

Knoxville - Volunteer Landing 37915. Phone: (865) 971-4440 or (800) 727-8045. www.cityofknoxville.org/parks/volunteer.asp Hours: Daylight hours. Admission: FREE. Note: The Star of Knoxville Riverboat and the Three Rivers Rambler train have depots near here. The FREE Knoxville Trolley has 4 different lines that take you to every possible site near or in downtown. Saves you the hassle of parking, especially weekdays and sport weekends.

Volunteer Landing offers attractions and eateries on the Tennessee River. At the Marina paddle, pontoon, and houseboats are available for rental (865-633-5004 or **www.volunteermarina.com**). There are numerous historical markers along the one-mile riverwalk, including interactive displays that tell of the historic significance of the river (waterfalls & fountains, too). The sprouting fountains on Neyland Drive are great for the kids to play in on hot summer days. You'll notice some families picnicking and others fishing from the docks. This is the place to start your visit in town because you really get a handle on the historical and fun attractions around town and in East Tennessee.

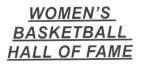

WOMEN'S BASKETBALL HALL OF FAME

Knoxville - 700 Hall of Fame Drive (I-40 exit 388, then Summitt Hill Dr. exit, near Volunteer Landing) 37915. www.wbhof.com Phone: (865) 633-9000. Hours: Monday-Saturday (summers). Tuesday-Friday 11am-5pm & Saturday 10am-5pm (rest of year). Closed on winter Sundays & Mondays except during special game event days. Closed on Christmas Day, Thanksgiving Day and Easter with abbreviated hours on some holidays. Admission: $7.95 adult, $5.95 senior (62+) & child (6-15).

The world's most interactive Hall of Fame brings college, Olympic and Pro teams' history to life. The facility features three indoor courts, an interactive locker room where visitors can hear a coach's halftime talk or "In the Huddle" pep talk with the coach (great photo ops). Put yourself in a Hall of Fame's induction pics or sit on benches amongst players. See the world's largest basketball or try your skills on the Ballgirl Athletic Playground. Dioramas feature an early basketball scene and the Red Heads actual touring car. Tip-Off Theater's inspirational film packs all the emotion of more than 100 years of history of women's basketball into 15 minutes. A very inspiring and exciting museum!

DID YOU KNOW? The world's largest basketball is located on the north end of the Hall, weighs 10 tons and sits on top of a glass staircase that resembles a basketball net.

IJAMS NATURE CENTER

Knoxville - 2915 Island Home Avenue (south of Fort Loudon Lake) 37920. Phone: (865) 577-4717. **www.ijams.org** *Hours: Monday-Friday 9:00am-4:00pm, Saturday Noon-4:00pm, Sunday 1:00-5:00pm. Grounds open 8:00am until sunset. Admission: FREE*

The regional environmental education center is surrounded by more than

150 acres of beautiful forests, meadows, ponds and gardens connected by 5 miles of trails. Special events include evening walks in the park, canoe trips, junior naturalist workshops, Bug Night, Invasive Species Movie Marathon and Music in the Park. We noticed unique exhibits like the Bird's Nests (even spider nests!), a live beehive and the Conservation Cottage (great ways to apply new recycle habits to your home as you walk thru the pretend house).

Of the Hiking Trails, we liked the Tennessee River boardwalk best. The winding boardwalk runs along the River Trail on the banks of the Tennessee River. You'll find many little critters, even Great Blue Herons, and even a small cave. Jo's Grove is a whimsical nature playscape with a fairy house and knome home.

MARBLE SPRINGS STATE HISTORIC FARMSTEAD

Knoxville - 1220 W. Gov. John Sevier Highway (at the corner of Gov. John Sevier Highway and Neubert Springs) 37920. **www.marblesprings.net** *Phone: (865) 573-5508. Hours: Wednesday-Saturday 10:00am-5:00pm, Sunday Noon-5pm. Limited winter hours for tours of buildings. Admission: Yes, varies with event. Tours: begin at top of hour at the Trading Post gift shop. $4 for tours.*

John Sevier, Tennessee's first governor, built this house when he came to the state capital in 1796. Marble Springs continued to be his home during his six terms as governor and two terms as a US Rep. This working farmstead, log structures and farm animals are used to educate the public about the life and times of the Governor.

The docents love what they do and offer group or family tours during posted hours. You'll hear about the magic carpet rules and how more than one dozen kids lived in one house, sleeping in one room…together.

HISTORIC CANDY FACTORY AND WORLD'S FAIR PARK SITES

Knoxville - 1060 World's Fair Park Drive 37996. Phone: (865) 546-5707. www. worldsfairpark.org.

A collection of shops and galleries featuring the works of local and regional artists. Also, home to a working chocolate factory (watch the ooey-gooey folks dipping chocolates by hand), near a children's playground called Fort Kid. Food cafes with light lunchtime snacks available. Also, the Art Museum Sunsphere and playful water fountains are in this square block area.

KNOXVILLE MUSEUM OF ART

Knoxville - 1050 World's Fair Park Drive (near US 441 & US 11/70, I-40 exit 388, follow signs) 37996. Phone: (865) 525-6101. www.knoxart.org Hours: Tuesday-Saturday 10:00am-5:00pm (later on Fridays), Sunday 1:00-5:00pm. Closed major holidays. Admission: $5.00 adult (age 18+). FREE child. Note: In the World's Fair Park is the Sunsphere, the 266-foot tall steel tower with a golden globe that was built for the 1982 World's Fair. Across the street is Fort Kid playground.

Highlighted in the permanent collection are works of American art created during and after the 1960s. The museum also contains five galleries, a Sculpture Terrace, and a Creative Corner. In the Corner, "put your face on" or walk into portraits, work on paper, abstract paint and read art-related books and games. The space is designed for pre-kindergarten and elementary school groups during weekdays, and self-directed for parents and children on weekends and holidays.

UNIVERSITY OF TENNESSEE CAMPUS

Knoxville - (most off or near Volunteer Blvd running thru the heart of campus) 37996. www.utk.edu.

Some sites you want to see include:

FOOTBALL HALL OF FAME: (865) 974-5789. 1704 Johnny Majors Drive, Neyland Thompson Sports Center. Monday-Friday 8:00am-5:00pm. FREE. The museum stands as a tribute to the student athletes who shaped 100+ years of Volunteer Football.

MCCLUNG MUSEUM: (865) 974-2144. 1327 Circle Park Drive, next to Visitors Info & Parking. **http://mcclungmuseum.utk.edu**. Monday-Saturday 9:00am-5:00pm, Sunday 1:00-5:00pm. Closed holidays. The Geology and Fossil History of Tennessee exhibition focuses on the many years of the state's geologic past and explores, thru graphics and animation, formations and drift. Special features are six life-size dioramas of life forms at various times with actual fossils of creatures, a replica of a giant dinosaur marine lizard or T-Rex, and actual dino eggs.

Also, Ancient Egypt and a Freshwater Mussels exhibit. Look for the many unusual fossils, both on display or under "walk-on windows" at your feet. A video portrays the journey of Cherokee through the ages. A new service is the monthly series of FREE Stroller tours!

GARDENS: (865) 974-7324. Neyland Drive at the Agriculture Campus. Daily sunrise to sunset. FREE. More than 1400 varieties of herbs and woody landscape plants, the All-America Flower Trials and TenneSelect program.

MCKENZIE SCULPTURE OF ATHLETES: (865) 974-1250. 1801 Volunteer Blvd., Thornton Athletic Student Life Center. FREE. 8:00am-4:00pm, Monday-Friday. Over 100 sculptural works including statuettes, bas-reliefs, medals, portrait medallions and plaques, which celebrate athletic achievement.

UNIVERSITY OF TENNESSEE ATHLETICS: NCAA baseball, basketball, cross-country, golf, swimming, track, volleyball & football. (800) 332-VOLS.

SAM HOUSTON SCHOOLHOUSE

Maryville - 3650 Old Sam Houston School Road (Hwy 33 north of town, follow signs) 37804. www.blountweb.com/samhouston/about_school_house.htm Phone: (865) 983-1550. Hours: Tuesday - Saturday 10:00am-5:00pm, Sunday 1:00-5:00pm. Admission: $1.00 adult, FREE child.

The oldest one-room log schoolhouse in the state (1794). Built two years before Tennessee became a state, the schoolhouse in Blount County is named for former Tennessee Gov. Sam Houston who opened the schoolhouse and served as one of its enthusiastic instructors. Students, ranging in age from 6 to 60, paid $8.00 to attend classes.

Visitors will find benches for students, the teacher's desk (and 19th century readers) and a fireplace used to warm the room. Look for the unique window covers that also served as tables.

..."Now Daniel, WHAT happened to your homework?"

Houston was attorney general and a two-term congressman while in Tennessee. In his younger years, he was adopted by the Cherokee and named "the Raven". Years later, after relocating to Texas, he became governor and president of the Republic of Texas, making him the only individual serving as governor of two states. He boldly fought for the rights of Indians in the West left after the Trail of Tears...trying to make an Indian state just for them.

Be sure to ask for the audio self-guided tour. It's very well done and easy for kids to follow.

BIG RIDGE STATE PARK

Maynardville - 1015 Big Ridge Road (From I-75 exit 122, take Hwy. 61 east approx. 12 miles) 37807. www.tennessee.gov/environment/parks/BigRidge/index.shtml Phone: (865) 992-5523. Hours: Daily 8:00am-10:00pm. Nature Center closes at 4:30pm. Admission: FREE

The heavily forested, 3,687-acre park lies on the southern shore of TVA's Norris Lake. In the Nature Center natural, historical and cultural exhibits depict scenes in the Big Ridge area including a display of mounted fauna of the Big Ridge area. The cabins are rustic in style. Everything is located mainly in one big room. Cabins have hardwood floors, kitchen, linens, many w/ fireplaces/firewood, and screened in porches. There is no air conditioning, televisions or phones. Five cabins sit lakeside. Fourteen sit on the ridge. Other activities include: camping, boating, hiking (15 miles of them for hiking only), fishing and playground/sport field areas.

MUSEUM OF APPALACHIA

Norris - Highway 61 (I-75 exit 122) 37769. www.museumofappalachia.org Phone: (865) 494-7680. Hours: Year Round during daylight hours, generally at least 9:00am-5:00pm. Closed only on Christmas. Admission: $18.00 adult (13-64), $15.00 senior (65+), $6.00 child (5-12). Educators: lessons for Living Hitory Tour Guides and written activities online under- www.museumofappalachia.org/school-amstudies.html.

Discover the pre-WWII heritage of the area at this 65-acre Appalachian history complex. John Rice Irwin's open-air museum is called "the most authentic and complete replica of pioneer Appalachian life in the world."

The museum contains over 250,000 pioneer everyday relics including 30 log structures - a chapel, a schoolhouse, cabins and barns. There's even a restaurant and craft center.

Of special interest to kids is the Mark Twain Family Cabin, Uncle John's dirt floor cabin (used as Daniel Boone's TV Home), and the Children's Corner in the Hall of Fame building. Look for a shoe carved from coal and a lot of whittlers and fiddlers who used their spare time to create famous works or just plain weird works of art? (i.e. A ukulele made from matchsticks or a "ukuweewee" – a "bed pan" banjo). A great, leisurely day trip…with lots to look see.

NORRIS DAM STATE PARK

Norris - 125 Village Green Circle (From I-75, take exit 128 and go 2.5 miles south on Hwy. 441 to the entrance of the park) 37769. Phone: (865) 426-7461. ***www.tennessee. gov/environment/parks/NorrisDam/index.shtml*** *Hours: Park Hours: Summer 8:00am - 10:00pm. Winter 8:00am - sundown. Lenoir Museum Hours: Wednesday-Sunday 9:00am-5:00pm.*

The first dam built in the TVA system, this area provided part of the electricity for the now historic Manhattan Project. The park recreation center is located at the Village Green Complex. A fee paid outdoor pool (only open June - early August), badminton, volleyball, basketball and many other activities are available to park visitors. Norris Lake is a sportsman's paradise offering 800 miles of shore-line for camping, boating, fishing and more. The park has 19 rustic vacation cabins and 10 three-bedroom deluxe cabins. All are located

in quiet, wooded settings and are completely equipped for housekeeping including electrical appliances, cooking and serving utensils, and linens. Guided activities include a nice morning lake cruise, wildlife tours, critter scavenger hunts and crafts or owl/bat walks.

18TH CENTURY RICE GRIST MILL - Originally constructed in 1798 along Lost Creek, this mill was operated by four generations of the Rice family. At times, the mill was also rigged to power a sawmill, a cotton gin, a trip hammer, and even to operate a dynamo that supplied electrical lights for the Rice home in 1899. Clear Creek Trail runs along the stream feeding the mill...very scenic...look for trout.

LENOIR MUSEUM - display of pre-industrial revolution equipment and products. When you visit the Museum, make sure and get a close look at the antique barrel organ. The organ plays ten different tunes with 110 wood pipes to make the music. In all, 44 figures are in action. These figures include dancers dancing, a clown clowning, foot soldiers marching, a woman churning and a blacksmith hard at work. Also, ask about the collection of antique mouse traps.

AMERICAN MUSEUM OF SCIENCE AND ENERGY

Oak Ridge - 300 South Tulane Avenue (I-75S exit 122, Hwy 61 turns into Hwy 95, Oak Ridge Pkwy to traffic light #10. OR, I-40 exit 376, Rte. 162N) 37830. Phone: (865) 576-3200. **www.amse.org** *Hours: Monday-Saturday 9:00am-5:00pm, Sunday 1:00-5:00pm. Closed Christmas, thanksgiving and new Years. Admission: $5.00 adult, $4.00 senior (65+) and $3.00 child (6-17). Note: Best for kids nearing middle school age and older, mostly because they have studied some of the science behind atomic energy. FREEBIES: Ask for the Scavenger Hunt -search each exhibit area for clues. Science @Home - crazy experiments:* **amse.org/visitors/science-home/.**

About one-third of the museum is devoted to the World War II Manhattan Project that created the secret city of Oak Ridge…enriching uranium that is used in nuclear bombs. One-third highlights basic science and technology and one-third is devoted to fossil fuels and alternative energy sources. There are live demonstrations for audience participation, hands-on activities, and models and devices to explore, experiment and discover more about how the world works through science.

Key spots are the: Solar Energy Project, Cold War/Civil Defense - model of atomic plant, sample lab diorama, and try-on assembly lab equipment;

What a fun way to learn about science!

Real Robots, and the Science & Tech Career Centers - modern uses for old technology facilities.

Atoms and Atom Smashers is a regularly scheduled demonstration (2-3 times daily) that combines a discussion of basic atomic structure with a "hair raising" demonstration of static electricity. Volunteer to become a very positively charged person! Funny and fun!

CHILDREN'S MUSEUM OF OAK RIDGE

Oak Ridge - 461 West Outer Drive (SR 95 to SR 62NW to Outer Drive, east) 37830. http://childrensmuseumofoakridge.org Phone: (865) 482-1074. Hours: Tuesday-Friday 9:00am-5:00pm, Saturday 10am-4pm, Sunday 1-4pm. Summer open Mondays 10am-5pm. Admission: $7.00 adult, $6.00 senior, $5.00 child (3-18). Educators: Lesson   Plans-http://childrensmuseumofoakridge.org/index.php/education/ teachers.

The motto of the museum is "please touch". Learn new ideas, develop useful skills - there is something for all ages. Tour the simulated Amazon rainforest, complete with sound effects, a waterfall, a railed walkway, beautiful murals, an observation deck high in the forest canopy-and many trees, flowers, and wild animals.

Now, watch a large model train display, or visit The Homestead consisting of three re-constructed log houses furnished with artifacts from 1850 to 1880. Each cabin depicts life on the frontier. Students frequently participate by role playing here and at City Life / Country Life (two period rooms, circa 1910).

It is not unusual to watch children walking around in wooden shoes and another group "making music" on an African Balafon in the International Hall. Waterworks or the Discovery Lab add more "touch" science.

SECRET CITY SCENIC EXCURSION TRAIN

Oak Ridge - Hwy 58, East TN Technology Park 37830. Phone: (865) 241-2140. www. techscribes.com/sarm/sarm.htm Hours: Spring, Summer and Fall season schedules. See Seasonal & Special Events. Regular Trips June - September depart on the 1st & 3rd Saturday each month at 11:00am, 1:00pm, 3:00pm and 6pm Dinner Train. Admission: $19.00 adult, $15.00 child (3-12).

Ride the Atomic Train on a 12-mile tour through the once secret K-25 Manhattan Project site and enjoy the scenic beauty of the Blair Community. Each round trip travels approx. 14 miles and lasts about one hour.

Trains are pulled by 1950s vintage Also diesel locomotives. Seating is in air-conditioned coach and a dining car, both restored from the 1940s era of passenger railroading. An open-air concession car has souvenirs and snacks for sale.

They celebrate pretty much every holiday with a themed train ride so this might be a good attraction to plan ahead for, make reservations, in advance and take a few hours out of your journey to relax and let someone elase do the driving.

WWII MANHATTAN PROJECT SITES

Oak Ridge - 302 S. Tulane Avenue 37830. Phone: (865) 482-7821. **http://** **oakridgevisitor.com/history/secret-military-facilities/#k25**

The self-guided auto tour map and/or tape of World War II's Secret City gives you the opportunity to experience the important sites built by the government for the now historic Manhattan Project - the government code name for the development of the Atomic Bomb! When this small valley grew in 1942 it consumed 1/7th of the electricity in the United States, had the 4th largest bus transportation system and employed 75,000 workers.

The highlight is the **EAST TENNESSEE TECHNOLOGY PARK OVERLOOK** (Former K-25 WWII Manhattan Project Facility) Hwy. 58, Oak Ridge, (865) 574-9683. View the historic former Manhattan Project Facility in this overlook that features pictures, historic displays and video. Daily, 9:00pm-5:00pm FREE. Small fee for tape/CD tour.

SWEETWATER VALLEY FARM

Philadelphia - 17988 West Lee Highway (I-75 exit 68, SR 323 east to Hwy 11, turn left) 37846. **www.sweetwatervalley.com** *Phone: (865) 458-9192 or (877) 862-4332. Hours: Monday-Saturday 9:00am-5:00pm. Extended store hours seasonally. Tours: Monday-Saturday every hour 11am-3pm (March-October) for $6.00 per person. Note: If you just stop in you can watch a video and sample - 15 minutes.*

Sweetwater Valley Farms boasts the best farmstead cheese in the state with names like Tennessee Aged Cheddar and Volunteer Jack. Their cows and what they eat are part of their secret. Stop in and see how cheese is made while tasting delicious samples.

The phrase "curds and whey" turns into reality when visitors are able to observe cheesemaking thru a viewing window. "Cheddar" becomes a verb which describes

Ever seen curds and whey?

the process of pasteurization, culturing (ugh!), slabbing, draining, milling, blocking and aging.

If you opt for the farm tour, you'll get a close view of the Feed Shed. Cows have 4 stomachs and need lots of food (it takes 100 lbs of feed and 50 gallons of water to make just 10 gallons of milk). They serve them 8 different grain blends made from things like cottonseed and tofu! Very interesting agricultural tour!

DOLLYWOOD

*Pigeon Forge - 1020 Dollywood Lane (one mile off the parkway) 37863. Phone: (865) 428-9494 or -9488. **www.dollywood.com** Hours: Daily 9:00am until dark (June - mid August). Otherwise open 3-5 days/week (April, May, late August, September-December). Best to view website for details. Admission: $45.00-$57.00 per person (age 4+). Second day is half price. Add about $20.00 per day if combined with Splash Country.*

Note: There are 5 sit-down restaurants and over one dozen fast food spots throughout the park...most offer BBQ and southern buffet specialties. Festival of Nations runs

April-mid May: sample entertainment, crafts, cultures and foods from around the globe (many exotic, ethnic dances and music). Harvest Celebration & Gospel Jubilee in October. DreamMore Resort on property.

SkyZip: Your hour-long SkyZip™ adventure includes experiencing up to four treks ranging in length from 700 to nearly 1,000 feet. Plus teeter above the treetops on a 100-foot-long swinging bridge. Each tour offers a distinctive point-of-view as you venture from point to point on an elevated and inclined wire high above the ground. SkyZip Ziplines is $49.

...BIG waterfall fun!

Dolly Parton grew up with the Smokies as her playground, so she decided to theme her entertainment park after a combination of her childhood and the Appalachian Mountains. 22 thrilling rides (from a 70mph triple loop coaster to leaping over a mountain waterfall at 50mph) and over 40 shows (from new country to the '50s to gospel acts) are the big draw here. Explore unique areas where kids run and soak each other at Beaver. Adventures in Imagination includes an interactive museum of Dolly's life and a four-dimensional simulator ride on a journey through the Smoky Mountains (fun, but very jerky and bumpy). Browse thru dozens of Master Craftsmen's showcases where old-art like glassblowing, blacksmithing, wagonmaking, etc. are demonstrated. Each season brings a different theme but summertime brings popular icons of children's entertainment in a character show, extreme sports shows, street performers and many hands-on activities. Worried about hot summer days…most of the rides get you wet…or, at least windblown! Also, most of the rides are for all school-aged kids…just check with someone exiting the ride if you have concerns about the "scare" factor.

SPLASH COUNTRY, DOLLYWOOD'S

Pigeon Forge - 1020 Dollywood Lane (turn off parkway at stoplight #8) 37863. Phone: (865) 428-9488. **www.dollyssplashcountry.com** *Hours: Mid-May to early September. Daytime hours. See website for details. Admission: $35.00-$45.00 (age*

4+). Combo packages with Dollywood at a discount available. Note: Showers, changing rooms, lockers and concessions. Bring your own towels.

Located on 25 wooded acres, this waterpark provides life jackets and lifeguards for safety. There's a 25,000 sq. ft. Wave Pool (large enough to get a thrill in your tube with room to spare), 13 Water Slides (from mild to wild), a Lazy River (the longest and most pleasant we've seen!), and two interactive Child's Play areas. Raintree Hollow is a large area of the complex with two slides for the water blasters. Mountain Twist is a 3-slide complex with twists, turns and a 42-foot drop. RiverRush is a water roller coaster! Some areas are shady, some in the sun. Lots of places to lounge near every ride make the park very manageable for families.

FUN TIME TROLLEYS

Pigeon Forge - *37863. www.pigeonforgetrolley.org Phone: (865) 453-6444. Hours: Daily 8:00am - Midnight early March through October. Daily 10:00am - 10:00pm, November and December. Closed on Thanksgiving, Christmas Eve and Christmas Day. All Day Pass $2.50.*

Fun Time Trolleys takes you to more than 100 stops throughout the city…for only 50 cents per person. Just look for the bear and they will be there shortly. See the city of Pigeon Forge and the city of Sevierville in a safe and unique way. The Trolley driver will accept exact fare only. The Trolley driver cannot make change. The fares apply each time you board the trolley.

PIGEON FORGE THEATERS

Pigeon Forge - *Parkway 37863. Admission: Varies between $10.00-$30.00 per person.*

HATFIELD & MCCOY DINNER & SHOW - High-flying Country Dinner Revue, 5:00pm & 8:00pm, shows daily. (865) 908-7469 or (800) 985-5494. **www.hatfieldmccoydinnerfeud.com**.

THE BLACKWOOD BROTHERS - Great gospel to classic country music. Breakfast show 10am. (865) 908-7469 or **www.smokymtnopry.com/shows/blackwoods-morning-variety-show**.

AMERICAN JUKEBOX THEATER - Best of the '50s, '60s, & '70s music. Showtime 7:30pm. Opens in March. (865) 774-7469 or **www.americanjukeboxtheater.com**

COUNTRY TONITE THEATRE - the show's foundation is country music, from classics to contemporary. Award-winning cloggers. Opens in March. (865) 453-2003 or **www.countrytonitepf.com**

COMEDY BARN THEATER - Clean comedians, magicians, jugglers, fire-eaters plus funny Country Bands and barnyard animals. Shows nightly (except January/February) @ 8:15pm, some matinees on weekends, (865) 428-5222 or **www.comedybarn.com**.

BIBLICAL TIMES DINNER THEATER - The story is told through the prophet Samuel's eyes. It pairs live and filmed actors with holographic technology and computer-generated special effects to create a production that will appeal to all ages. www.**biblicaltimestheater.com**

SCENIC HELICOPTER TOURS

*Pigeon Forge - 2491 Parkway 37863. Phone: (865) 453-6342. www.scenichelicopters.
com Hours: Monday - Saturday 10:00am - Dark (weather permitting), Sunday Noon
- Dark (weather permitting). Admission: Flights begin as low as $28.00 per person
and go up in price.*

Spectacular views of the mountain area. You can say you "Flew over the
Smokies"!

RIVER ISLAND (8-9 miles) - $28.00 per person - This flight takes you over
the French Broad river and rolling hills of Sevier County, from 1000 feet
above where you can see the beautiful panorama of the area. With an air
speed at over 100mph, you will cover almost 8 miles.

DOUGLAS LAKE (10-12 miles) $33.00 per person - This flight soars up
over 1200 feet, above pretty Tennessee farm country, on the way to Douglas
Dam with a beautiful lake view.

BLUFF MOUNTAIN (14-16 miles) $66.00 per person - As you depart from
the heliport toward the lower foothills of Bluff Mountain at 1500 feet you
will be amazed at the view of the Smoky Mountains.

FOOTHILLS (22-24 miles) $46.00 per person - This seems to be the most
popular flight taken by couples and families who want to take advantage of
the opportunity to fly over beautiful mountains as well as enjoy a little city
view. You'll be snapping pictures the entire flight.

TITANIC

*Pigeon Forge - 2134 Parkway 37863. Phone: (865) 453-4777. www.
titanicpigeonforge.com Hours: Open 9:00am-8:00pm daily. Admission: $23 adult,
$12 child (5-12).*

Towering 100 feet above street level, this ship-shaped venue holds more
than 400 artifacts and historic treasure. It allows each visitor to encounter
the personal, heroic and magic stories of Titanic's passengers. Each guest is
assigned a passenger or crew member to follow on the timeline. Often, you
see items from that person during the tour. The museum does a wonderful
job to re-create many parts of the ship including the magnificent grand
staircase and the dining room. See where each class slept for the night or
try to stay afoot as the museum floor slopes down like the sinking ship. You

also have the opportunity to see what 28 degrees feels like (temperature of frozen water surrounding the ship). Younger kids may be a little scared when they get to the part of the ship sinking (noises). Staff are peppered throughout in period costume who are kind and very helpful.

Interactive Area and Tot Titanic PLay and Learn Room. Climb the decks of the siniking Titanic (watch, it gets pretty slanted), drive the ship around a massive virtual iceburg, type out Morse Code (mayday!), tie knots and then ride in a replica wooden life boat to safety. In the Titanic Play room, meet "polar" the bear. This virtual bear interacts with the children in a very Disney like experience! Btw, did your passenger survive?

TRACK FAMILY RECREATION CENTER, THE

Pigeon Forge - 2575 Parkway (traffic light #3) 37863. Phone: (865) 453-4777. ***www. funatthetrack.com*** *Hours: Open 9:00am or 10:00am until dark. Admission: $3.00-$9.00 per ride per person.*

The action-packed family recreation center features the ultimate in go-kart tracks, like the Wild Woody, a three-tiered go-kart/roller coaster hybrid. Themed miniature golf, splash 'em on bumper boats, or test your courage from the top of the bungee jumping tower. Other features: The Rio Grande Train, The Carousel, The Red Baron Plane Ride, Spin Tops, Swings, Ferris Wheel, and Noah's Lark Giant Swinging Boat. Clean, safe environment... easy to manage all the rides as a family.

WONDER WORKS

Pigeon Forge - 100 Music Road, Parkway 37863. Phone: (865) 868-1800. ***www. wonderworkstn.com*** *Hours: Daily 9:00am-midnight. General Admission: $22.99 adult, $14.99 child (4-12). Each activity extra. Combo pricing for dinner show and amusements combined.*

Tennessee's only upside down attraction is an amusement park for you mind. This unique attraction features over 100 interactive hands-on exhibits. This part science museum, part entertainment venue is located on the Parkway in the former Music Mansion Theater. As you move from room to room, you will encounter different theme zones including: Disaster Zone, Challenge Zone, Space Zone, Sound & Light Zone, Wonder Zone, Far Out Illusion Gallery and Lazer Tag & Arcade. Wonder of Magic evening shows performs sleight -of-hand tricks, comedy and audience interaction.

DIXIE STAMPEDE, DOLLY PARTON'S, DINNER & SHOW

Pigeon Forge - *3849 Parkway (near stoplight #8 on the parkway) 37868. Phone: (865) 453-4400 or (800) 356-1676. www.dixiestampede.com Hours: Year-round, almost daily at 6:00pm. Most Fridays, Saturdays and summer season also 8:30pm. Admission: $50 Adult, $25 Children (4-11yrs). Come hungry. Note: Meet the horses in the show from 10:00am until showtime on display along the horsewalk outside. Farm animal allergies? Be prepared with antihistamines.*

The Smokies most fun place to eat! I guarantee it, says owner, Dolly Parton. The very action-packed dinner and show features 32 magnificent horses, beautiful costumes, gallant heroes, incredible horsemanship, and a stand to-your-feet patriotic finale…all in the massive indoor arena. All this excitement while enjoying a fabulous four-course feast that you have to eat with your hands! The soup and chicken are wonderful and while you're finishing your main course, you may be asked (kids and parents) to participate in several races - don't worry, everyone laughs with you and cheers you on. You'll love the dancing horses and the pig and giant ostrich races! The comic, Skeeter, is the best! Before the show, kick back with live bluegrass music and comedy in the Carriage Room (snacks served there beforehand).

MEMORIES THEATRE

Pigeon Forge - *2141 Parkway (between stoplights #0 & #1) 37868. Phone: (800) 325-3078. www.memoriestheatre.com Hours: Tuesday-Saturday 8:00pm. Reduced hours during non-peak seasons. Admission: $25.00 adult, $20.00 teen, $5.00 child (7-12). Prices vary by season and event.*

Tributes to legendary music artists are featured in Memories' Salute to Elvis & Friends. "Elvis" is joined by other entertainers who pay honor and perform as Kenny Rogers, Roy Orbison, Buddy Holly, the Blues Brothers, Loretta Lynn, Patsy Cline and Tim McGraw. The "Friends" begin the show. Their amazing look-alikeness, mannerisms and vocal talent really impressed us! Good show to take kids to after they've visited Graceland or are fans of some of the famous performers that started back in the '70s and '80s.

RAINFOREST ADVENTURES

*Sevierville - 109 Nascar Drive (off Parkway, north at Walmart, west at Nascar Dr) 37862. Phone: (865) 428-4091. **www.rfadventures.com** Hours: Daily 9:00am-5:00pm, except Christmas day. Admission: $11.99 adult, $9.99 senior (55+), $6.99 child (3-12). Discounts online.*

One of the largest tropical zoos in the world is home to tropical birds, pythons and anacondas, tree frogs and giant tortoises...all indoors. Your Jungle Expedition begins once you pass through the recreated ancient ruins, past a 25 foot tall jungle waterfall, and enter the Rainforest. Favorites may be the animated parrots, cockatoos or Zabu, the Madagascan ring-tailed lemur. Fuzzy white Cotton Top Tamarins are some of the smallest, and rarest monkeys on earth. Each season, they list where to look for new arrivals - bouncing baby animals. Live shows are conducted daily on each of the odd hours of the day.

TENNESSEE MUSEUM OF AVIATION

*Sevierville - 135 Air Museum Way (I-40 exit 407, US 66 southwest, then North on US 441) 37864. **www.tnairmuseum.com** Phone: (866) AV-MUSEUM. Hours: Monday-Saturday 10:00am-6:00pm, Sunday 1:00-6:00pm. Closed Thanksgiving and Christmas. Admission: $12.75 adult, $9.75 senior (60+), $6.75 child (6-12).*

Experience warbirds in this ever-changing exhibit space. You might even witness a demonstration war plane fly-by. Dioramas with videos help explain the progress of flight and how planes were used in wartime. The flight simulator on combat missions is probably the most fun for kids. Worth it for big wartime aviation buffs... otherwise, somewhat pricey for the amount of family interest. Their special events (listed on their website) are the best time to visit.

FORBIDDEN CAVERNS

Sevierville - 455 Blowing Cave Road (I-40 exit 432A, Hwy 411S OR I-40 exit 407, Hwy 66S to US 411N) 37876. www.forbiddencavern.com Phone: (865) 453-5972. Hours: Monday-Saturday 10:00am-6:00pm (April-November). Admission: $10.00 adult, $9.00 senior, $5.00 child (5-12).

The one hour walking tour past shimmering formations, towering natural chimneys, numerous grottos and a crystal-clear stream is added to with special lighting effects, a sound presentation and information from tour guides. Look for the largest wall of rare cave onyx known to exist and remnants of moonshining apparatus.

MUSCLE CAR MUSEUM, FLOYD GARRETT'S

Sevierville - 320 Winfield Dunn Parkway (I-40 exit 407, southwest on US 66 9 miles) 37876. Phone: (865) 908-0882. www.musclecarmuseum.com Hours: Daily 9:00am-6:00pm (April-December). Closed Thanksgiving and Christmas. Admission: $11 adult, $5.00 child (8-12). FREE (age 7 and under).

Large, newer collection of American Muscle Cars (90+) including factory lightweights, rare engines, superstock cars and NASCAR items. Begin with Elvis' limo and Cadillac. Even see the famous TNN "Shadetree Mechanic" T-Bucket! Fun stop for racing fans on your way to the Smoky Mountains.

Plenty of horsepower here!

SMOKY MOUNTAIN DEER FARM & EXOTIC PETTING ZOO

Sevierville - 478 Happy Hollow Lane 37876. Phone: (865) 428-DEER. www. deerfarmzoo.com Hours: Daily 10:00am-5:30pm. Closed Thanksgiving and Christmastime. Admission: $10.99 adult, $6.99 child (3-12). Feed cups $2.50. Note: Pony rides and horseback riding ($7.00-$20.00 extra).

Start or end your Smoky Mountain vacation at the Smoky Mountain Deer Farm & Exotic Petting Zoo. You can do more than just look at the deer at the Deer Farm. You're offered a rare opportunity to walk among, pet and feed over 100 hand-tamed deer as well as being able to interact with many other animals from around the world. See and pet zebra, zonkeys, camels, reindeer, kangaroos, wallabies, prairie dogs, miniature goats, exotic cattle, miniature horses and donkeys, and emu. The mini-mini horses are adorable. Fawns are born in June and July - the Bucks' antlers growing April through August; in full rack September - March.

TENNESSEE SMOKIES BASEBALL

Sevierville (Kodak) - 3540 Line Drive (Smokies Park, I-40 East to Hwy. 66, Exit 407) 37764. www.smokiesbaseball.com Phone: (865) 286-2300. Tickets: $5-$10 per seat.

Take your family out to the ballgame in a new stadium for AA affiliate for the Chicago Cubs, the Tennessee Smokies. Concessions and Double Play Café restaurant.

CADES COVE

Townsend - 10042 Campground Drive (just off Hwy 321, head south out of Townsend) 37882. Phone: (865) 448-4108 Park or (865) 448-6286 Hayrides. www. smokymountains.org Hours: Basically, sunrise to sunset. Note: Many cabin resort rentals are nearby. Orientation Center has $1.00 book that explains every marker and stop. Plan to spend hours exploring here. Be sure to pack picnic. No food service.

Cades Cove's 11-mile loop road takes visitors back to the late 19th century (pass many historic structures). The Primitive Baptist Church is made of wood and has wonderful acoustics. There are many campgrounds, canoeing, horseback riding, hiking, biking and tubing opportunities thru various outfitters.

You'll want to photograph the scenery and wildlife (1,500 kinds of flowering plants and more than 500 black bears). The best time for wildlife viewing early morning or late afternoon. Cable Mill is a water-powered grist mill which demonstrates the grinding of corn into meal. There is a Visitors Center at

"Postcard-like" scenery everywhere...

the site with restrooms and a gift shop. Hayrides are a unique and fun way to see Cades Cove from June-October (fee of $6.00-8.00). Many of our readers have their favorite spots they go back to every year.

TUCKALEECHEE CAVERNS

Townsend - 825 Cavern Rd. (follow signs off US 321) 37882. Phone: (423) 448-2274. www.tuckaleecheecaverns.com Hours: 10:00am-6:00pm (April-October). 10:00am-5:00pm (last half of March and first half of November). Admission: $16.00 adult, Half Price child (5-11).

Indians initially discovered these caverns and used them as a hideout. Later two boys played around the area and re-discovered the cave. Then, walkways were build of concrete and lighting added. Tours of the stream passage, Fairyland, and many formations are conducted approximately every 30 minutes by a guide.

WOOD N STRINGS DULCIMER SHOP

Townsend - 7645 East Lamar Alexander Parkway (Hwy 321) 37882. Phone: (865) 448-6647. www.clemmerdulcimer.com Hours: Monday-Saturday 10:00am-5:00pm.

Note: Just west of Mike's place is the LITTLE RIVER RAILROAD & LUMBER COMPANY MUSEUM (open daily summer and October, weekends rest of spring and fall). The museum has a locomotive out front and is filled with FREE viewing of how the town was formed and the industry behind it.

Home of the "Clemmer Dulcimer" and "Ban-Jammer" (Mike Clemmer's inventions). The dulcimer is a wire-

A little country pickin'...

stringed, fretted musical instrument with its origin in the Appalachian Mountains. It means "sweet song" and Mike likes to make each instrument from specially chosen wood blends to continuously create that special sound. He'll show you the materials he uses and demonstrate many instruments with different sounds. If you're there on a Saturday (around 7:00pm), seasonally, they host a Pickin' Porch out front where locals can jam and spectators can enjoy. What a sweet sounding treat! (Be sure to purchase Mike's CD before you head over to Cades Cove, down the road).

FROZEN HEAD STATE PARK

Wartburg - 964 Flat Fork Road (US 27 north to SR 62 east to CR 116 north) 37887. www.tennessee.gov/environment/parks/FrozenHead/index.shtml Phone: (423) 346-3318.

This large wilderness, forest area is named for a 3,324 foot peak which is often covered in ice or snow. 50 miles of backpacking and day-hiking trails provide wildlife and wildflower-viewing. This is one of the finest trail systems in Tennessee. There are over 50 miles of very scenic and challenging foot trails throughout this wild and rugged 11,876 acre mountain park. The trails feature waterfalls, giant sandstone rock formations, bluffs, abundant wildlife and 14 mountain peaks over 3,000 feet in elevation. Other activities: camping, horseback riding and fishing.

SUGGESTED LODGING AND DINING

CALHOUNS ON THE RIVER. Knoxville. 400 Neyland Drive, Volumteer Landing. 37915. Phone: (865) 673-3355. **www.calhouns.com**. Try the "best ribs in America" and their chicken so you can get an idea of what the locals rave about. Then, move on to other temptations like Buffalo Wings or Fried Green Tomatoes, to the enticing steak or catfish with their own recipe flavors. Some unique signature items include: White Chili, Turkey Creek Salad, Creamy Country Slaw, Smoky Mountain Baked Beans and Spinach Maria sides. Land a sweet ending with freshly made seasonal Strawberry Shortcake or Key Lime Pie. Calhoun's is accessible by boat and has its own dock for mooring your vessel. There is an outside deck as well as an enclosed deck with a panoramic view of the Tennessee River. Daily lunch and dinner served.

BEST WESTERN CEDAR BLUFF. **Knoxville**. I-40/75 exit 378A. (865) 539-0058 or (800) 348-2562 or **www.bwcedarbluff.com**. They have reasonable, clean, spacious rooms with an outdoor pool and hot breakfast. Each room has a refrigerator and recliner. The king rooms also offer a microwave and a loveseat sofa bed. Located on the west side of town with loads of restaurants nearby. Family Vacation Pkg starts at $89.

HOLIDAY INN SELECT, **Knoxville**. 525 Henley Street, (865) 522-2800). If you want to be in the middle of it all…we suggest this hotel for a downtown location at Worlds Fair Park. They offer seasonal Family Packages (see **www.knoxville.org**) and have a mini-fridge in the room. Their indoor pool/whirlpool was clean and warm. Kids eat free with paying adults in their restaurant.

MAINSTAY SUITES - **Pigeon Forge**. (Near traffic light #6). 410 Pine Mountain Road, 37863. (888) 428-8350 or (865) 428-8350. **www. mainstaypigeonforge.com**. All suites include a small kitchen, continental breakfast and fantastic indoor/outdoor pools plus a tube mini-lazy river!

THE DINER - **Sevierville**. 550 Winfield Dunn Pkwy. 37876 (Hwy 66 next to Lowes). **www.thediner.biz**. This 50s diner is reasonably priced and has so much to choose from. Smiley fries. Cruise ins.

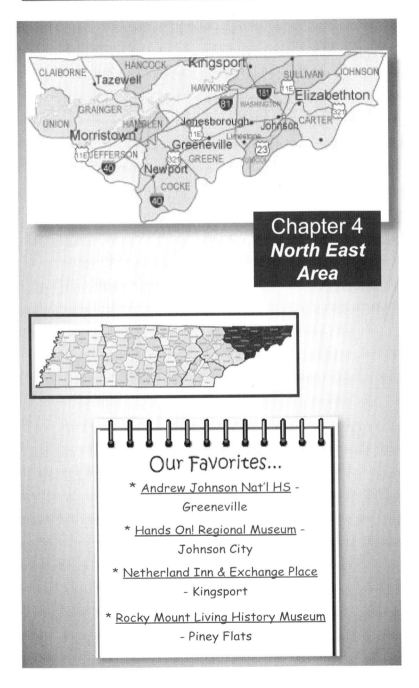

Chapter 4
North East Area

Our Favorites...

* Andrew Johnson Nat'l HS - Greeneville

* Hands On! Regional Museum - Johnson City

* Netherland Inn & Exchange Place - Kingsport

* Rocky Mount Living History Museum - Piney Flats

BRISTOL CAVERNS

Bristol - 1157 Bristol Caverns Highway (just off US 421S on Hwy 435) 37620. Phone: (423) 878-2011. www.bristolcaverns.com Hours: Monday-Saturday 9:00am-5:00pm, Sunday 12:30-5:00pm (mid March - October). Slightly reduced hours rest of year. Closed winter holidays. Admission: ~$10/person. Call for current prices.

Once used by Indians as an attack and escape route, the underground river that carved the chambers years ago remains an intriguing feature of this cavern. A guided tour (departs about every 20 minutes) of the caverns includes a walk along the banks of an underground river. Visitors can take the lighted asphalt trail that goes through several levels of the caverns.

BRISTOL MOTOR SPEEDWAY & DRAGWAY

Bristol - 2801 Bristol Highway 11E 37620. Phone: (423) 764-1161 tickets. www.bristolmotorspeedway.com

A motorsports and entertainment facility, esp. for NASCAR events. BMS boasts 147,000 grandstand seats plus luxury skyboxes. One of the classic speedways hosts races June-August with special events like NHRA Dragway races and the York Ice Rink (winter).

THEATRE BRISTOL

Bristol - 512 State Street (I-81N exit 3) 37620. www.theatrebristol.org Phone: (423) 968-4977. Note: Enjoy a look at the "Birthplace of Country Music" Mural (along State Street) and Museum (in the Mall).

The region's oldest children's theatre, The Discovery Series for children consists of five musicals (ex. Wizard of Oz, Sound of Music). Many selections are taken from required reading curriculum for Elementary students. Many of the regular shows have family themes, too. Some of the performances take place in the ARTspace, a multi-purpose, black box theatre which seats up to 100. Most of the performances take place in The Paramount Center for the Arts, a restored 756-seat movie palace which has been converted to use as a performing arts theatre.

CHRISTY MISSION

Del Rio - *1425 Chapel Hollow Road   37727. Phone: (423) 487-2648.* **www.** *discovercockecounty.com/_delrio/drattrac/drchrmis.htm   Admission: FREE, donations accepted.*

This is the actual location (Cutter Gap) where the book, plays and Broadway music, movie and television series "Christy" (by Catherine Marshall) was based on! A Story about a girl from North Carolina who came here to educate mountain children approximately one hundred years ago. Visit the original mission property (building is gone) anytime, or pick up a map of other sites along the road. The O'Teale Cabin is still available for touring.

SYCAMORE SHOALS STATE HISTORIC AREA

Elizabethton - 1651 West Elk Avenue (I-181 exit 31, take Rte. 321/67 to town) 37643. www.tennessee.gov/environment/parks/SycamoreShoals/index.shtml   Phone: (423) 543-5808. Hours: Tuesday-Saturday 9:00am-4:00pm, Sunday 1:00-4:30pm. Note: Visitors Center houses a museum, theater, and gift shop. Picnic area and 2-mile walking trail. Summer activities include Colonial Days & critter projects.

Step back in time to the turn of the 18th century with a visit to a Reconstruction of Fort Watauga as it stood in 1776. The original fort was excavated about a mile away on the shores of the Watauga River. The Overmountain Men mustered here in September 1780 before their march to fight the battle of King's Mountain. Here was established the first permanent American settlement outside the original 13 colonies and the Watauga Association - the first majority-rule system of American democratic government was formed in 1772. Playing in a fort is pretty fun.

CARTER MANSION - 1013 Broad Street (in downtown on Rte. 67/321), 543-6140. The oldest frame house in Tennessee, was the home of John and Landon Carter. Built (1775-1780) on lands bought from the Cherokee, the structure is open for tours. (mid-May - mid-August, Wednesday-Sunday and by appointment). Built on the Woodland burial mound, it's affiliated with the first government, the Wataugans. The oldest know paintings in Tennessee were uncovered here…probably done by a child or amateur.

ERWIN NATIONAL FISH HATCHERY & UNICOI COUNTY HERITAGE MUSEUM

Erwin - 1715 Old Johnson City Hwy./ 520 Federal Hatchery Rd. (Hwy. 107, Just off I-181) 37692. Phone: (423) 743-4712 hatchery or (423) 743-9449 museum. http://southeast.fws.gov/erwin/index.html   Hours: Hatchery Weekdays 7:00am-3:30pm. Museum: Daily 1:00-5:00pm (May-September), Weekends only (October). Admission: Donations

The hatchery produces rainbow trout in order to provide up to 15 million trout eggs to federal and state hatcheries for their trout stocking programs. Free hatchery group tours available by request. On the grounds of the hatchery, is a turn-of-the-century frame home of the former superintendent of the hatchery housing a Main Street representation, Indian artifacts, railroading, and Blue Ridge Pottery exhibits about the area.

ANDREW JOHNSON NATIONAL HISTORIC SITE

Greeneville - 101 North College Street (I-81N take exit 23 to Rt. 11E north to College & Depot Sts., downtown) 37743. www.nps.gov/anjo Phone: (423) 638-3551. Hours: Visitors Center Open 9:00am-5:00pm daily. Closed New Years Day, Thanksgiving and Christmas. Admission: FREE

Home of the nation's 17th President, the Andrew Johnson National Historic Site honors the life and work of the President and preserves his home, tailor

A tailor's tool…
a "goose iron"

shop, and grave site. He worked his way from tailor to President. His presidency, from 1865 - 1869, illustrates the United States Constitution at work following Lincoln's assassination and during attempts to reunify a nation that had been torn by civil war. The museum displays a 14-minute video at the Visitors Center (which is where you should begin…find out how dearly he cherished the Constitution). Children have the opportunity to try on period clothing and then view Andrew Johnson's original Tailor Shop and his tools. Try lifting an iron from those days. If you listen closely, you can hear Johnson cutting fabric. Also, each

For updates & travel games visit: **www.KidsLoveTravel.com**

visitor is given a replica of an 1868 impeachment ticket upon entering the Visitor Center. Visitors are encouraged to discover more about Andrew Johnson and the events leading up to his impeachment. What is the definition of impeachment? You can cast your vote to acquit or to find the president guilty at the "One Vote Counts" exhibit. Great intro to the political process and the enduring-ness of the Constitution.

ABRAHAM LINCOLN MUSEUM

Harrogate - Lincoln Memorial University (US 25E near the Cumberland Gap National Historic Park) 37752. www.lmunet.edu/museum/index.html Phone: (423) 869-6235. Hours: Monday-Friday 10:00am-5:00pm, Saturday Noon-5:00pm, Sunday 1:00-5:00pm. Admission: $5.00 adult, $3.50 senior, $3.00 child (6-12). Educators: Civil War Lesson Plans: www.lmunet.edu/museum/education/index.shtml

At the main entrance to the University stands the magnificent Abraham Lincoln Museum exhibiting many rare items - the silver-topped cane Lincoln carried the night of his assassination, a lock of his hair clipped as he lay on his death bed and two life masks made of Lincoln. The founding of this University by Union General Oliver Otis Howard fulfilled President Lincoln's desire to help the people of East Tennessee who had remained loyal during the Civil War. Even see the bed Lincoln slept in on his birthday in 1861.

HANDS ON! REGIONAL MUSEUM

Johnson City - 315 East Main Street (I-181 exit 32 west, between Market & Main, downtown) 37601. www.handsonmuseum.org Phone: (423) 434-HAND. Hours: Mondays 9:00am-5:00pm (June - August). Tuesday-Friday 9:00am-5:00pm, Saturday 10:00am-5:00pm, Sunday 1:00-5:00pm. Closed most major holidays. Admission: $8.00 (age 3+). Note: Programs are offered throughout the day.

Some favorite exhibits: The Discovery Room is a creative, hands-on exhibit allowing children to explore their creativity while learning about recycling; WKID-TV allows children to look at the "behind the scenes" workings of a TV station; The TVA/Water Play Dam - teaching about water power and electricity; Get Moving! features a Saturn automobile for children to explore both inside and out (including under the hood); The Ark focuses on exotic animals and touching the pelts provided. The amazingly large stuffed animals peeking out from windows of the Ark is so cleverly displayed!

Hands On! Regional Museum *(cont.)*

The Katie Ellen Coal Mine has tunnels for exploring that shows the impact of mining of the local areas; Alive & Well features live animals such as turtles, fresh water fish, lizards, and snakes - even touch a Chocolate Chip starfish!; Wings Airplane/Flight Simulator exhibit; and Kids Bank - A working kid's ATM and money trivia round out this educational exhibit. The volunteers' ideas and work here make it very unique.

TIPTON-HAYNES HISTORIC SITE

Johnson City - 2620 South Roan Street (I-181 exit 31, left on University, left on South Roan) 37605. www.tipton-haynes.org Phone: (423) 926-3631. Hours: Tuesday-Saturday 9:00am-3:00pm (April-mid November). Closed Thanksgiving and day after. Only open select winter weekdays. Admission: varies by season. It's best to call first before you plan a visit as they often are not open the full day.

Home of Col. John Tipton, John Tipton, Jr. and Confederate Senator Landon C. Haynes whose lives represent the history of Tennessee from pre-colonial times to Reconstruction. The site's first white resident was Colonel John Tipton, who built a substantial log house in 1784.

Tipton was a signer and a framer of the first Tennessee Constitution. In an area including this site, the Battle of Franklin was fought in 1788, the only armed skirmish between supporters of the proposed state of Franklin and their opponents, who were loyal to North Carolina. John Tipton, Jr. served in the Tennessee General Assembly from 1803 to 1819. In 1839, the estate was given as a wedding present to Landon Carter Haynes, who had the home enlarged and renovated. He also had built a free-standing office building, where he practiced law.

Haynes is chiefly remembered for his sponsorship of railroad-building and for his brilliant oratorical skills. Ten original and restored buildings and a newer museum are housed here. Often called Tennessee's most historic site because so much government-related activity occurred here.

WETLANDS WATER PARK

Jonesborough - 1523 Persimmon Ridge Road 37659. Phone: (423) 753-1553 or (888) 622-1885. www.wetlandsjonesborough.com Hours: Summers Monday-Saturday 10:00am-6:00pm, Sunday Noon-6:00pm. Admission: $12.00 adult, $9.00 senior (55+) & child (12 & under). Half price after 3:00pm.

A rampage down the 200 foot giant flume or a boardwalk stroll thru the natural wetlands combines fun and nature. There are also otter slides, a Lazy River, pool, children's play area, volleyball courts, concessions and picnic areas.

BAYS MOUNTAIN PARK & PLANETARIUM

Kingsport - 853 Bays Mountain Park Road (I-181, Kingsport exit, follow signs) 37660. Phone: (423) 229-9447. www.baysmountain.com Hours: Weekdays 8:30am-5:00pm, Weekends 1:00-8:00pm. Extended summer hours, reduced winter hours. Closed Thanksgiving, Christmas Eve and day, and New Years. Admission: $4.00 per carload. $1.50-$4.00 fee per person for programs, barge ride, shows.

A 3,000 acre nature preserve with more than 25 miles of hiking trails, barge rides on the 44 acre lake, wildlife habitats & programs (Wolf CAM & Howlings), saltwater tidal pool and marine aquariums, Planetarium theater and special sky-watching at the observatory - Saturday & Sunday & daily during the summer. Park hours: 8:30am-5:00pm. Extended hours during the summer.

MOUNTAIN HERITAGE FARMSTEAD MUSEUM - Houses a collection of artifacts depicting farm & home life from the 1800s through the early 1900s. Learn the hardships of mountain life. Open weekends 2:00-5:00pm; daily in summer, small admission.

NETHERLAND INN

Kingsport - 2144 Netherland Inn Road (I-181 exit 55 eastbound, turn right on Fairview, again right on Center) 37660. www.netherlandinn.com Phone: (423) 246-6262. Hours: Saturday-Sunday 2:00-4:00pm (May-October). Guided tours to the public. Admission: $3.50 adult, $2.50 senior, $1.50 student (age 6+).

The restored Inn faces the Old Stage Road and Holston River, which served as a migratory spot for settlers to build boats for their westward trip during the mid-1700s. The two rooms on the first floor accommodated the travelers on the 18 weekly scheduled stagecoach runs. There were some "wild times" in the tavern demonstrated by the bullet-riddled mantel. Many period pieces,

**Pioneer toys...
no batteries needed!**

flat boat cargo manifests and even graffiti of the age can be found here.

The Netherland Inn hosted many famous persons including Presidents Andrew Jackson, Andrew Johnson and James Polk. On the property is The 1773 Daniel Boone House (from Virginia). The popular features of this cabin are the games and toys used by children during the 1700 and 1800s. Look for the 200 year old rocking horse and the mechanical paddle…for the young and young at heart - really cute stuff!

Also, you'll find a ¼ scale replica of a flatboat built here...part of the new Museum of Pioneer Transportation in the Barn. Loads of interesting artifacts and stories here!

EXCHANGE PLACE

Kingsport - 4812 Orebank Road (SR 93 to Orebank Rd. exit) 37662. Phone: (423) 288-6071. www.exchangeplace.info Hours: Saturday-Sunday 2:00-4:30pm (May-October). Call ahead, though, as their schedule is dependent on weather and volunteer staff. Admission: FREE. Fee for special events.

This mid-1800s living farmstead derived its name from the exchange of currency and of horses when it served as a stagecoach stop. Visit with the animals (meet Billy or Oreo), feed the sheep or chickens, or put up hay. Visit the Spring - the very reason the farm was built here (original buttermilk paint, look out for precious water spiders); Gathering Room - Mammy's bench (allowed mothers to work & rock their babies), the log piece displayed in here has a replica carving where Daniel Boone shot a bear

...a replica piece of tree bark in which Daniel Boone carved some history...

on the property! Why did he always catch them near a beech tree?; Slave Cabin - where the family's favorite slave family lived; Or, the School Room - put on your apron or handkerchief and grab your slate! Once you cross the threshold doorway, be quiet and mind your manners! The volunteers here are passionate about this place!

WARRIORS' PATH STATE PARK

Kingsport - 490 Hemlock Road (I-81 exit 59, Rte. 36 north) 37663. www.tennessee. gov/environment/parks/WarriorsPath/index.shtml Phone: (423) 239-8531. Hours: 7:00am to 2 hours past dark.

Once the pathway for the Cherokee and pioneers, now with hiking, picnicking, horseback riding, fishing, swimming, and a pool. 134 campsites, RV, and primitive sites. The paved walking path around Duck Island is fully accessible, and other fully accessible trails are in the planning stages. Several other trails are also under development and one that includes a small boardwalk through the Sinking Waters wetland area. It is situated on the shores of TVA's Patrick Henry Reservoir on the Holston River.

DAVY CROCKETT BIRTHPLACE STATE PARK

Limestone - 1245 Davy Crockett Park Road (I-81N exit 23, then 3 miles off Hwy. 11E, follow signs) 37681. Phone: (423) 257-2167. www.tennessee.gov/environment/ parks/DavyCrockettSHP/index.shtml   Hours: Park: 8:00am-dusk. Museum: Wednesday-Friday 8:00am-4:30pm. Note: A short video about Davy Crockett can be viewed in the museum. August 17 is Davy Crockett Day. On premises is a swimming pool, picnic areas, fishing, hiking and many campsites.

The site of Davy Crockett's birth is now part of a state park. A replica of the log cabin where Crockett (celebrated frontiersman, warrior and backwoods statesman) was born (1786) is here on 105 partially wooded acres of land along the Nolichucky River. The cabin presents a typical frontier home much like the one in which Davy was born.

The Visitor center's museum exhibits tell of different aspects of Davy's life. The real Mr. Crockett was probably never called Davy, nor was he just a frontiersman. Actually, he was more refined and less of a giant (he was only 5'9"). Davy was a survivor, comical and a big talker. Check out the memorabilia from the 50s - King of the Wild Frontier.

Upset with the American government, he said (i.e. "forget you all..."), "I'm going to Texas". You'll find he was actually "Nature's Noblesman", not quite as wild as the tales...or was he? Come here to begin your discovery!

CROCKETT TAVERN AND PIONEER MUSEUM

Morristown - 2002 Morningside Drive (US 11E south, near US 25E, follow signs) 37814. Phone: (423) 587-9900. www.crocketttavernmuseum.org Hours: Tuesday-Saturday 11:00am-5:00pm (May-October). Admission: $5.00 adult, $1.00 child (5-18).

The reconstructed log building is located on the site where Davy Crockett's parents built a home for their nine children. The home also served as a wayside inn for early travelers. Crockett, known for his hunting skills, tall tales and courageous volunteer spirit, spent his boyhood here. This is where he learned to hunt. Visitors will explore the kitchen, the loom room, which features a loom and the necessary spinning equipment; the big room, which can be equated to the living room of the present day; and the loft, where the family slept. Travellers renting slept one family to a bed.

PANTHER CREEK STATE PARK

Morristown - 2010 Panther Creek Park Road (I-40 exit 394, Hwy 11E north) 37814. www.tennessee.gov/environment/parks/PantherCreek/features/biking.shtml Phone: (423) 587-7046. Hours: Daily 6:00am-dark.

Legend has it that both Panther Creek and Panther Springs received their names from the claim of a Colonel Bradley of Virginia who, while exploring the area, shot a panther that fell into the spring. Near Point Lookout, the highest place in the park, the elevation reaches 1,460 feet above sea level. Other activities: camping, fishing, boating and horseback riding.

ROCKY MOUNT LIVING HISTORY MUSEUM

Piney Flats (Johnson City) - 200 Hyder Hill Road (I-181/23 S exit 36, I-381 N, follow US 11E toward Bristol) 37686. Phone: (423) 538-7396 www.rockymountmuseum.com Hours: Tuesday-Saturday 11:00am-5:00pm (March - mid December). Closed MLK Jr. Day, Labor Day, Thanksgiving Day, and weekends in December. Admission:

For updates & travel games visit: **www.KidsLoveTravel.com**

$8.00 adult, $7.00 senior (55+), $5.00 child (5-17).

From October 1790 until March 1792, Rocky Mount served as the Territorial Capital of this region. Today this restored building, the only Territorial Capital on its original site in the United States, is a living history site. View the orientation video.

Mrs. Cobb and her grandson, Frederick do a wonderful job taking you back to 1791 (in first person character!). They engage the children with questions. Hear stories about the Cobb family, Governor Blount, Indian affairs, and the latest gossip of the territory. Some even get to taste dishes such as gingerbread or sausage muffins cooked over an open fire. Leaving the kitchen be sure to visit the garden (medicinal, culinary, and dye pot plants) and weaving room or sheep barn. On tour, check out the secret drawer, the "necessary", the reversible cradle, a snake gourd, a shoefly chair, or a beehive oven.

ROAN MOUNTAIN STATE PARK

Roan Mountain - 1015 Hwy 143 37687. Phone: (423) 772-0190 or (800) 250-8620. www.tennessee.gov/environment/parks/RoanMtn/index.shtml   Hours: 8:00am-4:30pm.

Park guests have opportunities to hike along creeks and ridges, fish for trout, play tennis, swim, cross-country ski, horseback ride, join rangers and naturalists for educational programs, and enjoy mountain music concerts. Guests who wish to stay overnight have a choice of RV and tent camping or 30 fully equipped cabins.

There are approximately 12 miles of hiking trails in Roan Mountain State Park and 2.25 miles of mountain bike trails. Difficulty levels range from easy to strenuous. Hikers can stroll along the Doe River or take a challenging trail up to a ridge with a great view. The 6285 foot peak offers breathtaking views of the Appalachian Mountains.The Appalachian Trail and famous Rhododendron Gardens of Roan Mountain can be accessed at Carver's Gap, an 8 mile drive from the park. (best display of blossoms, mid-June)

MILLER HOMESTEAD - a century old farmhouse, open summers, with tours, mountain music, storytelling, and traditional skills demonstrated.

TENNESSEE NEWSPAPER AND PRINTING MUSEUM

Rogersville - 415 South Depot Street 37857. Phone: (423) 272-1961. www. rogersvilleheritage.org/rha/details.asp?ID=17 Hours: Monday-Thursday 10:00am-3:00pm, other times by appointment. Please call before you visit to ensure someone will be in the office. Note: Grand Ole Opry star, Archie Campbell Complex, is on S. Main Street (423-235-5216) in town. Structures include the Ole Country Store, Gilleys Hotel, and the Archie Campbell Museum.

A quaint 1890 Southern Railway Depot contains the state's only newspaper and printing museum. This town was where Tennessee's first newspaper was printed November, 1791 and you can see printing presses dating from then until the time when newspapers went online. Also on exhibit are early newspapers of interest.

SUGGESTED LODGING AND DINING

COMFORT SUITES. **Johnson City**. - 3118 Browns Mill Rd. exit 19 off I-26, 37604. (423) 610-0010. **www.comfortsuites.com/hotel-johnson_city-tennessee-TN264**. Outdoor pool, large suite rooms w/ frig & micro & large continental breakfast. Very reasonable. Logans Roadhouse is adjacent to the hotel and Super Wal-Mart is located across the street.

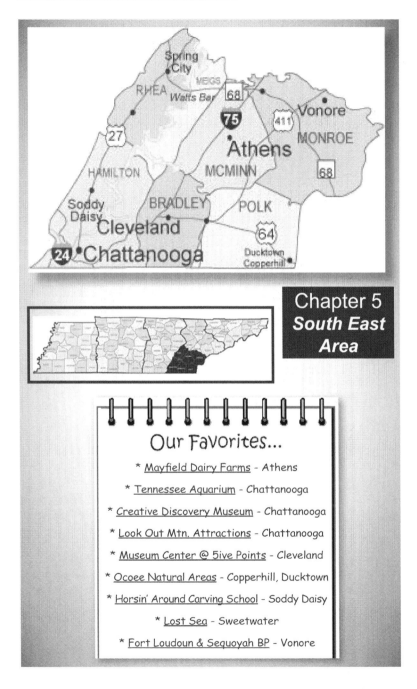

Chapter 5
*South East
Area*

Our Favorites...

* <u>Mayfield Dairy Farms</u> - Athens

* <u>Tennessee Aquarium</u> - Chattanooga

* <u>Creative Discovery Museum</u> - Chattanooga

* <u>Look Out Mtn. Attractions</u> - Chattanooga

* <u>Museum Center @ 5ive Points</u> - Cleveland

* <u>Ocoee Natural Areas</u> - Copperhill, Ducktown

* <u>Horsin' Around Carving School</u> - Soddy Daisy

* <u>Lost Sea</u> - Sweetwater

* <u>Fort Loudoun & Sequoyah BP</u> - Vonore

MAYFIELD DAIRY FARMS TOURS

Athens - *4 Mayfield Lane (I-75 exit 52, Mt. Verd. Turn east on Hwy 305 4.3 miles)*
37303. **www.mayfielddairy.com** *Phone: (423) 745-2151 or (800) Mayfield. Hours:*
Monday-Saturday 9:00am-5:00pm (March-August). Monday-Friday 9:00am-4:00pm,
Saturday 9:00am-2:00pm (September-February). Admission: FREE Tours: Tours
begin every 30 minutes or top of the hour, last about 40 minutes. Last tour is one
hour before closing. No tours on Wednesday. Wear comfortable, non-slip shoes. Some
stairs on tour. Note: Gift shop and ice cream parlor. FREEBIES: click on the link to
Fun & Learning to print some fun puzzles and games.

Get the "scoop" on the history of this dairy. Watch a film presentation
followed   by   a plant tour that includes how ice
cream treats are   made and how milk is bottled. Begin
by   donning   a      hair net and watch all the swirling
and twirling and   spinning and turning and churning of
jugs and cartons   of milk and ice cream. This fun
tour includes a   great look at how they make plastic
milk jugs, home-made, from a handful of tiny pellets...melted and molded.
It's amazing to see ice cream sandwiches made by one machine! After this
excellent guided visual tour - taste some of their ice cream creations for sale
(one scoop is only $1.00!). Try unique Yellow Brick Road or Turtle Tracks.
This is a must-see, easy to understand, colorful factory tour!

COOLIDGE PARK AND WALNUT STREET BRIDGE

Chattanooga - *Tennessee Riverpark (across the river from the Tenn. Aquarium) 37401.*
Phone: (423) 757-2142. **www.chattanooga.gov/PRAC/30_1096.htm** *Hours: Park:*
sunrise to midnight. Carousel: Monday-Saturday 11:00am-6:00pm, Sunday 1:00-
6:00pm. Fountains: Daily 8:00am-10:30pm (April-October). Admission: Carousel
rides: $1.00 adult, $0.50 senior and child (13 & under). Note: Park anywhere
downtown and pick up the trolley or walk to the Bluff View District - then
walk over the bridge with a picnic basket or take out lunch from one of the
assorted local cafes. *Bring a change of clothes for the kids if they want to*
Fountain Water Play!

Once downtown by the river, start your excursion by popping the top of a
cold cola and snacking on Moon Pies (locally made) while you walk the

Walnut Street pedestrian bridge over to Coolidge Park. (Check out the Sculpture Garden outside the HUNTER MUSEUM (**www.huntermuseum.org**) as you enter the bridge).

This is truly Americana at its best. Stroll across the world's longest pedestrian bridge, play in the Park's interactive water fountain and on the Walnut Wall

...the World's Longest Pedestrian Bridge...relaxing walk with a view!

Climbing Facility, or ride on the antique carousel. The carousel was made by another favorite, HORSIN AROUND CARVING SCHOOL in nearby Soddy Daisy. People will be seen walking, biking, Frisbee throwing, playing badminton or volleyball, splashing in the fountains or just picnicking on the grass. Water spurts from both ground-level jets and to the surprise and delight of their targets, the mouths and snouts of stone animals (lions, tigers & bears). The park hosts open-air performances and has a Chattanooga Theatre Centre presenting regular plays.

BLUFF VIEW ART DISTRICT

*Chattanooga - Corner of High & East 2nd Street (I-24, take Hwy 27 N, exit 1C to 4th St. to Art District) 37403. **www.bluffviewartdistrict.com** Phone: (423) 265-5033.*

Peer through the windows of The Chocolate Kitchen, the Courtyard & Pastry Kitchen, or the Bakery and Pasta Kitchen to get a sneak peek at the delicious concoctions being served at the District's fine restaurants. Now, grab a snack, dessert or meal at a café or restaurant in the area.

If you still want more art...head over to the Hunter Museum of Art to view changing and permanent exhibits of regional fame (along the Tennessee River Walk, 423-267-0968 or **www. huntermuseum.org**, Open daily, Admission). The "Big Julie" and the "Fundraiser" sculptures are of interest (one is a life-like in the main lobby…amazing). Much of the modern glassworks are colorful with unusual shapes.

TENNESSEE AQUARIUM

Chattanooga - One Broad Street (I-24 to downtown, follow I-27 N to exit 1C, turn left at 2nd light) 37401. Phone: (423) 267-FISH or (800) 262-0695. www.tnaqua.org Hours: Daily 10:00am-7:30pm (ET). Last admittance time is 6:00pm. IMAX shows begin at 11:00am. Closed Thanksgiving and Christmas. Extended hours on weekends, holidays and summertime. Admission: $24.95 adult, $14.95 child (3-12). Advance tickets can be purchased by phone or online. IMAX tickets extra $8-$10.

Tours: Have you ever wondered what it's like to fix meals for 9,000 animals every day? Have you ever thought about what it takes to clean a fish "bowl" containing 450,000 gallons of water? Behind-the-scenes tours tell all (extra fee). FREEBIES: Downloadable activities like penguin quizzes, a pirate treasure map, and scavenger hunts are printable from: www.tnaqua.org/Education/FunStuff.aspx. Educators: Exhibit & IMAX scavenger hunts & guides on specific themes: www.tnaqua.org/Education/TeacherTools.aspx.

River Gorge Explorer: This 70 passenger high-speed catamaran is the first of its kind in the Southeast. Aquarium visitors can extend their adventure by cruising into the Tennessee River Gorge aboard this sleek vessel. An Aquarium naturalist will lead you into this protected habitat, pointing out wildlife and historic points of interest along the way. (~$30 extra per person).

The Tennessee Aquarium tells the story of fresh water ecosystems. You follow the Tennessee River from its Appalachian beginnings through the swamp waters of the Mississippi River and into the Gulf of Mexico (lots of colorful fish), making side trips to some of the world's other great rivers. Our favorite area was Discovery Hall - pet a fish!-what does it feel like? Look for baby alligators in the nursery.

Along the way, visitors travel through a 60-foot canyon and two living forests. In the rivers, you'll see the only mammals on-site...river otters and their playful antics. A look at the creepy alligator snapping turtle (prehistoric) or side-necked turtles is a highlight, too.

The Tennessee Aquarium has expanded (as have most all the museums on the riverfront). The addition presents a saltwater adventure that explores the mysteries of the ocean. Ocean Journey is the place to touch sharks and sting rays. Immerse yourself in the Butterfly Garden (very friendly creatures) or dive into a secret cave reef and discover the weird world of boneless beauties. A funny sit is the live penguins on Penguin Rock. The jelly fish and giant crab were big hits with the kids.

CHATTANOOGA HISTORY CENTER

Chattanooga - 2 West Aquarium Way (TN Aquarium complex) 37401. www. chattanoogahistory.org Phone: (423) 265-3247. Hours: Monday-Friday 10:00am-5:00pm, Saturday & Sunday 11:00am-5:00pm. Closed Christmas. Admission: $4.00 adult, $3.50 senior, $3.00 child (5-18). Note: Check their website for grand reopening dates.

The Chattanooga Regional History Museum is the place you'll meet the region's peoples. Events are illustrated in five historical periods: Early Land, Early People; The Cherokee Nation; Growth & Conflict; The New South; and The Dynamo of Dixie. View the Marks On The Land orientation video about the history of Chattanooga. The Discover History Hallway makes the past accessible through hands-on interactive learning stations. Did you know Coca-Cola's bottling franchise, Moon Pies and Little Debbie's were first made here?

CHATTANOOGA DUCKS TOURS

Chattanooga - 503 Market Street (Corner of Market St. & 5th St behind Big Red Duck) 37402. Phone: (423) 756-DUCK. www.chattanoogaducks.com Admission: $22.00 adult, $20.00 senior, $11.00 child (3-12). Tickets are available at the Visitors Center

First it's a bus, then a boat, then a bus again...QUACK!

or on board. Tours: Best to call for reservations first. 60+ minute tours. Ducks leave hourly from 10am-dusk. Sundays Noon-8pm (May-October), weather pending. Note: Command Post Museum: Browse through this new exhibit and check out how East Tennessee heroes contributed to the largest wars in world history.

The Chattanooga Duck's are unique ex-military amphibious vehicles made for the US Army to land troops on beaches during wartime. The Ducks are equally at home on land as well as water. Begin downtown with a "quacky" tour of famous sites. Then, hit the water as they tell you about Maclellan Island, the Tennessee River and places of natural and historical interest...most only accessible by boat. Hopefully, you'll observe a Great Blue Heron or migrating Warblers. The birds live among squirrels, rabbits, raccoons, beaver, fox, ducks, geese and other waterfowl. Good tour

Capt. Daniel guides us safely on our journey!

to do before you explore the city...they point out many sites along the way that might interest you. Buy a "Duck Quacker" whistle before you tour so you can "quack all the day"!

CHATTANOOGA LOOKOUTS

Chattanooga - AT&T Field, 201 Power Alley (I-24 east to exit 178 on US 27 N, downtown. Take exit 1C onto 4th St, first left on Chestnut) 37402. Phone: (423) 267-2208 or (800) 852-7572. www.lookouts.com

Double A Professional Baseball Team. LA Dodgers affiliate. Join the Little

Lookouts club. Tickets are $3.00-$9.00.

CHATTANOOGA RIVERBOAT CO. SOUTHERN BELLE

Chattanooga - 201 Riverfront Pkwy, Pier 2 (Ross's Landing across from Aquarium) 37402. ***www.chattanoogariverboat.com*** *Phone: (423) 266-4488 or (800) 766-2784. Admission: (see brochure or online schedule) Sightseeing Cruises run $7.95-$14.95, Breakfast and Lunch Cruises run $12.95-$24.95. Family Nite Dinner Cruise and Monday nite Pizza Cruises are more. Tours: Boarding 30 minutes before departure (April-December). Basically 1-3 departures in the afternoon, one in the evening for dinner.*

Enjoy the informative commentary on the city's history as you float down the beautiful Tennessee River. Familiar sights like Lookout Mountain and Chattanooga's skyline are leisurely viewed as you snack or eat a meal. Entertainment on many evening dinner cruises includes magicians and dance

Unique views from the river...

bands. Look in Seasonal & Special Events for "themed" special events. If you're going on a meal cruise, be sure to bring along travel games (cards, coloring books, crayons) while the kids wait for food. The atmosphere is relaxed so it's a nice cruise for a lazy day along the river.

CREATIVE DISCOVERY MUSEUM

Chattanooga - 321 Chestnut Street (Riverfront District) (I-24 to downtown, then US 27 N to exit 1-C, 4th Street to Chestnut) 37402. Phone: (423) 756-2738. ***www.cdmfun. org*** *Hours: Daily 9:30am-5:30pm (summer). Monday-Saturday 10:00am-5:00pm, Sunday Noon-5:00pm (September-May). Closed Wednesdays (September-February). Last ticket sold one hour prior to closing. Closed Thanksgiving and Christmastime. Admission: $11.95 general (ages 2+) or $9.95 per person (show Aquarium ticket or military ID). Note: Great gift shop for educational toys.*

Specially designed for children ages 2-12, this museum is full of hands-on discoveries in art (where you can sculpt, print and puppet). See your face as a Dali or a Warhol painting. Let your kids' imaginations run wild digging for dino bones or making music. Play giant instruments. Sing in a canyon, a shower or a concert hall! This place has the widest variety of musical instruments to try. And, with each sound, a simple description of the people behind the music (this is our favorite part of the site and the best we've ever seen)! In the Inventors Clubhouse learn about local inventors, then make your own inventions.

Learning through play...Love It!

"RiverPlay" has a two story climbing structure consisting of nets, slides, a spiral staircase, and even a lift to provide access for visitors who use wheelchairs. A multi-level riverboat is nearby - a pilot's cabin and crane lift are there. Underneath the climbing structure is a watercourse where kids can sail boats, learn about dams and locks, create river currents, and use water pressure to spin wheels and tip buckets. Can you climb all the way to the crows nest and raise the mast... it's high!

Kids can visit the Little Yellow House or climb up to the Rooftop Fun Factory. Explore the world of simple machines as you enjoy sound, movement and fun high up on the rooftop.

BESSIE SMITH CULTURAL CENTER

Chattanooga - 200 East Martin Luther King Jr. Blvd. 37403. Phone: (423) 266-8658. www.bessiesmithcc.com Hours: Monday-Friday 10:00am-5:00pm, Saturday Noon-4:00pm. Admission: $7.00 adult, $5.00 senior & student, $3.00 child (6-12).

The exhibits begin with a "Wall of Respect", dedicated to African-Americans who have achieved first in their professional endeavors. After passing the "Wall", the visitor travels through an authentic African dwelling and a section with a variety of statues, tools and artifacts depicting the life, work, art and worship of Africans before they came to America. There are other displays of Chattanooga African-American Civil War involvement, their achievements in sports and performing arts, portrayals of family and professional life and even a focus on the Civil Rights movement. The achievements of Bessie Smith are remembered at the annual Riverbend Festival, too.

CHATTANOOGA ZOO

Chattanooga - 501 North Holtzclaw Ave (I-24 exit 4th Ave., turn right, then left on 23rd St.; turn right on Holtzclaw; left on McCallie Ave.; right into Warner Park) 37404. **www. chattzoo.org** *Phone: (423) 697-1322. Hours: 9:00am-5:00pm Closed: Christmas Day, New Year's Day, Martin Luther King Day, Thanksgiving Day. Admission: $8.95 adult, $6.95 senior (65+), $5.95 child (3-12). FREEBIES: Education page has activities to do while visiting zoo (scroll to bottom of page).*

A 5-acre zoo offering exotic animals and an animal contact area. The Warner Park Ranch Exhibit invites visitors to directly interact with the 'ranch' animals. The Gombe Forest features chimpanzees, the Himalayan Passage features red pandas, the highly endangered "Bali-Mynahs", and Asian Elongated tortoises, and the Zoo's newest exhibit, the Cougar Express, features Mountain Lions. Newer exhibits feature lively chimps, a spider monkey habitat, and an African Aviary home to Crowned Cranes and Pygmy Goats kids can pet. Want to try a camel encounter? Hope they don't spit!

INTERNATIONAL TOWING & RECOVERY HALL OF FAME MUSEUM

Chattanooga - 3315 Broad Street (north of Lookout Mtn. Incline) 37408. Phone: (423) 267-3132. www.internationaltowingmuseum.org Hours: Monday-Friday 10:00am-4:30pm, Weekends 11:00am-5:00pm. Shorter winter hours on weekdays. Closed major holidays. Admission: $8.00 adult, $7.00 senior (55+) and $4.00 child (6-18).

Enjoy restored antique wreckers and equipment, industry-related displays of tools, unique equipment, and pictorial histories of manufacturers who pioneered a worldwide industry. Model T's & Model A's with cranes and wreckers are fun to see. Chattanooga was chosen as the museum's home because the industry's first wrecker was fabricated in town. Understand the engineering behind a  wrecker with exhibits like the drapery rod example. Tons of toy & collectible tow trucks are on display and available to purchase - a little boy's dream.

LAKE WINNEPESAUKAH AMUSEMENT PARK & SOAK YA WATERPARK

Chattanooga - Lakeview Drive (I-24 East to the Moore Road (exit 184) and go straight to the 2nd traffic light and turn right onto McBrien Road) 37412. Phone: (877) LAKEWIN. www.lakewinnie.com Hours: Weekends 10:00am- 8:00 or 10:00pm (April-mid-September). Open Wednesday-Friday (May-early August). Admission: $18.00 (age 3+, includes 14 ride tickets).$10.00 seniors & babies gate admission. $26.00 unlimited rides wristband. Individual Ride Tickets are available for .95¢ each. (rides range from 2-5 tickets). Educators: Teachers Guides to physics online.

Free concerts featuring Christian, Country or Rock music artists are regular items on the Lake Winnie calendar of events. Thirty rides with exciting rides like the Cannon Ball Roller Coaster and the Pipeline Plunge, an intense water ride featuring a five-story maze of pipes that lead to a wet and wild final splash. Kiddie Land at Lake Winnie has dozens of attractions designed for the youngest of your family members. Wholesome and old-fashioned.

BOOKER T. WASHINGTON STATE PARK

Chattanooga - 5801 Champion Road (I-75 exit 4, Hwy 153. Take exit Hwy 58, go 5 miles) 37416. Phone: (423) 894-4955. Hours: 7:00am-dark. www.tennessee.gov/ environment/parks/BookerTWashington/index.shtml

Named for famous educator, Booker T. Washington, this 352-acre park is located on the shores of TVA's Chickamauga Reservoir. They have a year-round lodge and seasonal boat-launching ramp. The park has a large Olympic-size pool with diving board and a childrens' wading pool. The pool is open from early summer through Labor Day. Park recreation activities include hiking, field games, playgrounds, basketball, badminton, horseshoes, volleyball and board games.

CHATTANOOGA NATURE CENTER & REFLECTION RIDING

Chattanooga - 400 Garden Road (I-24W to exit 175, turn left onto Brown's Ferry, go to Cunnings Hwy, turn left; follow signs) 37419. Phone: (423) 821-1160. www. chattanature.org & www.reflectionriding.org Hours: Monday-Saturday 9:00am- 5:00pm. Sundays, April through October: 1 pm - 5:00pm. Admission: $10.00 adult, $7.00 senior (65+) and child (4-11). Note: While visiting the Center, children *can learn what it's like to be a real naturalist by checking out one of the Discovery Forest Backpacks (rental $3.50). Packed with study and field guides, binoculars, a microscope, and more...your child's next visit will become much more than a walk through the woods. We'd recommend attending during special events.*

DISCOVERY FOREST TREEHOUSE is a structure built among the arms of a 100-year-old Overcup Oak in the heart of the   Nature Center's lowland forest wetlands. Stained glass works and many more pieces make it one of the most unique treehouses in the world.

WILDLIFE   WANDERLAND EXHIBIT AREA: The centerpiece of this area is the Red Wolf exhibit where daily programming educates visitors. Unlike a zoo, the Wanderland holds only native birds and animals that are unable to be released because of their injuries and/or extensive human contact.

REFLECTION RIDING GARDEN AREA (by car, bike or walking). The three-mile driving road (which gives the Riding its name) invites visitors to "ride" through the changes each season. Labels and signs tell of the horticulture, geology, history and geography of the area.

RACCOON MOUNTAIN CAVERNS

Chattanooga - 319 West Hills Drive (1.3 miles off Interstate 24. Exit Lookout Valley (Tiftonia), #174, Scenic US 41) 37419. Phone: (423) 821-CAVE. **www. raccoonmountain.com.** *Hours: Vary by season. Call first. Admission: Crystal Caverns Tour: $13.95 adult, $6.50 child (5-12). Note: Hiking trails, campground, swimming pool, playground, batting cages, and Go-Carts. They even have panning for gems with specialty Gold or Fossil Panning bags for purchase that almost guarantee a find.*

Walk into the majestic Crystal Palace Room - one of the largest cave formation chambers in the Southeast. You will stroll along a smooth, circular walkway with gentle slopes and just a few steps as you view an assortment of stalactites, stalagmites, rim stone pools, fossils, and even evidence of past earthquakes. Wild Cave expeditions are tours with trained cavers guiding you through the vast underground network of chambers, canyons, tunnels, small streams, and large waterfalls that are beneath Raccoon Mountain.

TENNESSEE VALLEY RAILROAD

Chattanooga - 4119 Cromwell Road (Grand Junction depot: near the Jersey Pike Exit off Highway 153 (past airport); 1 mile from I-75) 37421. Phone: (423) 894-8028 or (800) 397-5544. www.tvrail.com Admission: $16.00 adult, $10.00 child (age 3-12). Tours: Trains run Wednesday-Sunday March-October; Weekends through Thanksgiving, December special theme trains only. Departures 2 to 5 times daily. Approx. one hour trip. Special longer Dixie Land Excursions posted throughout the year. Concessions: The Station has a full deli with indoor or picnic seating.

Note: Hey Kids -- Bring your parents to a Day Out With Thomas™ (usually the first two weekends in May). Activities pay tribute to everyone's favorite #1 engine with coloring pages, storytelling, Thomas & Friends™ videos, performances by clowns, appearances by Sir Topham Hatt™, and the highlight is a 25-minute ride on a full-sized, vintage train pulled by Thomas the Tank Engine!

"Missionary Ridge Local Service" is a six-mile, 50-minute roundtrip from Grand Junction Station to East Chattanooga Depot, crossing Chickamauga

...watch the engine turn around...

Creek, CSX mainline (ex-W&A), Tunnel Boulevard and Awtry Street bridges and passing through the pre-Civil War Missionary Ridge Tunnel (over 950 ft. long built in 1858). If you ride the last car, you can stand out on the porch when going thru the tunnel for the best view. Passengers detrain in East Chattanooga for a layover which includes watching the locomotive rotate on a turntable and a tour through the railyard. Visit the restoration shop to see works in progress before reboarding the train for the return trip. This stop looks just like a giant Thomas depot on the Island of Sodor! In the depot, a conductor may help you send a message.

AUDUBON ACRES

Chattanooga (East Brainerd) - 900 Sanctuary Road (From I-75, take Exit 3A to E. Brainerd Rd. East) 37421. Phone: (423) 892-1499. Hours: Monday - Saturday 9:00am - 5pm, Sunday 1:00pm - 5pm. Admission: $4.00 adult, $2.00 child (5-12).

For updates & travel games visit: **www.KidsLoveTravel.com**

Over 100 acres of wildlife sanctuary with 4 miles of trails, a pedestrian suspension bridge over the South Chickamauga Creek and a reconstructed Cherokee cabin (dates back to the 1700s and is said to be the birth place of Cherokee naturalist, Spring Frog). Little Owl Village is the location of a Mississippian Era Native American village in the 1400s and 1500s. This village is believed to be the location of the first contact between local Native Americans and Spanish explorers. It is being slowly restored as records indicate it was burned to the ground when the explorers invaded in the 1500s.

ROCK CITY

*Chattanooga (Lookout Mtn) - 1400 Patten Road (I-24 exit 178 south, follow signs to Lookout) 30750. **www.seerockcity.com** Phone: (706) 820-2531 or (877) 820-0759. Hours: 8:30am - 5:00pm every day except Christmas. Open later in the summer and peak shoulder seasons. Admission: $19.95 adult, $11.95 child (3-12). Combo prices with other Lookout Mountain attractions offered. Note: Cornerstone Station soda fountain. Educators: **www.teachrockcity.com***

The Grand Corridor welcomes you to unusual rock formations carved by nature. Look for the quiet, enchanted gnomes and elves around many corners... There's a wonderful outdoor family adventure ahead! Start at the Needles Eye - narrow passage.

Deer Park - observe rare white Fallow deer in the wild – descendants of species transported here from Europe in the 1930s (our family thought they looked right out of a storybook!).

...top of the world to 'ya!

Swing-A-Long Bridge - provides visitors with both a challenge and a breathtaking view. This engineering marvel stretches a full 180 feet through the blue sky.

Lover's Leap - do you believe the stories of Indian braves and

...See 7 States

maidens thrown from this cliff?

Seven States Flag Court - from the time of the Civil War, people noted you could see 7 states from this lookout - Alabama, Georgia, Kentucky, North Carolina, South Carolina, Tennessee, and Virginia.

Fat Man's Squeeze - think thin! And, the 1,000 Ton Balanced Rock - how does it stay up? Amusing Gnomes hang out near Fairytale scenes. Garnet Carter and his wife first developed this land and, because of some construction delays, ended up inventing miniature golf and creating a "rock" park!

BATTLES FOR CHATTANOOGA ELECTRIC MAP & MUSEUM

Chattanooga (Lookout Mtn) - 1110 E. Brow Road (I-24 W exit 178, Lookout Mtn., to Broad St. S (Hwy. 41), follow signs) 37350. Phone: (423) 821-2812 or (423) 821-7786 (Point Park). www.battlesforchattanooga.com Hours: Daily 9:00am-6:30pm (summer). 10:00am-5:00pm (rest of year). Admission: $8.00 adult, $6.00 child (5-12).

The kids' favorite feature will be the three-dimensional electronic battle map presentation of Chattanooga's Civil War history. It features 5,000 miniature soldiers, 650 lights, sound effects and exceptional details of the major battles which were fought here in November of 1863. Hear and see about Chattanooga's "Battle Above the Clouds" and Sherman's assault on Missionary ridge before his historic March To the Sea. This is just long enough to help you visually see the battle from afar and understand the strategies involved without getting boring.

...lights tell the story of the battles

CHICKAMAUGA AND CHATTANOOGA NATIONAL MILITARY PARK

Chattanooga (Lookout Mtn) - East Brow Road (atop Lookout Mountain) 37350. Phone: (706) 866-9241 Ranger or (423) 821-7786 Visitor Center. www.nps.gov/chch Hours: Daily 8:30am-5:00pm except Christmas. Admission: $3.00 per each adult (age 16+) for Point Park and again for Cravens House. Pay by the honor system. Note: Hiking and horse trails. Ranger guided talks and Civil War era demonstrations are conducted during the summer season.

In the fall of 1863, two armies clashed in an effort to gain control of vital transportation hubs. The battle was fought over a four square mile area that was covered with dense woods and thick underbrush, unlike most battles that occur in open fields. Both sides were winning at different points.

After you learn about the battles, be sure to take a walk over to **POINT PARK** - the site of the famous "Battle Above the Clouds". Learn why it's called that (there were two kinds of fog that day). See preserved/interpreted portions of the Chickamauga battlefields - the battles that sealed the fate of the Confederacy. The Visitors Center is home to the

...see the sites of the "Battle Above the Clouds"

large mural, the "Battle of Lookout Mountain" with audio presentation that helps you visually locate the details of this enormous mural painted by an eye-witness. Cravens' House (open for touring) was the site of some of the fiercest fighting, serving as headquarters for both sides. Why did soldiers and reporters take the house apart to stay warm?

LOOKOUT MOUNTAIN INCLINE RAILWAY

Chattanooga (Lookout Mtn) - 827 E. Brow Road/3917 St. Elmo Ave. (Lower Station) (near I-24, 3 blocks south of Hwy. 11, 41, 64 or 72 on Hwy. 58) 37350. Phone: (423) 821-4224. www.ridetheincline.com Hours: Monday-Friday 9am-6pm, Saturday/ Sunday 9am-7pm. Last round trip leaves one hour before closing time. Closed Christmas Day only. Admission: Tickets may be purchased at either the Lower or Upper Station and at the Chattanooga Visitors Center. Round trip $15.00 adult, Half *price child (3-12). $1.00 discount for one way fares. Senior pricing is child pricing (December-February only). Combo prices with other Lookout Mountain Attractions offered. Tours: Approximately 10 minutes, one way. Note: Candy Connection, Snack Shoppe at Upper Station. Seasonal gift shop at Lower Station.*

"America's Most Amazing Mile" delights guests as the Incline climbs historic Lookout Mountain. Chattanooga's surrounding mountains and valleys come in full view as the trolley-style railcars carry you high. The 72.7% grade of the

track near the top gives the Incline the unique distinction of being the steepest passenger railway in the world. The free observation deck at the Upper Station is the highest overlook on Lookout Mountain.

While at the upper station, be sure to visit the Incline's machine room where the giant gears and cables are put into motion. Be sure to check out the Incline Centennial Exhibits, too. And while you are traveling on the Incline, you will pass another Incline car on the single track. At the halfway point of the track, the two Incline cars pass along side each

...looking out the back of the car, down the steep hill we're climbing...

other. The "switch" allows the two cars to travel on a single track system. Make sure you wave to the folks in the other car.

At 600 steep feet per minute, this is really cool!

RUBY FALLS

Chattanooga (Lookout Mtn) - 1720 S. Scenic Hwy. (I-24 exit 178 or 174, follow signs) 37409. Phone: (423) 821-2544. www.rubyfalls.com Hours: Daily 8:00am-8:00pm. Closed Christmas Day. Admission: $17.95 adult, $9.95 child (3-12). Combo prices with other Lookout Mountain Attractions offered. ZipSTream zipline - $20-$35. Tours: Minimum time for caverns tour is 1 1/2 hours. Guided tours take you on a one mile easy hike. Note: Lookout Mountain Tower (stairs), the Fun Forest Playground, and gift shops/snack bar. Be sure to have the kids use the restroom before touring - only one way in and out. Educators Downloadable lesson plans including vocab, *quizzes, and crosswords: www.rubyfalls.com/pages/Field-TRip_Planning/*

The thundering 145 foot waterfall inside historic Lookout Mountain is the world's highest underground waterfall. A powerful earthquake, or more likely a series of them, caused the layers of rock in the Mountain to bend or fold upwards... cracks or crevices then occurred. Take a descending elevator tour that opens to cave paths of the Lookout Mountain Caverns. Look for rock formations that resemble steak and potatoes, an elephant's foot or an angel's wing. These caves were once used by Native Americans and Civil War troops for  living space and as a hideout for the outlaws. The 1/2 hour wait is worth it as you enter the Falls room! The "light & sound" show that magically, spiritually occurs once you're by the Falls is awesome! Lots of oohs and aahs here...

MUSEUM CENTER AT 5IVE POINTS

Cleveland - 200 Inman Street East (I-75 exit 20 or 25, follow US 11 to Inman St. east) 37311. Phone: (423) 339-5745. **www.museumcenter.org** *Hours: Tuesday-Friday 10:00am-5:00pm, Saturday 10:00am-3:00pm. Closed holidays. Admission: $5.00 adult, $4.00 senior & students. FREEBIES: Ask for a treasure hunt paper you complete using clues numbered throughout the museum.*

A regional history museum of the Ocoee Region. "The River of Time" core exhibit includes seven time periods dating from prehistory to today and interprets how people of this region lived, worked and played. Using video and displayed artifacts, you can meet "Fallen Sky" (an aging Cherokee), a traveling missionary, a child (petrified pants, stiff shoes, swinging washer and butter churn), a railroad conductor (progress), a black teacher, or a TVA carpenter. Great stories with hands-on activities at each station. Did you know Cleveland, Tennessee is the stove capital of the world?

RED CLAY HISTORIC PARK

Cleveland - 1140 Red Clay Park Road S.W. (I-75, take exit 3-A, (E. Brainerd Rd.) - head East about 10 miles. 37311. Phone: (423) 478-0339. www.tennessee.gov/ environment/parks/RedClay/index.shtml Hours: 8:00am-Sunset (March-November). Open until 4:30pm (December-February). Visitors Center closed December 20-January 1. Park closed Christmas.

Being a historic park, Red Clay is dedicated to the preservation and interpretation of Cherokee history. The James F. Corn Interpretive Center, located near the park entrance, houses the park administrative offices, a theater, a resource reading room, and exhibits. This facility contains artifacts and documents that emphasize the 19th-century Cherokee history and culture. Replicas of a Cherokee farmstead (many were farmers) and Council House of the period show how the area might have looked 150 years ago. This site is used for modern Indian festival grounds. The Blue Hole spring is located near the Council House and is accessible by a paved trail designed to accommodate the handicapped. The Blue Hole spring is about 15 feet deep, and produces over 504,000 gallons of water a day.

CHEROKEE NATIONAL FOREST

Cleveland - 2800 North Ocoee Street (Forest supervisors office) 37320. Phone: (423) 476-9700. www.fs.fed.us/r8/cherokee/

Best known for its rivers along with several lakes which offer more than enough for a vacation of whitewater rafting, floating, canoeing, sailing, fishing and water skiing. Spread throughout the region are trails for biking, horseback riding and hiking trails, with many areas perfect for wildlife watching at designated Watchable Wildlife locations. Also within the forest are several campgrounds and picnic/swimming areas (several nice beach areas near each of the 3 Ocoee Dams).

At **COKER CREEK**, view the falls (FS Road 2138) along the trail that connects to the John Muir Trail (423-261-2157). In town at **COKER CREEK VILLAGE** you can ride horses or try your hand at gold panning (423-261-2310). The Ocoee River is the site of the Class 3 & 4 rapids (ages 12+). The Hiwassee River has outfitters that rent funyaks, tubes and rafts or people can canoe and kayak on their own. The Hiwassee River is ideal for beginners and families with Class I and 2 rapids. The call (gobble) of the wild turkey in the

East Tennessee mountains is an unforgettable sound. Male turkeys (gobblers) usually begin actively attracting female (hen) turkeys by gobbling in early March through mid-May. This thunderous sound is a sure sign that spring is in the air.

CLEVELAND SPEEDWAY

Cleveland - 2420 S. Lee Hwy 37320. **http://clevelandspeedway.com/** *Phone: (423) 479-8574.*

1/3 mile semi Banked Red Clay Oval in Tennessee race Super Late Models every Saturday night, March-August. The other racing divisions at the track include the Claimer Late Models, the Hobby division, the Pony Stock division and the "Anything Goes" Street division. Admission. (kids are usually only $3.00)

OCOEE WHITEWATER CENTER

Copperhill - Rte. 1, Box 285, Hwy. 64 37317. Phone: (423) 496-5197 or (877) 692-6050. **www.fs.fed.us/r8/ocoee/** *Hours: Monday-Sunday 9:00am-5:00pm (midMarch-mid-November). Weekends only 8:30am-4:30pm (December-March). EST Note: Conservation Center has various kids programs in the summer.*

Home of the 1996 Olympic Whitewater Competition, visitors can also try their hand at rafting the Olympic Race Channel (only 20x/year-level 3 & 4 rapids). There are 10 miles of hiking and bike trails plus a Native Garden. Swim the "blue hole", just dip your feet in wading pools or walk out onto the rocks when there aren't rapids running. The Visitors Center features video footage of the Olympic races, examples of the construction (before & after) and how they created "faux" rock. Can you tell the difference?

DAYTON PARKS

Dayton - Highway 27 37321. Phone: (423) 775-6171.

CHICKAMAUGA LAKE - offers a variety of sport fishing, outdoor camping, and family water activities.

LAUREL-SNOW POCKET WILDERNESS & BUZZARD POINT Walnut Grove Road, (423) 775-7801, This is the first National Recreation Trail in Tennessee. It provides 10.5 miles of wilderness trail guiding you to waterfalls, forest and unique rock formations. They offer trails for hikers.

HIWASSEE / OCOEE STATE PARK

Delano - *Spring Creek Road (U.S. Hwy. 411, the Ocoee river on U.S. Hwy. 64) 37325. www.tennessee.gov/environment/parks/Hiwassee/index.shtml Phone: (423) 263-0050 or (423) 263-0060. Miscellaneous: Stop by the Webb Brothers Store in Reliance to shop at a 1936 era general store, post office, refreshments and local gossip. Raft and funyak rentals.*

Hiwassee (Sugarloaf Mountain) State Park is situated at the foot of the Ocoee #1 Dam. This state park contains the scale model for the 1996 Olympic Race Course. Especially great to view before you hit the rapids or in lieu of rafting them. Restrooms, picnic area, campsites and canoe put-in. This stretch of river offers canoeing, rafting, fishing, hiking and nature photography. A scenic portion of the John Muir trail winds through the river gorge. The Ocoee River is a premier white-water river in the Southeastern United States possessing Class III, IV, & V rapids.

DUCKTOWN BASIN MUSEUM

Ducktown - *(Hwy 64) 37317. www.tnhistoryforkids. org/places/ducktown_basin Phone: (423) 496-5778. Hours: Monday-Saturday 10:00am-4:00pm. Closed Sundays, Thanksgiving, Christmas, & New Years. Admission: $1.00-$3.00.*

As you drive into the area, look for the copper-colored hills everywhere. Located on the grounds of the historic Burra Burra Copper Mine (best view is from museum's observation platform), the museum exhibits help visitors understand the environmental and cultural history of Tennessee's only copper district. They use a slide show and simulated hard rock copper mine walkthrough. In 1843, a

Inside a giant ore bucket

gold prospector discovered rock he thought was gold. It turned out to be red copper oxide. Prospectors, land speculators, and engineers poured into the area from everywhere. By 1860 there were 1,000 people employed here. Today, instead of copper, now companies produce sulfuric acid instead. Ever heard of roasting rock?

L & N DEPOT MUSEUM

Etowah - P.O. Box 390 37331. www.etowahcoc.org/qualityoflife/lndepot.asp Phone: (423) 263-7840. Hours: Tuesday-Saturday 9:00am-4:30pm, Sunday 1:00-4:00pm. Closed major holidays. Admission: Donations accepted.

This 1906, two-story Victorian rail station has an exhibit "Growing Up With The L&N: Life and Times in a Railroad Town," that tells the story of this town built as a planned community by the Louisville & Nashville Railroad. The museum traces the working class history of the people focused on the railroad business. Also, large artifacts from the depot when it was used as a Canteen during WWII are displayed.

An active rail yard is outside where visitors enjoy trains switching, changing crews and passing through. The best view is from the Portico Room observation deck- the circus trains passing thru are a local favorite! Hopefully, a local will be around to tell you some personal stories (lots of townspeople like to hang out here). The town's Visitor Center is located in the depot also.

HARRISON BAY STATE PARK

Harrison - 8411 Harrison Bay Rd. (I-75 exit 4, Hwy 153. Exit Hwy 58 N, go 10 miles) 37341. www.tennessee.gov/environment/parks/HarrisonBay/index.shtml Phone: (423) 344-2272. Hours: 8:00am-10:00pm.

Located along miles of the Chickamauga Reservoir, the park has one of the most complete marine facilities available on any TVA lakes. Many also come for the wildlife viewing. There are three hiking trails at the park. There is a 4.5 mile trail, a .5 mile trail and 1 mile trail. Trails are open year-round. There is a biking trail available at the marina. The park has an Olympic-size swimming pool and a wading pool for small children. The pool is open from Memorial Day through late summer.

FORT MARR

Ocoee - (along US 64) 37317. www.tennesseeoverhill.com Phone: (423) 263-7232.

Built in the early 19th century, its most notorious function was during the Cherokee Removal, when it was part of a larger stockade. The Blockhouse, which remains today, can be seen here. Nancy Ward, Beloved Woman of the Overhill Cherokees, is buried nearby, along with her son, Five Killer. The graves overlook the pastoral landscape along the Ocoee River.

HORSIN' AROUND CARVING SCHOOL

Soddy Daisy *- 8361A Dayton Pike (Rte. 7W exit off I-75, TN 153W turns into Rte. 27 North, Soddy Daisy) 37379. Phone: (423) 332-1111.* **www.horsin-around.net** *Hours: Monday-Friday 9:00am-5:00pm, Saturday 9:00am-6:00pm. Please call ahead to schedule tours. Otherwise, you'll catch students working by chance. Admission: Group tours are $3.00 for adults and Free for children with adult.*

This cute, little baby elephant wanted to go home with us...

The Coolidge Park Carousel features more than 50 animals including horses, tigers, fish, dinosaurs, and even a giraffe! All the animals were hand-carved by students of Horsin' Around carving school. Many people ride by and visit. Some talk to Bud or one of his students who finds it relaxing to craft wooden animals. With sawdust everywhere, you'll see the carousel animals in many stages starting from regular pieces of unfinished wood. With the tap, tap, tap of wooden mallets on chisel handles, pieces of wood fall away to reveal the shape of their creator's vision. Because the work is done by different artists each animal has unique characteristics. Be careful, though, you may fall in love with these animals and want to come back as a student soon!

WATTS BAR DAM AREA

Spring City *- Highway 68 (trails are off of Shut-in Gap Road, northwest of city) 37381. Phone: (888) 238-3263 PIN 1318.*

PINEY RIVER TRAIL, STINGING FORK POCKET WILDERNESS, & TWIN ROCKS NATURE TRAIL - Natural wilderness areas with waterfalls, forests, unique rock formations, deep gorges. Swimming and fishing are the predominate recreation activities in the area.

WATTS BAR RESORTS - That family vacation you thought was gone still happens here as you stay in one of the resort cabins, situated on the 39,000 acre lake along the Tennessee River, they are good spots for fishing, boating, water skiing, house boating and picnicking from your rented pontoon boat or bring your own. Several restaurants allow you to dine while you view gardens, lake and wildlife.

LOST SEA

Sweetwater - 140 Lost Sea Road (I-75 exit 60, Rte. 68, between Madisonville & Sweetwater) 37874. ***www.thelostsea.com*** *Phone: (423) 337-6616. Hours: Open daily 9:00am until 5:00pm (winter), until 6:00pm (September, October, March, April), until 7:00pm (May, June, August), until 8:00pm (July). Closed Christmas Day. Admission: $17.95 adult, $7.95 Child. Note: Cavern Kitchen, General Store, Trading Post, Blacksmith Shop, picnic facilities and a nature trail. Level walkways on dirt floors, however some steep hills. Stroller/ wheelchair accessible. Asthmatic persons may experience breathing difficulty. More Adventuresome? Ask about the Wild Cave tour (4 hours) or Overnights.*

A giant, metal, bright yellow tunnel...not a usual cave entrance!

Walk thru a metal tunnel into the unbelievable site of the giant Indian council chamber (600 ft x 120 ft). Indians used the calcium deposits as toothpaste and Confederate soldiers mined the cave for saltpeter. "America's Largest Underground Lake" is home to rare Cave Flowers and cascade formations. The earliest known visitor to the cave was a saber-toothed tiger, whose fossilized remains are now in the Museum of Natural History.

A guided walk to the bottom of the cavern is rewarded upon entering the lake room, where you will board large glass bottom boats for a trip into the Lost Sea. While on the trip, you will observe some of the largest rainbow trout in the United States (but, why do they taste like liver?) and learn about the 4-acre lake underground. It's hard to believe what you see here!

CHEROHALA SKYWAY

Tellico Plains - 250 Ranger Station Road (Rte. 165) 37385. Phone: (423) 253-2520. www.cherohala.org Hours: Daily, all day. Remember, the roads are winding and snow is common from mid-November thru mid-April, especially in higher elevations. Admission: FREE

The bulletin board welcomes visitors with general information about the Skyway. It crosses through the Cherokee National Forest into North Carolina. Covering portions of what was once a Cherokee Indian trading route, this 40+ mile, two-lane blacktop road passes crystal-clear rivers and stops at scenic overlooks.

Paralleling the Tellico River, the Skyway winds along the river at 1,000 ft. elevation offering canoeing and fishing (mile post 2 & 4). From at least 1650 AD, the Cherokee resided here until 1838 (Removal), when the area was opened for Euro-American settlement. Tellico ("tel-li-quo") means "plains" in Cherokee.

At mile post 5, the Skyway begins its ascent through hills and valleys. Stop at mile post 14-16 to view Turkey Creek overlook. Closer to mile post 18, the Skyway passes by a black bear refuge and offers views of many rugged "rock" mountains. Near the Ranger Station (service road 210), you can view Bald River Falls without leaving your car as water cascades over 100 feet onto the rocks below. Further along this road is a state-operated trout hatchery.

FORT LOUDOUN STATE HISTORIC PARK

Vonore - 338 Fort Loudoun Road (Rte. 72 South, off I-75, to Highway 411 North until it intersects Hwy. 360 South.Turn onto 360 South) 37885. www. tennessee.gov/environment/ parks/FortLoudoun/index. shtml Phone: (423) 884-6217. Hours: 8:00am-Sunset. Visitors Center is open daily from 8:00am-4:30pm except Thanksgiving, Christmas or New Years. Admission: Donations. Note: We recommend Garrison Weekends-A living history program featuring the lives of the soldiers and civilians who originally

occupied the fort. While here, the garrison group carries out the activities common to frontier outpost. Musket drills, artillery training, cooking in the fireplaces and the bake oven, the sights and smells of frontier America.

This site is the location of one of the earliest British fortifications on the western frontier, built in 1756. Today, the fort and the 1794 Tellico Blockhouse overlook TVA's Tellico Reservoir and the Appalachian Mountains.

It's like a giant "playground" of Redcoats and Indians inside the fort. It will inspire children's imagination to play as they wander inside the palisade walls! An interpretive center offers information on the area's history and artifacts that were excavated prior to the Fort's reconstruction. A 15-minute film adds to the visitor's understanding of the period. Kids gravitate to the Redcoat "Muppet" display and the diorama showing whites living inside the fort, with Cherokee peering behind bushes on the outside.

Also, fishing, hiking and boating recreation opportunities. Feeding the giant carp at the Fort Loudoun Marina is lots of family fun (the carp are numerous and absolutely gigantic and well fed on Calhoun's scraps). Fort Loudon Marina, the largest marina on the Tennessee River, also offers both jet ski and pontoon boat rentals.

SEQUOYAH BIRTHPLACE MUSEUM

Vonore - P.O. Box 69, Citico Road (across from Fort Loudoun St. Pk., off Hwy 411 North, follow signs) 37885. www.sequoyahmuseum.org Phone: (423) 884-6246. Hours: Monday-Saturday 9:00am-5:00pm, Sunday Noon-5:00pm. Closed Thanksgiving, Christmas, & New Years. Admission: $3.00 adult, $1.50 child (6-12). Note: Nearby are monuments commemorating the Overhill towns of Chota and Tanasee, namesake for the State. Begin with the video introduction...a good overview. Many easy videos & "Hear Phones" are located throughout at different stations.

Nearly everywhere you walk around here is prehistoric & historic Indian land. The museum illuminates thousands of years of native lifeways in the Little Tennessee River Valley and honors Sequoyah, the inventor of the Cherokee alphabet. Unlike the white soldiers during the war of 1812, Sequoyah and other Cherokees weren't able to write letters home, read military orders, or record events as they occurred. With years of work, he finally reduced the thousands of Cherokee thoughts to 85 symbols representing sounds. He made a game of this new writing system and taught his little girl Ayoka how to make symbols. By the 1820s, Cherokee were reading and writing documents.

...the "Talking Leaves"

The museum also tells of the history of the Cherokees in their family life, customs, beliefs and sadness when the Trail of Tears began. Boys love the demos of the blowgun and bow & arrow used to kill small animals. The one band of Indians that didn't leave on the Trail of Tears still has a reservation just over the border into North Carolina. Very interesting, educational museum about the Cherokee. You'll love the gift shop - everything is hand-made by Cherokee!

SUGGESTED LODGING AND DINING

CHATTANOOGA CHOO CHOO HOLIDAY INN RESORT -
Chattanooga. 1400 Market Street. Phone: (423) 266-5000 or (800) TRACK-29. **www.choochoo.com**. "It's a train. It's a song. It's a hotel." This is the hotel made famous in the Glenn Miller song (hear it on their website). The 30-acre vacation family complex includes a 1900s train station (now a lobby and restaurant), three pools (one indoors) with waterfalls and slides, casual restaurants (like the Silver Diner car) and snackeries, shops, an arcade and overnight lodging in regular rooms, suites or actual Victorian parlor cars on the property. They have a trolley ride ($0.50) you can take thru the complex and the kids will like the largest model railroad museum in the South display (very small admission). The water garden is filled with more than 400 fish. Try the Station House Restaurant where your server is taking your order one minute, on stage singing the next. Maybe make it more special by ordering a Shirley Temple for the kids with dinner. Their pools and train station environment make this the perfect family stay in Chattanooga! Admission: Rooms and great family packages from $99.00 - $229.00, depending on time of year and type of room, plus amount of perks included. Miscellaneous: The FREE shuttle bus to downtown is right next door and highly recommended for any downtown site visits.

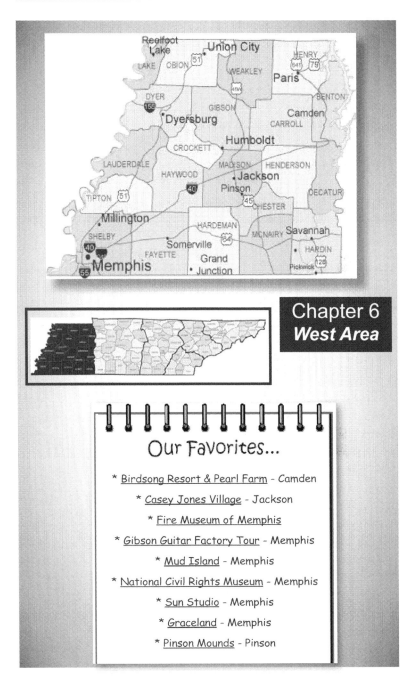

Chapter 6
West Area

Our Favorites...

* *Birdsong Resort & Pearl Farm* - Camden

* *Casey Jones Village* - Jackson

* *Fire Museum of Memphis*

* *Gibson Guitar Factory Tour* - Memphis

* *Mud Island* - Memphis

* *National Civil Rights Museum* - Memphis

* *Sun Studio* - Memphis

* *Graceland* - Memphis

* *Pinson Mounds* - Pinson

WEST TENNESSEE DELTA HERITAGE CENTER

Brownsville - 121 Sunny Hill Cove (I-40 exit 56) 38012. Phone: (731) 779-9000. Hours: Monday-Saturday 10:00am-4:00pm. Admission: FREE

Counties in the area have furnished displays to highlight destinations in the region. Other featured sites include the Cotton Museum. Visitors can see and experience the evolution of cotton farming from the time everything was done by hand to today's ultramodern methods of farming. Young and old alike enjoy the hands-on exhibit of the stages of field cotton to ginned cotton. The West Tennessee Music Museum spotlights Carl Perkins, Tina Turner and Sleepy John Estes (even the small home of Sleepy John, famous blues musician, is on site) with music and pictures. The Hatchie River Museum focuses on the fragile watershed of the last untouched river west of the Tennessee River in all of the state.

PARIS LANDING STATE PARK

Buchanan - 16055 Hwy 79N (east of Paris on US 79) 38222. www.tennessee.gov/ environment/parks/ParisLanding/index.shtml. Phone: (731) 641-4465 or (731) 642-4311 Inn. Miscellaneous: Nearby in Paris is a large replica of France's Eiffel Tower, standing proudly with an American flag at the top.

Paris Landing State Park is named for a steamboat and freight landing on the Tennessee River, dating back to the mid-1800s. From here and other landings on the Tennessee River and Big Sandy River, supplies were transported to surrounding towns and communities by ox cart. The 841-acre Paris Landing State Park is situated on the western shore of what is now Kentucky Lake, one of the largest man-made lakes in the world. The 100-plus room Inn has a restaurant, outdoor swimming pool, volleyball and tennis courts and a boat dock. There is a swimming area and beach on Kentucky Lake (along with loads of water recreation). 10 fully-modern cabins and camping facilities are available, too. Summer weekend Music in the Park live entertainment outdoor amphitheater concerts are offered.

BIRDSONG RESORT & PEARL FARM

Camden (Kentucky Lake) - 255 Marina Road (I-40 exit 133 on Scenic Hwy 191N or Rte.70, Hwy 191S) 38320. Phone: (731) 584-7880 or (800) 225-7469. www.

For updates & travel games visit: **www.KidsLoveTravel.com**

birdsongresort.com Admission: The mini-theatre & museum are open for walk-in traffic daily, FREE. Best weekdays (45 minutes long). Packages from $40-$55.00 for 2 to 5 hour guided tours. Kids rates run $5.00-$25.00. Note: There are 11 cabins on the property with picnic tables, outdoor grills, full kitchens and some with screened porches & fireplaces. Other resort activities include swimming, basketball, volleyball, shuffleboard, ping-pong, fishing, boating and rentals.

Yes, a freshwater pearl farm (one of a kind in the U.S.) right in Western Tennessee!

<u>MINI PEARL OF A TOUR</u> (April-November) - Look just below the surface of Kentucky Lake where mussels incubate to eventually process pearls. Freshwater pearl farmers explain how man manipulates the natural process of pearl production with skill and patience *(they have to wait 5 years!)*. During the tour, you'll take a boat out to the farm to

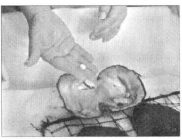

...the pearl is the prize!

visit with divers. You'll witness implantation demonstrations and see how mussels are cared for during the cultivation process. The biggest secret - the thickness of the shell grown here. Kids like to help dissect a mussel to get a pearl out! 5 hour tours include a visit to the <u>Tennessee River Folklife Museum</u> & <u>Pilot Knob Civil War Lookout</u> *(logging, pearl button industry and mussel farming artifacts)* and a catered BBQ meal. Did you know the pearl is the official state gemstone?

Every visit is a wonderful memory of this relaxed area. Have fun boating, swimming or tubing. Stay in spacious cottages (Families can stay at America's only freshwater pearl farm for just over $100 nightly), and enjoy good food (the Catfish Place in town – get it Cajun or fried). Learn new things about aquatic nature. We highly recommend calling ahead to reserve a tour and overnight stay (cottages, RV or camping). If you just pop in, at least look through the museum and watch the video. Be careful ladies, it's hard to resist buying a set of uniquely natural pearls (great prices for the real stuff!). This place is absolutely amazing fun…and so-o-o unique!

NATHAN BEDFORD FORREST STATE PARK

Eva - 1825 Pilot Knob Road (9 miles east of Camden on Hwy 191) 38333. www. tennessee.gov/environment/parks/NBForrest/index.shtml   Phone: (731) 584-6356 or (800) 714-7305 cabins. Hours: 7:00am-10:00pm. Center: Daily 8:00am-4:30pm. (closed for lunch).

This park was named for General Nathan Bedford Forrest, the intrepid Confederate cavalry leader, who on November 4, 1864, attacked and destroyed the federal supply and munitions depot at (Old) Johnsonville at the mouth of Trace Creek. Also fishing, boating, group lodge and modern cabins.

TENNESSEE RIVER FOLKLIFE MUSEUM: When TJ Whitfield retired from a career of musseling on the Tennessee River, he probably never thought his boat, "Old Betsy" would come to rest at this high point. The boat is now a centerpiece of an exhibit on the River Folklife Center atop Pilot Knob. The museum houses an antique brail boat (used for musseling prior to the invention of the electric motor), artifacts from the pearl button factories that once lined the river banks, pearling and diving industry exhibits, and many Civil War items of interest. On the deck outside the building is the "Liar's Bench" where recorded interviews can be heard with the press of a button. Listen to the tall-tales and legends of the river people.

NATIONAL BIRD DOG MUSEUM & WILDLIFE HERITAGE CENTER

Grand Junction - 505 W Hwy 57 38039. Phone: (731) 764-2058. Hours: Tuesday-Friday 9:00am-2:00pm, Saturday 10:00am-4:00pm, Sunday 1:00-4:00pm. www.birddogfoundation.com Admission: FREE

"Bird dogs make great friends!"

You can't miss the museum…kids squeal at the bronze dogs outside. Recognizing over 40 breeds of bird dogs, the museum features numerous exhibits, sporting dog art, wildlife murals, artifacts, and game bird specimens. Among the portraits and exhibits contained in the museum, you will find the National Champions (like the famous Count Noble in full point) which have found glory on the Ames Plantation near Grand Junction (4275 Buford Ellington Road, 731-878-1067 or **www. amesplantation.org**).

WILDLIFE ROOM - displays stuffed wildlife - many you may have never seen. See all the predators that naturally might like a bird for dinner. Even touch many skulls and skins. What happened to the two deer that occupied the interlocked horns? Why are female birds drab in color?

CHICKASAW STATE PARK

Henderson - 20 Cabin Lake (SR 100) 38340. Phone: (901) 989-5141. **http://state. tn.us/environment/parks/Chickasaw/** *Hours: Daily 6:00am-10:00pm. Lodge open April-October. The restaurant is open Thursday through Sunday. Note: Cabin Reservation: (800) 458-1752.*

This park and forest was once part of a vast area belonging to the Chickasaw Nation prior to the Jackson Purchase of 1818. Parents like the Bear Trace Golf Course designed by Jack Nicklaus. Miles of roads and trails wind thru the scenic timberlands touching Lake Placid. The park offers vacation cottages, camping sites, group lodge, hiking trails, tennis, badminton, basketball and volleyball courts, a playground, and archery range, ball fields and horseback riding in the summer. A park recreation director, on duty during the summer months, conducts group games, arts and crafts, evening, campfire programs and hayrides. Country dances are held on holiday week-ends.

ALEX HALEY HOUSE AND MUSEUM

Henning - 200 S. Church Street 38041. Phone: (731) 738-2240. **www. alexhaleymuseum.org** *Hours: Tuesday - Saturday 10:00am-5:00pm. Tours are 30 minutes. Admission: $6.00 adult, $4.00 student.*

This is the boyhood home of Alex Haley, Pulitzer Prize-winning author of "Roots". Visit the burial site of Haley and well-known family members including Chicken George. The front porch of this home is where young Alex heard the stories of his ancestors. "The front porch of this home is, in fact, the birthplace of Roots," said Haley. This ten-room bungalow, constructed from 1918 to 1921 by Haley's grandfather, Will E. Palmer, has been restored to model the home as it was when Haley was born. Some of the 1919 furniture which decorates the home belonged to the Haley's family. Haley's book received international acclaim and spurred millions to research their own ancestry.

FORT PILLOW STATE HISTORIC PARK

*Henning - Rte. 2, 3122 Park Road (Hwy 87, off Hwy 51, west of town) 38041. www.
state.tn.us/environment/parks/FortPillow/index.shtml Phone: (731) 738-5581.*

During the spring and early summer of 1862, the Union Navy bombarded Fort Pillow from its mortar boats. Few casualties resulted, but with the increasing danger of being cut-off from the main army, the Confederate Army evacuated Fort Pillow in June of 1862. Union forces immediately occupied the fort and held it for almost two years.

The Museum is where visitors will find Civil War artifacts and interpretive displays. There is a 12-minute video on the 1864 Battle shown by request. Fort Pillow State Historic Park has been designated as a Wildlife Observation Area. Interpretive signs identify certain species and their habitat. The park provides sanctuary for deer and turkey, and is frequented by bird watchers. Nature and recreational programs are presented during the summer months or upon request. Other Activities: Playgrounds, Volleyball, Tennis, Horseshoes, Softball, tent camping, canoeing and fishing. The Mississippi River Bike Trail winds its way thru here. Hours: 8am-4pm (closed for lunch).

CYPRESS GROVE NATURE PARK

*Jackson - US 70 W   38301. Phone: (731) 425-8364. Hours: Daily 8:00am-
5:00pm (November-March), 8:00am-dusk (April-October). Admission: FREE. www.
jacksonrecandparks.com/leagues/custom_page.cfm?clientid=3046&leagueid=0&pageid
=558*

Established to preserve part of Jackson's natural river bottom habitat, the park consists of 165 acres of Cypress forest and features trails, a couple miles of elevated boardwalk, a pond and a lake. The site also features a Raptor Center, a haven for birds of prey that have been injured and cannot survive on their own in the wild. Picnic facilities are here, too.

NC & ST. L DEPOT AND RAILROAD MUSEUM

*Jackson - 582 South Royal St. (I-40 exit 80A, south on Hwy 45 bypass) 38301. www.
jacksonrecandparks.com/leagues/custom_page.cfm?clientid=3046&leagueid=0&
pageid=1112 Phone: (731) 425-8223. Hours: Monday-Saturday 10:00am-3:00pm.*

For updates & travel games visit: **www.KidsLoveTravel.com**

Admission: FREE.

The N.C. & St. Louis Railroad brought passengers to Jackson's Depot to partake of the town's mineral waters, eat popcorn supplied by a local character named "Popcorn Johnny" and listen to the music. The Depot features a museum, Amtrak dining car, two cabooses, and an elaborate model railroad display reflecting the town's history as West Tennessee's railroad hub.

CASEY JONES VILLAGE

Jackson - 56 Casey Jones Lane (I-40 exit 80Aat US 45 bypass) 38305. Phone: (731) 668-1223 or (877) CASEY-100. www.caseyjonesvillage.com Hours: Daily 6:00am-10:00pm (except Easter, Thanksgiving & Christmas). Museum has regular business hours. Admission: Fee charged for train ride and mini-golf (summers 10:00am-9:00pm). Fee for House/Museum tour ($6.50 BOGO ticket if you have receipt from Old Country Store).

All aboard for Casey Jones Village where your kids will run to climb on Engine 382 to ring the bell. Train engineer Casey Jones, heroically stayed with his train and died in a wreck outside Vaughan, Miss.

The Casey Jones Home & Railroad Museum is the historic 1900s home of America's most legendary railroad man. His story was told in one of the most popular ballads ever written. The Museum includes railroad artifacts, original steam locomotive engines and a model railroad exhibit. How did he get the name, Casey? Learn how Casey loved the challenge of running faster times on the railroad. If he was behind,

All aboard the mighty 382...

he was skilled to make up time. See a video & mini model RR showing exactly how the accident happened…the crash heard round the world. Why was he a hero?

A miniature train ride and miniature golf operates seasonally. What a family-friendly place with something for everyone! Stretch your legs leisurely wandering through the many shops, railroad cars and museum and a game of mini-golf.

A great place to sit a spell...

Casey Jones Village *(cont.)*

Save your appetite, because you'll have to try at least one of the Old Country Stores Southern buffets. A great value (kids pay 50¢ times their age), the food here is so fresh. Every meal serves up something from the griddle. Say hello to the owners: Clark (usually makin cracklin' corn bread at the griddle) or Juanita in the gift shop. Tell them *Kids Love Tennessee* sent 'ya.

Now, if you're enjoying yourself too much, how about an overnight (for reasonable cost) in one of their cabooses or rail cars? Because they're real railroad cars, space is limited, but what fun!

WEST TENNESSEE DIAMOND JAXX BASEBALL

Jackson - Pringles Park, 4 Fun Place (I-40 exit 85) 38305. Phone: (731) 644-2020. www.diamondjaxx.com Hours: Schedule includes 70 dates between April and August each year. Most games are Monday-Saturday at 7:05pm or Sunday at 2:05pm. Admission: $2.00-$9.00.

The West Tenn Diamond Jaxx, a Class AA professional baseball team affiliated with the Seattle Mariners, plays in the 6,000-seat Pringles Park. It also offers a variety of amusements and attractions sponsored by Pringles Potato Chips, made in Jackson.

MEMPHIS MOTORSPORTS PARK

Memphis (Millington) - 5500 Victory Lane 38053. Phone: (901) 358-7223 or (866) 407-7333. www.racemir.com.

Hosts NASCAR series, Craftsman Truck Series, as well as NHRA Drag Racing Series. Weekly racing and special events. All drag race seating is general admission except for the Nitro grandstand. Children 12 and under are FREE with a paid Adult. General admission around $15.00. Events spring - early autumn. NASCAR events packages are more and must be purchased in advance.

BEALE STREET WALKING TOURS

Memphis - Beale Street Information Center 38103. Phone: (901) 527-3427. Hours: Handy House: Tuesday-Saturday 10:00am-5:00pm (summer) and Tuesday-Saturday 1:00-4:00pm (winter). Admission: Handy House: $2.00 per person.

Lining this famous street are some big-name nightspots including B.B. King's Blues Club, and Hard Rock Café, on Beale Street. Besides hearing music most every evening and some late afternoons, you can also visit various specialty shops or the home of W.C. Handy, who launched his career from here. The small wood-frame house depicts the humble beginnings of the "Father of the Blues".

Another popular stop is A. Schwab's, a century-old family-operated dry goods store, where you can find everything from tools to toys. Also check out the Beale Street Police Substation and Museum to see relics from old time police days. On Main Street (intersects with Beale), take a $1 trolley up north towards Mud Island or the Fire Museum.

CIRCUIT PLAYHOUSE

Memphis - 1705 Poplar Ave. 38103. www.playhouseonthesquare.org Phone: (901) 726-4656. Hours: Performances for different shows run Thursday-Sunday.

Professional live theater offering Broadway and off-Broadway performances at affordable prices ($15.00-$30.00). Theatre for Youth feature each year plus many Playhouse performances are geared towards families (Purple Purse, Wizard of Oz, Peter Pan).

FIRE MUSEUM OF MEMPHIS

Memphis - 118 Adams Avenue (downtown, a few blocks east of the Mud Island Walkway) 38103. Phone: (901) 320-5650. www.firemuseum.com Hours: Monday-Saturday 9:00am-5:00pm. Closed Sunday. Admission: $6.00 adult, $4.00 senior (60+) & $5.00 child (3-12).

This downtown museum is housed in the old Fire Station No. 1 and contains a collection of artifacts, including stories and photos of the city's most devastating fires. However, most of the features are for kids beginning with an animated "talking" horse that narrates a video about the role horses played in fire fighting;

Interactive games that teach fire safety and simulate real fires through devices such as hot air, thick smoke, and wrap-around video screens (this will get your attention!); and a 1967 Pumper or modern fire truck cab that children can actually get in and play "fire fighter." Dress up in uniform, turn on the siren or simulate fighting a fire in a skyscraper. There's even a firefighters video arcade to play games on.

This is our favorite Kids Fire Museum in the nation!

GIBSON GUITAR FACTORY TOURS

*Memphis - 145 Lt. George W. Lee Avenue in the Beale Street Entertainment District, just a half a block south of Beale Street and Highway 61 (a.k.a. Third Street) 38103. Phone: (901) 544-7998. **www2.gibson.com/Gibson/Gibson-Tours.aspx** Admission: $10.00 (ages 5+ only). Tours: last approx 45 minutes, manufacturing not guaranteed but there will always be Luthiers present.*

See Gibson guitars made on a docent-led tour of 16 work stations on the factory floor. Knowledgeable "honest to goodness" musicians lead you along

...learn the steps behind Gibson's legendary sound...

as master craftspeople use the latest technology to hand-craft a guitar from a block of wood. Learn about Gibson's 100-plus years of history as you get an up-close view of skilled artisans as they design, carve, paint, polish and ship one-of-a-kind instruments. You won't believe how they can shape and carve wood into those smooth guitar lines! The Les Paul and B.B. King's Lucille are just two of the many prestigious guitars manufactured on-site.

MEMPHIS REDBIRDS (AUTOZONE PARK)

Memphis - 8 S Third Street (Union at Third Street, Riverside Dr. exit, downtown) 38103. Phone: (901) 721-8050 or 721-6000 box office. **www.memphisredbirds.com** *Hours: Games April-August. Admission: $7.00-$20.00.*

After you dine at Rendezvous, head over to AutoZone ballpark for good, old-fashioned minor league baseball with a modern twist. Redbirds Baseball, the AAA affiliate of the St. Louis Cardinals. Dominating the park's entry plaza is the 37-foot tall "Nostalgia Man". Kids can join the Kids Club.

The Boardwalk is a family-oriented games and amusement area & P.D. Parrot's Playhouse Perch is a playground and fun zone located next to the Bluff. From the "pinball" chute to the playground…you're guaranteed an exciting and entertaining ballgame…and for a reasonable price.

We watched a 10-inning overtime winning game with a solo homerun in the bottom of the 10th! The place went wild with fireworks celebrating the big victory. Minor league baseball is a great way to afford a game as a family, without all the Big League celebrity hoopla.

TOURS: Take a peek "behind the scenes" of the state-of-the-art press box, lighting and see where the players workout. Tours are $5.00 per person at 10:00am & 1:00pm on non-game days.

MEMPHIS RIVERKINGS

Memphis - (DeSoto Civic Center, I-55 towards Jackson, MS. Take the Church Road Exit (#287). Turn right onto Church Rd. then turn left onto Venture Dr) 38103. Phone: (662) 342-1755. **www.riverkings.com**

Pro hockey championship team season runs October-April. Tickets prices start as low as $5.00. Affiliation as a primary AA affiliate in the SPHL.

MEMPHIS ROCK N SOUL MUSEUM

Memphis - 191 Beale Street at FedEx Forum Plaza (in the Beale Street District on Beale Street and Third St, I-55N exit 12B, east on Beale) 38103. Phone: (901) 205-2533. **www.memphisrocknsoul.org** *Hours: Daily 10:00am-7:00pm Admission: $11.00 adult, $9.00 senior, $8.00 child (5-17).*

"In the quest to identify the roots of America's music, all roads lead to Memphis". The Smithsonian's exhibit tells the history of musicians working in the Delta and Memphis area from the 1930s to 1970s and the style of music they developed…from Blues & Gospel To Rock-And-Roll And Soul. Kids like the CD headset that they can program themselves and customize their tour by listening to songs from certain eras. Start in the cotton fields, then to radio studios and jukebox eras. Then, enter Sun Records and Elvis Rockabilly (white man's words to black man's music) along with Johnny Cash, Carl Perkins or Jerry Lee Lewis…Rebel music crossing the sounds of the blues, soul and country.

MEMPHIS ZOO

Memphis - 2000 Prentiss Place, Overton Park (midtown, off N. Parkway) 38103. Phone: (901) 276-WILD. www.memphiszoo.org Hours: Daily 9:00am-5:00pm. Winter hours close at 4pm. Closed some holidays. Admission: $15.00 adult, $14.00 senior (60+), $10.00 child (2-11). Parking $5.00.

Over 3,000 animal residents occupy areas such as: Cat Country; Primate Canyon; Animals of the Night; Once Upon a Farm; Tropical Bird House; and the new China Exhibit.

Memphis is one of only four US cities with its own pair of rare animals – Le Le and Ya Ya, a pair of giant pandas. Why are they so precious? The entire China exhibit utilizes educational graphics, murals, video, traditional music and artifacts to enrich the experience as it engages each visitor in the culture, history and wildlife of China.

While at the zoo, be sure to visit Cat Country. With its shaded boardwalks and easy viewing areas (most animals like to "rest" right near the viewing windows) – it's a hit with kids. Check out the Capybara (giant guinea pigs)!

MISSISSIPPI RIVER MUSEUM

Memphis - 125 N Front Street (Mud Island) 38103. Phone: (901) 678-7230. www. mudlisland.com Hours: Tuesday-Sunday 10:00am-5:00pm (mid April to Memorial Day & September, October). Admission: Includes monorail roundtrip & guided River Walk tour, plus museum: $10.00 adult, $9.00 senior (60+), $7.00 child (5-11).

This museum of the natural and cultural history of the Lower Mississippi River Valley tells a story. The search for more efficient transportation and the economic impact of river transportation played a vital role in the development of trade routes and the growth of river cities.

Walk on a steamboat and hear stories from passengers and crew about life on the river - even go up to the pilothouse. Meet a gallery of famous Showboat folks (Mark Twain, Mike Fink). Now, enter the full-size cannon room of an ironclad and then go on land and fire back.

The Theatre of Disasters Gallery has an audio visual presentation of river tragedies, including the great earthquake of 1811, the yellow fever plagues, and steamboat disasters. Next, relax listening to river music.

Finally, exit thru the River Room's 4000 gallon aquarium full of river fish (look out for the giant catfish!). Very well done!

MUD ISLAND RIVER PARK

Memphis - 125 N Front Street (walkway or monorail over from Riverside Drive, downtown) 38103. www.mudisland.com Phone: (901) 576-7241 or (800) 507-6507. Hours: Daylight hours. Admission: FREE. Fee for boat and bike rentals. Note: Monorail ($4.00 per person fee) and Walkway access from downtown riverfront. There are also canoe, kayak, airboat, pedal boat and bicycle rentals. 3 food concession areas.

This combination public park, museum, and entertainment center lies between the Mississippi River and the Wolf River Harbor.

The <u>RIVER WALK</u> is a five-block-long scale model of the Mississippi from north to south. Along your journey, you'll revisit historical events and learn about geographical transformations. Walk along the banks or actually wade in the "River" - great family fun! The "1,000" mile journey concludes at the Gulf of Mexico, a

...wading down the river...fun!

one acre enclosure that holds 1.3 million gallons of water. There, visitors can enjoy a leisurely pedal boat ride.

The <u>MEMPHIS BELLE PAVILION</u> is home to the WWII famous bomber airplane with a self-guided tour (901-412-8071), and the <u>RIVER MUSEUM</u> (901-576-7230) is on the island (see separate listing).

On occasion the Queen Line of famous riverboats docks here.

NATIONAL CIVIL RIGHTS MUSEUM

Memphis - 450 Mulberry Street (downtown, a few blocks from Riverside Dr, look for the large Lorraine Motel sign) 38103. Phone: (901) 521-9699. **www.civilrightsmuseum.org** *Hours: Monday-Saturday 9:00am-5:00pm, Sunday 1:00-5:00pm. Closed Tuesdays. Open until 6:00pm (May-August). Admission: $12.00 adult, $10.00 senior and student, $8.50 child (4-17). Free Time (Mondays): 3:00 pm-6:00pm.*

...the actual site...so emotional

The enhanced experience of actually being at the original Lorraine Motel, site of Dr. Martin Luther King, Jr.'s assassination, is enough in itself.

Begin with an easy video to understand the movement. Kids and parents get goosebumps seeing where Dr. King died and all the use of the word "Colored". The letters "C" and "W" were recognized even by the illiterate.

The walk-thru exhibits are very touching - esp. getting kicked off a bus or seeing the actual motel room and balcony where Martin Luther King was shot! The Exploring Legacy exhibit focuses on more recent Civil Rights struggles as well as revealing additional facts & artifacts surrounding the assassination (previously classified documents and evidence). Inspiring feelings of love of freedom here! Warning: strong themes and message might scare or intimidate young ones under 7.

SLAVE HAVEN UNDERGROUND RAILROAD MUSEUM (BURKLE ESTATE)

Memphis - 826 N 2nd St. 38103. www.slavehavenundergroundrailroadmuseum.org Phone: (901) 527-3427. Hours: Monday-Saturday 10:00am-5:00pm (summer), Monday-Saturday 10:00am-4:00pm (winter). Admission: $10.00 adult, $8.00 student (4-17).

This former waystation on the Underground Railroad has a secret cellar and trap doors that reveal the escape route and hiding room of runaway slaves. Learn hidden code designs sewn into quilts. Get to know Harriet Tubman as she encouraged slaves to follow her. Mommas had to silence their babies when hiding in the cellar. Startling (a little disturbing for young ones) displays of ads, auctions and artifacts help tell the story of slavery and the escape to freedom.

SUN STUDIO

Memphis - 706 Union Avenue (I-40 exit Rte. 51S, head east on US 70/79/51/64, seven blocks from the River) 38103. Phone: (901) 521-0664. www.sunstudio.com Hours: Daily 10:00am-6:00pm Admission: $12.00 general. FREE for children under ages 3-11. Children on tour must be at least 3 years old. No strollers as there are stairs on the tour. Tours: given at the bottom half of the hour. Note: With computers and CD music to back you up, you can produce your own little song ($20-$30.00) that says "Recorded at the Legendary Sun Studio Memphis".

This tiny studio (with added museum cafe and gift shop) is where the Rock n' Roll sound started. Elvis Presley, Carl Perkins, Johnny Cash, Jerry Lee Lewis and Roy Orbison all got their start here and stars like U2 and BB King still record here.

They made a new sound in this Studio and the walls still feel like they sing and talk to you. Owner Sam Phillips would record anything, anytime, anywhere. Your tour guide showcases memorable moments, out-takes from sessions and you can even touch Elvis' first microphone and hear his first recording as a shy boy with a new sound! Kids like listening to

...singing into Elvis' microphone!

Elvis goofing off on tape and hearing the first radio play of Elvis' "That's All Right". Also, hear the first Rock n Roll song - "Rocket 88" - recorded with a new "distorted" sound, by accident *(a broken amplifier)*.

You must visit this site as part of your exploration of Elvis and rock n roll!

CHILDREN'S MUSEUM OF MEMPHIS

Memphis - 2525 Central Avenue (1-240 East to Airways Exit #23 and travel North to Central Avenue, continue East on Central to Hollywood) 38104. Phone: (901) 320-3170. www.cmom.com Hours: Daily 9:00am-5:00pm. Closed some major holidays. Admission: $12.00 general. Splash Park (seasonal summers) $8-$10. Combo: $17.00. FREEBIES: www.cmom.com/about/just-for-kids/ Educators: Traveling Exhibit Resources - www.cmom.com/traveling-exhibit-resources/ Note: Toddlers Playscape area. Kids Coke Corner vending machines. Jasons Deli and a great gift shop. The special events here are probably the best of Children's events anywhere!

Hands-on fun here at a museum designed as a miniature city. Sit in a flight

...Capt. Daniel says "Clear for Take off"

simulator and a real airplane cockpit, explore a Mississippi River model, climb thru the arteries of a giant heart, ride a bicycle...on Mars, don a lab coat and play dentist in Smile, hop on a real fire engine or shop for groceries. Create performances on stage using the gobs of outfits you can wear and "act" with on a real stage with changing backgrounds.

The ever-popular WaterWORKS area is water play while you're learning. Let it Rain room simulates a storm and flood - how do you survive erosion? Homes has endless possibilities of ways to try to build and design your own home or climb up a giant skyscraper!

New and upgraded components and activities to the Garage exhibit include: Build-a-car – a computer program allows visitors to build their own car; Tire-changing/jack demo; Drive train – a partial "transmission" displayed with the crankshaft, gears driveshaft and rear axle; Brake demo; career dress-up – information on careers related to auto design, engineering, manufacturing and repair; Minivan – allows kids to role-play driving (includes the gas pump nearby for fill-ups); Real Engines and Happy car/sad car.

MEMPHIS BROOKS MUSEUM OF ART

Memphis - 1934 Poplar Avenue, Overton Park (just west of East Parkway and south of North Parkway, and adjacent to the Memphis Zoo) 38104. Phone: (901) 544-6200. ***www.brooksmuseum.org*** *Hours: Tuesday-Friday 10:00am-4:00pm, Saturday 10:00am-5:00pm, Sunday 11:00am-5:00pm. Admission: $7.00 adult, $6.00 senior, $3.00 student (6+).*

The state's oldest and largest fine-arts museum, Brooks offers works dating from ancient times to the latest modern. Throughout the year, the museum hosts a series of Family Days in conjunction with special exhibitions. These fun-filled days are free for everyone and include hands-on art projects and other exciting activities such as: live music, costume contests, films, storytelling, and food. Everyday, families can enjoy self-guided discovery tours and special audio tour stops.

NATIONAL ORNAMENTAL METAL MUSEUM

Memphis - 374 Metal Museum Drive (I-55 exit 12C) 38106. Phone: (901) 774-6380 or (877) 881-2326. ***www.metalmuseum.org*** *Hours: Tuesday-Saturday 10:00am-5:00pm, Sunday Noon-5:00pm. Closed Christmas to New Years. Admission: $5.00 adult, $4.00 senior (62+), $3.00 student. Note: Riverbluff picnic pavilion w/ sculpture garden overlooking Mississippi river.*

The only facility of its kind in the country, the museum not only contains a collection of American and European ironworks, metal sculpture, medieval armor and unique

...my metal garden friend

metal jewelry, but also presents traveling exhibits, as well. Walk around the garden with one area full of animal sculptures.

Metal Art is interesting to look at, but the kids gravitate to the studio workshop where artists perform their craft. Demonstrations on weekend afternoons are fun to watch. Check out the colorful "Four Tops" and "Cornstalk Fence" on your way out.

SOULSVILLE: STAX MUSEUM OF AMERICAN SOUL MUSIC

Memphis - 926 E. McLemore (east of downtown off Crump Blvd, south on Mississippi, east on McLemore) 38106. www.soulsvilleusa.com Phone: (901) 946-2535. Hours: Monday-Saturday 9:00am-4:00pm, Sunday 1:00-4:00pm (March-October). Open at 10:00am, Monday-Saturday (November-February). Closed some holidays. Admission: $10.00 adult, $9.00 senior (62+) and military, $7.00 child (9-12). Under 8 years old FREE.

They celebrate soul music here...the Memphis music made famous by Otis Reading, Isaac Hayes, Al Green, Aretha Franklin, Earth, Wind & Fire and the like. Stax Studios is where it happened in the 1960s and 1970s and this site follows the music's development from local churches to the international stage. Interact with exhibits in the Soul music record label, STAX building. As well as being a historical music mecca, this funky little neighborhood also has some of the best soul food in the world...from the Big S Grill to Ellen's Soul Food.

CHUCALISSA MUSEUM

Memphis - 1987 Indian Village Drive (I-55 exit 9, at edge of Fuller State Park, off Mitchell/Winchester Road, west of Graceland) 38109. Phone: (901) 785-3160. www. chucalissa.memphis.edu Hours: Tuesday-Saturday 9:00am - 5:00pm. Shorter winter hours. Admission: $5.00 adult, $3.00 senior and child (4-11). Note: Guided tours,

 *crafts, workshops and storytelling offered on a seasonal basis. Lots of activity at Pow Wows held here every few months.*

Built on a Native American Temple Mound complex, this museum and outdoor exhibit features artifacts, an authentic reconstructed pre-Columbia village (w/ thatch roof huts representative of 500 years ago) and an interpretive nature trail. Meaning "abandoned house" (Choctaw), Chucalissa was inhabited by various Indian tribes, who mysteriously deserted the face of the earth in the 1500s. Begin by exploring windows of the ages (starts B.C.)...all the artifacts they found are examples of the periods of different civilizations.

Outside, the dioramas inside the huts appear as if you're visiting a family or chief. Can you guess which is the chief's house? You can easily turn your child into an ancient mystery solver here.

T.O. FULLER STATE PARK

Memphis - 1500 Mitchell Rd. (off Hwy 61, south of Memphis) 38109. Phone: (901) 543-7581. www.state.tn.us/environment/parks/TOFuller/index.shtml Hours: 8:00am-sunset.

The park was named after Dr. Thomas O. Fuller who had spent his life empowering and educating African-Americans during the late 1800s and early 1900s. Provides: golf, swimming, camping and hiking opportunities.

LICHTERMAN NATURE CENTER

Memphis - 5992 Quince Rd. 38111. www.memphismuseums.org/nature.htm Phone: (901) 767-7322. Hours: Monday-Thursday 9:00am-4:00pm, Friday-Saturday 9:00am-5:00pm, Sunday Noon-5:00pm. Admission: $6.00 adult, $5.50 senior (60+), $4.50 child (3-12).

Lichterman now welcomes you with a large visitors center that has an orientation room (with exhibits and closed-circuit viewing of wildlife) and a nature store. On the premises are greenhouses, a backyard wildlife center (interactives, a cutaway pond and meadow habitats, and an elevated boardwalk into the forest), and 3 miles of boardwalks and trails.

MEMPHIS PINK PALACE MUSEUM

Memphis - 3050 Central Avenue (I-240 North to Union Ave. exit east. Go to Hollywood, turn right (south), next light (Central) turn left (east) 38111. Phone: (901) 320-6362. www.memphismuseums.org Hours: Monday-Saturday 9:00am-5:00pm, Sunday 1:00-5:00pm. Closed on Thanksgiving Day, Christmas Eve, Christmas Day and New Year's Day. Admission: $11.75 adult, $6.25 child (3-12). IMAX and Planetarium are extra or may buy combo package at a discount. Note: IMAX Theater (901-763-IMAX) with new films every 4 months (IMAX Discovery Room, adjacent, has fun, interactive experiences related to current films). Sharpe Planetarium seasonal sky shows and special Elvis and Holiday laser shows. Educators: Teachers Guides-www.memphismuseums.org/guides

The Pink Palace Mansion was Piggly Wiggly founder's dream home, though he never lived in this estate built of pink Georgia marble. The Mansion exhibits tell the historical story of Memphis with name-droppers like Mayor

Boss Crump and the King, Elvis to events like the Age of Discovery or the Trail of Tears. See the role wars, women and entrepreneurs played. And then, some exhibits are just plain "to see it is to believe it" (shrunken woman's head and miniature circus). View lifelike dioramas of each time period.

The exact replica of the first Piggly Wiggly grocery store is fun to play pretend in. You'll delve into natural regional history, too, as your tykes peer thru microscopes at some tiny things out of the lower Mississippi River Valley. See life-size dinosaur replicas and footprints, mastodon skeletons and teeth, tusks and a display of fossils.

They also operate an 1830s historical home, MAGEVNEY HOUSE, downtown (198 Adams Avenue, 901-528-4464, FREE, closed Sundays & Mondays & January & February) which was home to one of Memphis' first schoolteachers with original furnishings.

The other museum is the COON CREEK SCIENCE CENTER (2985 Hardin Graveyard Rd, Adamsville 38310, 901-636-2362) but is limited to organized groups.

MEMPHIS SYMPHONY ORCHESTRA

Memphis - 3100 Walnut Grove Road, Ste. 501 (performances at Cannon Center) 38111. Phone: (901) 324-3627. ***www.memphissymphony.org***

Family Concerts and Pops Series interest children the most. Catch Grammy award singers or an evening of Elvis. Also, Memphis Youth Symphony and pre-concert activities occasionally offered.

MEMPHIS BOTANIC GARDEN

Memphis - 750 Cherry Road (Interstate 240, take exit 20-B) 38117. Phone: (901) 685-1566. ***www.memphisbotanicgarden.com*** *Hours: Monday-Saturday 9:00am-6:00pm (March-October). Only open until 4:30pm (November-February). Admission: $8.00 adult, $6.50 senior (62+), $5.00 child (3-12).*

As you stroll through 96 acres of gardens, in the heart of East Memphis, you see horticulture at its best. Check out the Japanese Garden of Tranquility, Sensory, and Hyde & Seek Prehistoric Trail (dinos, fossil pit, play structure). Festivals are probably the best time for families to come and actively learn about and use natural materials to craft special works. At the heart of the park is the Red Drum Bridge arching over a koi-filled lake (a kid favorite).

DAVIES MANOR PLANTATION

Memphis - 9336 Davies Plantation Road (I-40East exit 20 north) 38133. Phone: (901) 388-0715. **www.daviesmanorplantation.org** *Hours: Tuesday-Saturday Noon-4:00pm (April-early December). Admission: $5.00 adult, $3.00 student.*

An Indian chief built Shelby County's oldest log house in the early 1800s. Later, the Davies moved in and turned the property into a plantation. The plantation house is a two-story pioneer home and your 30 minute tour shows you the entry, kitchen, bedrooms and other parts of the house.

SHELBY FARMS

Memphis - 7171 Mullins Station or 500 Pine Lake Drive (I-40 exit 12 or I-240 exit Walnut Grove Rd) 38134. **www.shelbyfarmspark.org** *Phone: (901) 382-0235. Hours: Visitor Center open weekdays 8:00am-4:30pm.*

This 4,500-acre park offers a little nature and a little sporting. Patriot Lake Trail is 12 feet wide and 1.67 miles long. This multi-purpose trail, winding around Patriot Lake, is enjoyed by walkers, joggers, cyclists and inline skaters. Chickasaw Trail is a 3.3-mile long path traveling through the northern portion of the park. It meanders through pine and hardwood forest areas and past three lakes. Walkers, Joggers, bikes and inline skaters are allowed on the Chickasaw Trail.

From horseback riding and hiking, canoeing and wind-surfing, to wildlife watching or bison roaming on the animal range.

The Showplace Arena is where equestrian and other type of events are held. DUCKS UNLIMITED international headquarter's scenic waterfowl propagation lake is here as well as, the AGRICENTER INTERNATIONAL which displays advances in farming technology.

MEMPHIS GRIZZLIES

Memphis - (home games played at the Fed Ex Forum) 38173. Phone: (901) 888-HOOP or (866) 479-4667. **www.grizzlies.com**

Catch this NBA team in action each October through April. Grizz Kids Fan Club includes stickers, posters and magazines. Learn about the legend of Grizz and Super Grizz mascots, too. Tickets range $30.00+.

MEMPHIS RIVERBOATS

Memphis - 45 Riverside Drive (park at Memphis Harbor, foot of Monroe & Union Avenues at trolley stop) 38173. www.memphisriverboats.net Phone: (901) 527-5694. Admission: Sightseeing: $10.00-$20.00 (age 4+). Dinner & Music: up to $50.00 per person.

Two hour riverboat cruises on the Mississippi. Take a step back in time with the narrative of past and present river life. A riverboat cruise is a quiet way to learn a little about the river era of Native Americans, explorers, riverboat men like Mark Twain and Mike Fink, highlights of local Civil War river battles and the heritage of the Mississippi River bluffs and delta, plus today's commerce on the river.

GRACELAND

Memphis - 3734 Elvis Presley Blvd. (I-55 exit 5B, Elvis Presley Blvd) 38186. Phone: (901) 332-3322 or (800) 238-2000. www.elvis.com Hours: Monday-Saturday 9:00am-5:00pm, Sunday 10:00am-4:00pm (March-October). Daily 10:00am-4:00pm, except holidays (November-February). Admission: Platinum Tour (all 4 attractions): $37.00 adult, $33.30 senior (62+)/student, $18.00 child (7-12). Mansion Only: $33.00 adult, $30 senior/student, $15.00 child. Other Exhibits: $8.00-$12.00 adult, $7.00-$10.00 senior/student, $5.50-$6.00 child. Note: A few cafes and grills are in the complex for casual dining. Arrive early if you want to tour the home first. Plan a 2 -4 hour visit.

Experience Elvis' home with the Mansion audio tour (featuring comments from Elvis himself and Lisa Marie) and some new artifacts, not on display until recently. The tour now includes never-before-seen items like the desk from Elvis' personal office and an extensive collection of his stage costumes.

Start in the Plaza (across the street) with a *Walk A Mile In My Shoes*, presented at the Bijou Theater in the middle of the plaza, this 22-minute film takes guests through highlights of the exciting, fascinating career of Elvis Presley (presented on the hour and the half-hour).

After the shuttle takes you over to the home, you'll be one of many to see the insides of the antebellum-style house,

...inside Elvis' living room

including the dining room where Elvis often took a late evening dinner with friends, the kitchen, the TV room and several others. Look for the "Teddy Bear" chair in the Jungle Room. His career is completely unfolded and his "relax time" revealed. You'll go from excitement in the Racquetball Room to the sad story of his last days. Then walk out to his grave before you leave.

Later, cruise through the ELVIS PRESLEY AUTO MUSEUM, filled with Elvis' exclusive limited edition and rare vintage vehicles. Wild and colorful cars to look at and even all the golf carts he used to have on the property. See his custom jets...the "Lisa Marie" &

T.C.B. with "Lisa Marie"

...signing the stone wall

"Hound Dog II". Get a more intimate glimpse at Elvis' personal life & family in the 68 SPECIAL exhibit full of candid photos & home-movie clips. You can even touch some of his '70s sample artifacts or watch videos from his tours and see many homemade gifts sent to him. You will leave here knowing so much more about his personal life and really catch "Elvis Fever"!

MEEMAN-SHELBY STATE PARK

Millington - 910 Riddick Road (13 miles north of Memphis, off US 51) 38053. Phone: (901) 876-5215 or (800) 471-5293. www.state.tn.us/environment/parks/ MeemanShelby/index.shtml Hours: 7:00am-10:00pm.

More commonly known as Shelby Forest, this state park sits atop the Chickasaw Bluffs. Bordering on the Mississippi River, the park consists of bottomland hardwood forests and two lakes. Besides hiking trails, camping, and an Olympic-sized swimming pool, the park offers fishing and boating on its Poplar Tree Lake. The park's Nature Center has several exhibits and offers guided tours.

TENNESSEE NATIONAL WILDLIFE REFUGE

Paris - *3006 Dinkins Lane (along the TN River and Kentucky Lake) 38242. Phone: (731) 642-2091.* **http://tennesseerefuge.fws.gov/**

The Tennessee National Wildlife Refuge combines 25,000 acres of water, 19,000 acres of woodland and 5,000 acres of farmland and pasture to offer irresistible resting and feeding opportunities for migrating waterfowl on one of the nation's major flyways. In addition to being a home to wildlife, the refuge offers many recreational opportunities such as: hunting, fishing, boating, canoeing, wildlife viewing, and photography. Public use areas are open during daylight hours, except as modified by seasonal refuge regulations.

PARKER'S CROSSROADS BATTLEFIELD

Parker's Crossroads - *(I-40 and Hwy 22, exit 108) 38388. Phone: (731) 968-4225.* **www.parkerscrossroads.org** *Hours: Daily 9am-4:30pm. Admission: FREE*

This is the site of the famous December 31, 1862 battle by Confederate General Nathan Bedford Forrest. The self-guided driving tour brochure (available at Log Cabin Info Center) takes about one hour, with stops at important points of interest. Every two years (even number years), the association recreates a living history presentation of the battle.

PICKWICK LANDING STATE PARK

Pickwick Dam - *Park Road (I-40 to SR 22 south thru Shiloh, then SR 142 south to SR 57 east) 38365. Phone: (731) 689-3129 or (731) 689-3135 inn.* **www.state. tn.us/environment/parks/PickwickLanding/index.shtml** *Hours: Daily 8:00am-10:00pm.*

Excellent fishing (the Catfish Capital of the World), a golf course, a marina and great accommodations (lodge and cabins) are all available at this State Park.

Pickwick Landing was a riverboat stop dating from the 1840s. In the 1930s, during the depression, the site was chosen for one of the Tennessee Valley Authority's dams on the Tennessee River.

The new Inn & Restaurant overlook beautiful Pickwick Lake (offering for skiing, boating, canoeing, swimming and camping). All 119 rooms have a picturesque view of the lake. The Inn also has a new gift shop, exercise room with Nautilus equipment, an indoor and outdoor pool, laundry facilities and tennis courts. Each cabin has four double beds, for a capacity of eight people. Linens, dishes, cookware, even firewood for the fireplace are all provided. Fishing, food and a close-up look at a large dam and lock system.

PINSON MOUNDS STATE ARCHAEOLOGICAL PARK

*Pinson - 460 Ozier Road (Hwy. 45 S to Pinson, turn left at the park sign, SR 197 and then follow the signs) 38366. Phone: (731) 988-5614. **www.state.tn.us/environment/ parks/PinsonMounds/index.shtml** Hours: Monday - Saturday 8:00am-4:30pm, Sunday 1:00-5:00pm. Closed winter weekends (November-March). Park trails and picnic shelter are open until dark.*

Pinson Mounds consist of at least 15 earthen mounds, a geometric enclosure and surrounding habitation areas. It is the largest Middle Woodland period mound complex in the Southeast and dates to about 1-500 A.D. The Native Americans that built the mounds lived long before historically known Native American tribes, and used the site for ceremonial purposes and burials (see the many skeletons they found).

As you enter the building, you walk right into a recreated mound!

The museum attempts to replicate a mound with displays, videos and interpretive programs. Families like the open feeling of the grounds, picnic areas, playground, and the six miles of hiking trails with a boardwalk along the Forked Deer River.

Fieldwork is normally conducted in the summer, and visitors are welcome to watch the archaeologists at work. If they're not digging outside, you can learn and see how a dig is conducted by video and the excellent "Archeology in the Field" exhibit. In this diorama, you'll see a dig with each part of the process separately lit to highlight different features. Can you solve the mystery?

BIG HILL POND STATE PARK

Pocahontas - *984 John Howell Road (SR 57) 38061. Phone: (731) 645-7967.* **www.state.tn.us/environment/parks/BigHillPond/index.shtml** *Hours: 6:00am-9:00pm.*

The park is located on the junction of the Tuscumbia and Hatchie State Scenic River. Park highlights include:

THE BOARDWALK AND DISMAL SWAMP - (8/10th) of a mile long, through the scenic Dismal Swamp

THE OBSERVATION TOWER - 70 feet tall, this refurbished fire tower offers a panoramic view of Travis McNatt Lake and Dismal Swamp.

CIVIL WAR EARTHWORKS - railroad guard post built by Union Soldiers.

NATURE WATCHING - waterfowl, including osprey, migrations in spring and fall, some year round residence, abundant wildlife.

SALTILLO HISTORIC DISTRICT & FERRY

Saltillo - *Main Street 38372. Phone: (731) 925-2364 Hardin County CVB.*

Enjoy a ride on one of Tennessee's remaining river ferries to the charming town of Saltillo, an early river town with homes dating from the 1840s. Styles of architecture range from Greek Revival and Italianate influences to country farmhouses. Two cemeteries and a church pre-date the Civil War. The Saltillo Ferry is open Monday-Saturday 7:00am-4:00pm. Fee charged for ferry crossing. Driving tour map available from Hardin County CVB.

TENNESSEE RIVER MUSEUM

Savannah - *495 Main Street (US 64, downtown) 38372. Phone: (731) 925-2364 or (800) 552-3866.* **www.tennesseerivermuseum.org** *Hours: Monday-Saturday 9:00am-5:00pm, Sunday 1:00-5:00pm Admission: $3.00 adult, FREE for children. Note: On Rte. 128S (just a mile south of Rte. 64), you might want to grab a bite to eat for lunch or dinner @ Darryl Worley's (of fame: "Have You Forgotten?") Worleybirds casual restaurant.*

The museum has displays of paleontology, archeology, war on the river and the steamboat era. In the exhibits are items from the ironclad gunboats "Cairo" to the riverboats, to musseling (pearl buttons came from mussels, long ago)

plus other items concerning the river and its influence on the heritage of the Tennessee Valley. The world famous "Shiloh Effigy Pipe" of a man kneeling is the central archeological item.

Be sure to ask for the scavenger hunt sheet - it makes the museum more interesting to follow clues. Hands-on areas include the walk-thru battleship and trying to lift a 6 lb. Cannonball. The collection of fossils is wonderful… many you can touch.

SHILOH NATIONAL MILITARY PARK

Shiloh - 1055 Pittsburg Landing Road (Hwy 22 between SR 57 & US 64, on the west bank of the TN River) 38376. ***www.nps.gov/shil/*** *Phone: (731) 689-5696. Hours: Daily 8:00am-5:00pm. Closed Christmas. Admission: FREE. Note: During fall and spring, ranger-led programs are available on weekends. Right across from the Military park is Shilohs Civil War Relics. Browse through the displays and hear some stories, then purchase a relic - some are just $1.00 dug from nearby Civil War campsites*

(daily, except Tuesday, until 5:00pm, ***www.*** ***shilohrelics.com*** *or 731-689-4114).*

After bloody Shiloh, fought here in April, 1862, "The South never smiled again". Tours begin with an orientation movie at the visitor center. Now, let the kids touch and try on soldier uniforms (great photo ops). After looking over the museum exhibits, walk outside through the National Cemetery and to Pittsburg Landing on the Tennessee River. Understand and learn about the Hornets nest and temporary hospitals. Along the ten-mile, self-guided auto-tour, stop at each of the fourteen wayside exhibits (audio tour tapes available at the museum). Summertime: Daily rifle firing demos or ranger lead talks meeting at different tour stops. There are also hiking and biking trails in the 4000 acres and <u>SHILOH INDIAN MOUNDS</u> on the bluff overlooking the river. The mounds of Woodland/ Mississippian culture prehistoric Indians is one of the best preserved in the Tennessee River valley.

REELFOOT LAKE STATE PARK

Tiptonville - Rte. 1 (SR 22 & 78) 38079. Phone: (731) 253-7756. www.state.tn.us/
environment/parks/ReelfootLake/index.shtml Note: Reelfoot Lake State Park has
three hiking trails that are very popular and an auto tour that circles the lake.

Created by a series of earthquakes in 1811, this 13,000 acre lake offers great fishing
and waterfowl viewing (plus American bald eagles) in the winter.

BALD EAGLE TOURS - Eagles can be seen perching, flying/soaring and
often snatching fish from the lake. Nearby is the Reelfoot National Wildlife
Refuge & the Reelfoot Lake Waterfowl Festival Duck & Goose Calling
Contest.

PONTOON BOAT CRUISES (May through September, Fees required) -
Offered by naturalists, these trips allow visitors to experience the beauty of
Reelfoot Lake and learn about this unique area. Three-hour cruises depart
daily at 9:00am and short cruises are offered on weekends and holiday
afternoons. Sunset cruises are offered several times per month and moonlight
cruises are offered during the full moon (full moon rising through Cypress
Trees is an awesome sight).

MUSEUM (731-253-9652, 8:00am-4:30pm daily) - exhibits include large
aquariums with native fish and a discovery room with a variety of reptiles
and amphibians. The boardwalk is especially popular with bird watchers,
photographers, and fishermen.

DAVY CROCKETT CABIN - (901-665-6195, 219 N Trenton Street, Hwy
45W) Davy Crockett came to Gibson County in the fall of 1822, where he
farmed and reportedly killed 105 bears in one winter! The cabin has logs from
the original structure plus pieces of furniture from the Crockett Family.

NATCHEZ TRACE RESORT STATE PARK

Wildersville - 24845 Natchez Trace Road (I-40, exit 116) 38388. www.state.tn.us/
environment/parks/NatchezTrace/index.shtml Phone: (731) 968-8176. Miscellaneous:
In nearby Lexington, explore many other lakes (Beech, Pine, Sycamore, Dogwood &
Redbud) for outdoor recreation (731-968-6191). The Beech River Cultural Center &
Museum houses local geology, settler lifestyle and war history (731-967-0306).

Named for the western alternative route of the famous Nashville to Natchez,
Miss. Trail of the 18th and 19th centuries. The park includes Pin Oak and

Cub Lake and part of the Natchez Trace State Forest. Along with scenic woodlands, the park offers four lakes, miles of hiking trails, a wrangler camp inn, boating, resort lodge, restaurant, playgrounds, a ballfield, 250 miles of horse riding trails, a park store, archery range, and cabins. Picturesque Pin Oak Lodge is situated on the wooded shores of Pin Oak Lake. Support facilities include an exercise room, playground, tennis courts, and adult and kiddie swimming pools. The restaurant at Natchez Trace park over looks the pool and beautiful Pin Oak Lake.

SUGGESTED LODGING AND DINING

HEARTBREAK HOTEL. **Memphis**. 3677 Elvis Presley Blvd. (across from Graceland Mansion, I-55 exit Elvis Presley Blvd.) Phone: (901) 332-1000 or (877) 777-0606 **www.heartbreakhotel.net** Just the mere fact that it's across from Graceland is enough, but, this hotel has many family-friendly features. From the "Broken-heart" shaped outdoor swimming pool (how fun - great photo ops), to free in-room Elvis movies (all day), to free deluxe continental breakfast to a refrigerator and microwave in every room...this is a fun, comfy place to stay. The Jungle Room Café offers sandwiches and salads...even the famous recipe Peanut Butter and Banana grilled sandwich -
YUM! (we asked for lite on the PB). The hotel offers the Elvis Experience that includes package rates to Graceland at a discount. If you're really into it, rent an Elvis theme suite. After spending a night or two here, you'll be as hooked on Elvis as we were!

ARCADE RESTAURANT. **Memphis**. Just a couple of blocks south of Beale Street is the Arcade Diner (540 South Main) where Elvis loved to come for home-cooked breakfasts and their famous cheeseburgers. They even have one booth (in the back) you can sit in that was Elvis' favorite. $3.99 kids menu and they have old-fashioned shakes, too. (daily 7:00am-3:00pm, 901-526-5757, **www.arcaderestaurant.com**)

RENDEZVOUS RESTAURANT. **Memphis**. If you arrive into town near dinner, parents (and kids 10 and older) must first initiate themselves to Memphis with a visit to Rendezvous ribs! Their dry rub ribs are so tasty and unique, who needs sauce! *(Note: these are my favorite ribs ever! However, the flavor of the rub and sauce may be too spicy for the kids to love as much but they have other items on the menu).* No salads, no desserts - just barbeque meat and sides! They're located in an alleyway near Peabody Place. Ask a local for directions. If you want, just pop in and order carryout – no need to call ahead – they always have ribs ready. "for most people – locals and tourists alike – the Rendezvous' dry ribs are the very essence of Memphis barbecue." (901) 523-2776 or **www.hogsfly.com**. Serving dinner Tuesday-Saturday, lunch on Friday and Saturday.

PEABODY HOTEL. **Memphis**. Right across from Rendezvous ribs alleyway is the most magnificent grand old hotel in town - the Peabody. Known especially for their ducks - 4 ducks that have their own residence on the roof. Each morning, a duck butler leads the ducks from their "nest" as they waddle to follow him down the elevator to the main lobby where they spend their afternoons splashing in the foyer fountain.

Even non-guests can watch the parade of ducks each late morning and early evening!

If you are a guest, this is the perfect spot to overnight to be in the middle of the action! The rooms are high ceiling, spacious, luxurious but comfortable with hi-def tvs and super beds. A little ritzy for kids but if yours are well behaved a fun treat.

Chapter 7

Seasonal &
Special Events

JANUARY

COUNTRY DANCE WORLD CHAMPIONSHIPS

M – Nashville. Gaylord Opryland Resort & Convention Center. **www. ucwdcworlds.com**. Public is invited to the vendor area and free live music stage. Passes are available to purchase for the competition and Learn to Dance workshops. (First week of January)

WILDERNESS WILDLIFE WEEK

ME – Pigeon Forge. www.mypigeonforge.com. Outdoor lovers' activities including guided tours and workshops about the Smoky Mountains and its history. Casual tours or more strenuous hikes. Admission for guided tours. (9 days beginning week after New Years in January)

ELVIS PRESLEY BIRTHDAY CELEBRATION

W – Memphis. Elvis Presley's Graceland. **www.elvis.com**. Fun-filled days and nights feature events in celebration of Elvis' birthday. Birthday cake to all Graceland visitors on January 8th. Admission. (5 days leading up to January 8th)

FEBRUARY

SADDLE UP!

ME – Pigeon Forge. Music Road Hotel and various theatres. **www. mypigeonforge.com**. Features cowboy poetry, Western music and dancing, songwriting workshops and chuckwagon dinners. (Second long weekend in February)

SMOKY MOUNTAINS STORYTELLING FESTIVAL

ME – Pigeon Forge, Country Tonite Theatre & Grand Resort Hotel. **www. mypigeonforge.com**. Master storytellers carry on the Appalachian tradition of spinning tales indoors, theater-style, or outdoors alongside a blazing bonfire. Evening trolley rides. Admission. (mid-February long weekend)

MARCH

OLD-TIME FIDDLER'S CHAMPIONSHIP

M – **Clarksville**. **www.tnfiddlers.com**. Admission (12+). Annual state championship that features authentic old-time music. (Last Friday & Saturday in March)

APRIL - (EASTER EVENTS)

EASTER EGG HUNTS

ALL AREAS – Tennessee State Parks (most all). Three age divisions for children ages Toddler thru 10 years old. Grand prize (savings bond) & little treats can be found. **www.state.tn.us/environment/parks**. (Easter Saturday)

EASTER BUNNY TRIP

M – **Nashville**. Tennessee Central Railway. **www.tcry.org**. Departs at 9:00am to Watertown, 90 mile trip. Ride along with the Easter Bunny and join the egg hunt during the layover in Watertown. Admission. (Two Saturdays before Easter Sunday)

EGGSTRAVAGANZOO

M – **Nashville**. Nashville Zoo at Grassmere. **www.nashvillezoo.org**. Games, egg hunts, and children's activities. Bunny Breakfast by reservation only. (Easter Saturday)

EASTER SUNRISE SERVICE

ME – **Gatlinburg**. Ober Gatlinburg. (865) 436-5423. Free tram rides, a breakfast buffet offered, Easter egg hunt for children ages 2-10, and a special sunrise worship service. FREE. (Easter morning beginning at 6:30am)

SPRING COLORS / EASTER TRAINS

ME – **Oak Ridge**. Secret City Scenic Excursion Train. **www.techscribes. com/sarm/srm_scs.htm**. Admission. (Easter Saturday, 1:00 & 3:00pm)

EASTER BOAT CRUISES

SE – Chattanooga. Southern Belle Riverboat. **www.chattanoogariverboat.com**. Easter cruises with families are available on Easter weekend. Kids love their breakfast cruise, which includes a visit from the Easter Bunny. Admission. (Easter weekend in April)

BREAKFAST WITH BENNY THE BUNNY

W - Memphis. Children's Museum of Memphis. **www.cmom.org**. Children pet live rabbits, decorate Easter hats and bags, make bunny ears and surprise eggs, get their faces painted, have fun with carnival games, and meet Benny the Bunny at this "eggs-tra" special event. Children can also get their photos taken with Benny the Bunny for an extra fee. Breakfast snacks will be served. Admission (includes museum admission that same day). The event is appropriate for children ages 2-8 years old. (Saturday morning of Easter weekend)

APRIL

NATIONAL CORNBREAD FESTIVAL

EM– South Pittsburg. Downtown Historic district. **www.nationalcornbread.com**. Celebrate cornbread and small town hospitality at this event that includes a Championship cookoff, carnival, puppet shows, magicians, cloggers, storytellers, entertainment and trolley rides. (Last weekend in April)

SOUTHEASTERN LIVING HISTORY RENDEZVOUS

M – Castalian Springs, Bledsoe Fort Park. Some 500 folks from various places portraying life 1740-1840. Traders row. Admission. **www.srlab.net/bledsoe/events.html**. (first nine days in April)

HERITAGE DAYS

M – Goodlettsville. Mansker's Fort. Travel back in time to 18th century times complete with music, food, crafts and games. **www.manskers.historicallifestyles.com**. Every artist and merchant must adhere to 1750-1790 attire. Watch artisans demonstrate their craft. Purchase colonial foods such as pork chops w/ sizzle sauce, bratwurst, roast corn, beans, or fried pies cooked over a fire. Also, Scottish dancing, live music, puppets, beggars, preachers and Indians. Admission. (mid-month weekend in April)

WORLD'S BIGGEST FISH FRY

W – Paris. **www.worldsbiggestfishfry.com**. More than 10,000 pounds of catfish will be served along with large parades, auto shows, a rodeo, all-you-can-eat dinners and catfish races. Admission. (Last full week of April)

MAY

SPRING HOMECOMING

M – Clarksville. **www.historiccollinsville.com**. Celebration that features musical entertainment from world-renowned gospel, country and bluegrass musical groups. You'll also see pioneer activities, appearances by local music groups, and historic village tours. Weekend passes and day rates available. (Third weekend in May)

TENNESSEE RENAISSANCE FESTIVAL

M – Nashville (Triune). Castle Gwynn, a full size replica of a 12th century castle. **www.tnrenfest.com**. Step back in time to 16th Century England and enjoy the colorful pageantry of costumed villagers, musicians, and artisans. Games of human skill, full armored joust and man-powered rides. Admission varies. (Every weekend in May)

STRAWBERRY FESTIVAL

M – Portland. Downtown. Parade, storytelling, bluegrass music, games and the Middle TN Strawberry Parade. At the peak of the strawberry business, this small town was shipping out 30 railroad carloads a day. You can still visit local strawberry patches. **www.portlandtn.com/strawberry_festival.htm** (Mid-May for five days)

SCOTTISH FESTIVAL & HIGHLAND GAMES

ME – Gatlinburg. Mills Park. **www.gsfg,org**. More than 60 clans gather with activities including pipe & drum bands, pro and amateur Highland athletics, Highland dancing, border collie demos, entertainers and food. Admission. (Third long weekend in May)

DAY OUT WITH THOMAS™

SE – Chattanooga. Tennessee Valley Railroad. **www.tvrail.com**. Welcome Thomas the Tank Engine – ride on a vintage, full-size train led by Thomas himself, meet with Sir Topham Hatt, watch Thomas & Friends videos, coloring books, funny clowns and lots of extra food and entertainment. Admission (age 1+). (First and second long weekends in May)

STRAWBERRY FESTIVAL

SE – Dayton. Main Street. **www.tnstrawberryfestival.com** Pie and cake baking contests, carnival, parade, block party, children's area, entertainment, local entertainers, the Strawberry Crunch Demo Derby (rodeo grounds in Evensville), and Strawberry Shortcake at the Courthouse. (Mid-May for ten days)

STRAWBERRY FESTIVAL

W – Humboldt. 1200 Main Street. **www.wtsf.org**. Includes parades, walking horse show, car show, carnival, gospel singing, country western dancing, checker's tournament, and Strawberry Recipe Contest. The Festival Museum includes memorabilia of past festivals dating back to 1934 and displays of local culture (authentic strawberry packing shed, early telephone switchboard). FREE. (Mid-May for 8 days)

ITALIAN FESTIVAL

W – Memphis. Marquette Park. **www.memphisitalianfestival.com** Authentic Italian cuisine, arts, crafts, games and music. Includes a spaghetti gravy contest. (Memorial Day weekend)

MEMPHIS IN MAY

W – Memphis. Tom Lee Park & various locations. (901) 543-5303 or **www.memphisinmay.org**. This is a celebration of business and fun with events including the Beale Street Music Festival, International Fest, and World Championship Barbeque Cooking Contest (all shapes and sizes of cookers made to resemble everything from fire trucks to piggy banks – 90,000 pork lovers sample and view demos of BBQ). Check schedule. (Entire month of May)

JUNE

RC & MOON PIE FESTIVAL

M – Bell Buckle. Town Square. A day of crafts, carnival, live music, games, the world's largest Moon Pie, Moon Pie toss, synchronized wading, Superman and Wonder Woman of Bell Buckle contest. **www.bellbucklechamber.com/ rcmoon.html**. (Third Saturday in June)

FAN FAIR, THE WORLD'S BIGGEST COUNTRY MUSIC FESTIVAL

M – Nashville. Downtown venues, Nashville Convention Center and Riverfront Park. (866) FAN-FAIR or **www.fanfair.com**. Over 40 hours of live entertainment but the real fun is the picture and autograph sessions with the stars. Admission varies – call or visit website for details. (First long weekend in June)

NATIVE AMERICAN FESTIVAL & MUSTER

NE – Elizabethton. Sycamore Shoals State Historic Area. (423) 543-5808. **www.thewataugans.org**. An emphasis on Cherokee culture includes native music, dance, encampments, musket drills, tomahawk throwing, flint-napping and campfire cooking. Admission. (First weekend in June)

RIVERBEND FESTIVAL

SE – Chattanooga. Ross Landing & Downtown. **www.riverbendfestival. com**. This nine-day festival draws hundreds of thousands of spectators each year. It features country, blues and rock musical performances, sporting events, family activities, food and a spectacular fireworks display. Admission. (Second week of June)

JULY

JULY 4TH CELEBRATIONS

Our Nation's Birthday Party featuring live music, exhibits, concessions and fireworks show.

M – Nashville. Riverfront Park. (615) 862-8400. Nashville's largest one-day event. Science of fireworks and chemical reactions at Adventure Science Center.

July 4th Celebrations *(cont.)*

ME – Gatlinburg. Strike of Midnight Parade. The first Independence Day parade in the nation each year.

ME – Kingston. Fort Southwest Point & Walt's Bar. Lakefront. **www.southwestpoint.com**. Living history, boat races.

ME – Knoxville. Volunteer Landing. Star of Knoxville rides. Admission for rides. (865) 215-4248.

ME – Pigeon Forge. Patriot Festival. (800) 251-9100.

NE – Elizabethton. Roan Mountain State Park. (423) 772-0190.

SE – Chattanooga. Coolidge Park. Creative Discovery Museum & Winnepesaukah Amusement Park. **www.chattanoogacvb.com** or (423) 424-4430. Fireworks downtown and at Winnepesaukah. Red, White, & Blue Day, scavenger hunt, crafts, ice cream.

W – Memphis. Beal Street & Tomlee Park. (901) 529-0999. Fireworks on the Mississippi River. Memphis riverboat cruises.

OFFICIAL STATE & NATIONAL CHAMPIONSHIP SMITHVILLE FIDDLERS' JAMBOREE

EM – Smithville. Town Square. **www.smithvillejamboree.com**. State and National championship in 24 categories plus seven categories for beginners. Jam sessions and crafts. (First weekend in July)

NORTH TENNESSEE STATE FAIR

M – Clarksville. Clarksville Fairgrounds Park. www.northtnstatefair.webs.com. Agricultural & livestock exhibits, tractor & truck pulls, carnival rides, demolition derby, beauty pageant. Adm. (mid-July)

For updates & travel games visit: **www.KidsLoveTravel.com**

UNCLE DAVE MACON DAYS FESTIVAL

M – Murfreesboro. Cannonsburgh Village. (615) 893-2361. Visit the free village with buildings open to view/discuss with period-costumed docents. Take your picture by the World's Largest Cedar bucket, then listen in on the Championship old-time banjo, clogging and buckdancing performances. This festival is broadcast on the original Opry radio station, WSM, where Uncle Dave developed his roots in music. FREE. (Second weekend in July)

WATAUGANS OUTDOOR DRAMA

NE – Elizabethton. Sycamore Shoals Historic Area. (423) 543-5508. **www. thewataugans.org**. 18th Century settlement comes to life thru local outdoor drama. Watch them form the Watauga Association, the Transylvania Purchase, the siege of Fort Watauga, and the Muster of the Overmountain Men before the Battle of Kings Mountain. You might learn some 18th century lingo or get to know interesting regional characters. Admission. (Last three weekends, Thursday-Saturday, in July. Performances begin at 7:30pm)

FUNFEST

NE – Kingsport. Fort Henry Drive/Memorial Drive. **www.funfest.net**. Begin with Farm Fest @ Exchange Place. Now, check out the top-name contemporary concerts or Kids Central at the elementary school. Strolling magic shows, balloon animals, obstacle course, splash dance, petting zoo, moonwalk, gymnastics demos, and a fishing derby. FREE admission. Some activities require a fee. (Third week of July)

SCOPES TRIAL PLAY & FESTIVAL

SE – Dayton. Rhea County Courthouse, downtown Hwy 27. **www. scopesfestival.org**. This restored courthouse was the scene of the Scopes Monkey Trial. The Scopes Evolution Trial started after the passing of a statute by the Tennessee legislature which made it unlawful for any teacher in any public school "to teach any theory that denies the story of the divine creation of man as taught in the Bible, and to teach instead, evolution". Local businessmen and one teacher conspired a publicity stunt. Up to 10,000 reporters and onlookers came to this small town to observe the most famous lawyers and orators of the time debate the case against the alleged teacher's violation. How does it end? Admission for play, FREE for festival. (July)

NO TILL FIELD DAY

W – Milan. West Tennessee Agricultural Museum, US 45E/70 & 79. (901) 686-8067. **http://milan.tennessee.edu/MNTFD/**. The nation's largest such event, this is a good opportunity to visit the Ag Museum and the extensive collection of farming tools spanning two centuries of farming development. FREE. (July)

CATFISH DERBY KIDS FISHING RODEO

W – Savannah (Pickwick Dam). Pickwick Landing State Park. (800) 552-3866 or (731) 925-8094. Join other anglers (age 4-16) at the "Catfish Capitol of the World." and fish for prizes for the biggest catfish. Record fish from these waters have exceeded 100 lbs! (Third Saturday in July)

AUGUST

TENNESSEE WALKING HORSE NATIONAL CELEBRATION

M – Shelbyville. Calsonic Arena. **www.twhnc.com**. The premier showcase for the Tennessee Walking Horse breed. The champion is crowned plus hosting of horse shows, rodeos and concerts. The history of the breed and horse industry is featured in exhibits and videos at the Tennessee Walking Horse Museum. Admission. (Ten days in August)

CELEBRATE FREEDOM! – PIGEON FORGE SALUTES AMERICA'S VETERANS

ME – Pigeon Forge. **www.mypigeonforge.com**. This award winning festival is a tribute to all Americans that have served in the armed forces. Historical exhibits, military book fair, special guest speakers, and star entertainment. (Previous performers have been Lee Greenwood, Aaron Tippin) (Second Saturday in August)

CHEROKEE DAYS OF RECOGNITION

SE – Chattanooga. Red Clay State Historic Area. (423) 478-0339. Authentic Cherokee food, crafts, dance, & music. FREE admission. **www.tennessee.gov/environment/parks/RedClay/pdf/cherokeedays.pdf**.   (First weekend in August)

INTERNATIONAL ROCKABILLY REUNION

W – Jackson. 531 Riverside Dr. **www.rockabillyhall.org**. Celebrate the heritage and continued interest in rockabilly music throughout the world. Features national and international stars from current years and the past. (Second weekend in August)

SOUTHERN INDIAN HERITAGE FESTIVAL

W – Memphis. Chucalissa Village. **www.chucalissa.org**. Bring the family and come watch a pot being made, or point being flint-knapped, throw a spear with an atlatl or shoot a blowgun. Listen to a storyteller or watch a traditional dance. Admission. (First weekend in August)

ELVIS WEEK

W – Memphis. Graceland. **www.elvis.com**. Elvis fans from around the WORLD gather to remember the music, the magic and the memories associated with the legacy of Elvis Presley. A full week of music, dance, sports and charitable events. Candlelight vigil on August 15. Admission. (Week of Elvis' death in mid-August)

MUSIC & HERITAGE FESTIVAL

W – Memphis. Center for Southern Folklore. **www.southernfolklore.com**. Celebrating the arts, music and food of the region. (Labor Day weekend)

SEPTEMBER

CORDELL HULL FOLK FESTIVAL

EM – Byrdstown, Cordell Hull Birthplace and Museum State Park. **www.cordellhullmuseum.com**. A day filled with music, storytelling, crafts, demonstrations, museum and birthplace tours, as well as guided hikes to Bunkum Cave, Reptile Programs and a birds of prey show. Also a youth corn maze, corn shuck doll making and a petting zoo. Feel free to dress in late 1800s attire. (third weekend in September)

September *(cont.)*

SOUTHERN HERITAGE DAY

M – Burns. Old Spencer Mill (30 miles west off I-40 exit 182). **www. oldspencermill.com**. Civil War demos with period food and music. Tours of grist mill, living history demos (broommaking, basketweaving, weaving, spinning), farm animals. (Saturday after Labor Day in September)

RIVERFEST

M – Clarksville. McGregor Park, Cumberland River Walk. **www. clarksvilleriverfest.com**. Celebrate Clarksville's river heritage. Children's activities, arts and crafts, entertainment, boat races. Admission. (weekend after Labor Day)

AFRICAN STREET FESTIVAL

M – Nashville. TSU Main Campus. (615) 299-0412. Exotic food concessions. Stage show featuring gospel, reggae, rap, blues, jazz, R&B and drama. Children's storytelling. Free admission. (Third long weekend in September)

APPLE FESTIVAL

M – Nashville. Nashville Farmer's Market. (615) 880-2001. Apple samples, square dancing, and country music singing contest. Kids will also enjoy a farm animal petting zoo, craft projects, and games. Free admission. **www. nashvillefarmersmarket.org**. (Second Saturday in September)

GREEK FESTIVAL

M – Nashville. Holy Trinity Greek Orthodox Church. **www. holytrinitynashville.org** Enjoy music and dancing, exhibits, shopping, and the fabulous Greek food and drink. Admission. (First long weekend in Sept)

TENNESSEE STATE FAIR

M – Nashville. Tennessee State Fairgrounds. **www.tnstatefair.org**. See over 10,000 livestock, agricultural and creative arts exhibits, free concerts from stars, Midway KidsTown free children's area (age 12 and under). Admission. (9 days – begins weekend after Labor Day).

FALL HERITAGE FESTIVAL

ME – Townsend. Smoky Mountain Convention and Visitors Bureau. **www. smokymountains.org**. The festival is a family-oriented event that includes a variety of events that celebrate Appalachian heritage and culture, including bluegrass music, arts and crafts, storytelling ("old cornstalk, hillbilly stories") and historic re-enactments. FREE. (Last weekend in September)

SYCAMORE SHOALS CELTIC FESTIVAL

NE – Elizabethton. Sycamore Shoals State Historic Area. **www.facebook. com/SycamoreShoalsCelticFestival** Come celebrate Celtic heritage that fills our lives in the mountains of East Tennessee. Clans and Family Societies will be on hand to help with family history. Enjoy dance, music, food, vendors, demonstrations, reenactments of 18th & 19th Century heritage, lectures, and a special musical concert on Saturday evening all with a focus on our Celtic culture. Admission. (Mid-September)

OVERMOUNTAIN VICTORY TRAIL CELEBRATION

NE – Elizabethton. Sycamore Shoals State Historic Area. (423) 543-5808. **www.thewatuagans.org**. Annual encampment by the Company of Overmountain Men celebrating and re-creating the muster of the Overmountain Men before the battle of King's Mountain in 1780. Witness the historic march crossing the river. (Third wkend in Sept)

CULTUREFEST

SE – Chattanooga. (423) 267-1218. **www.rivercitycompany.com/events/ culturefest.asp**. Held at Coolidge Park, this event celebrates cultural, ethnic and national diversity in the city and the arts. Enjoy and engage in performances, food and art indigenous to various cultures within the community. (September weekend)

SEQUOYAH FALL FESTIVAL

SE – Vonore. Sequoyah Birthplace Museum. **www.sequoyahmuseum.org**. Native American festival interpreting history, crafts, food, dance, painting and clothing. Cherokee Artist demos. Admission. (weekend after Labor Day in September)

18TH CENTURY TRADE FAIRE

SE – **Vonore**, Fort Loudoun Historic Park. **www.state.tn.us/environment/ parks/loudoun/events.htm** The park's largest event hosts about 200 re-enactors and 5000 visitors at the recreation of the Trade faires of old. Visitors walk the streets of the faire and shop for period wares, sample food and enjoy entertainment of the times. Indian Camp. Admission. (Weekend after Labor Day)

TENNESSEE RIVER FOLKLIFE AND MUSIC FESTIVAL

W – **Eva**. Nathan Bedford Forrest State Park. **www.tennessee.gov/ environment/parks/NBForrest/** Includes crafts, food, live music, folk heritage demos, children's games and the annual Patsy Cline sing-a-like contest. (Third Saturday in September)

ARCHEOFEST

W – **Jackson**. Pinson Mounds State Park. **www.state.tn.us/environment/ parks/pinson/archfest.htm**. A celebration of Native American culture and archeology. Traditional Native American storytellers, music, dancers, and artisans. Hay wagon tours, demonstrations, and films are available. (Third weekend in September)

MID-SOUTH FAIR

W – **Memphis** Fairgrounds. **www.midsouthfair.com**. Regional state fair with over 60 rides, over 150 food vendors, 200 exhibitors, free mainstage concerts, rodeo, livestock shows, creative arts and student competitions. Admission. (Last ten days of September)

INTERNATIONAL GOAT DAYS

W – **Millington**. USA Stadium & Arena. Rustic fun featuring goat shows, contests, & games. Rural craft demos reflect gentler times of the past. **www. facebook.com/InternationalGoatDaysFestival?ref=ts&fref=ts**. (First full weekend in September)

SEPTEMBER / OCTOBER

SANGO MILLS FARM

M – **Clarksville**. 154 Towes Lane, Madison St. Extension. (931) 358-2637. Apples and sorghum on a working farm. Watch the sorghum cooking process or view fresh cornmeal being ground. FREE. (September-October, Tuesday-Saturday, daytime)

AMAZING MULE MAZE

M – **Spring Hill**. Rippavilla Plantation, 5700 Main Street (Hwy 31 south). **www.rippavilla.org**. 2.5 miles of twisting, turning fun. It's challenging in the daylight…but we dare you to try it after nightfall, in the shadows of the tall corn and faint light of a flashlight or glow stick. Admission. (Friday thru Sunday, September-October)

SMOKY MOUNTAIN HARVEST FESTIVAL

ME – **Gatlinburg**, Pigeon Forge, Sevierville. (800) 251-9100. City and businesses decorate in autumn themes with a decorating contest, craft shows, pumpkins, fall flowers, cornstalks, scarecrows and a gospel jubilee. **www.smokymountainharvestfestival.com**. (Mid-September thru October)

AMAZING CORN MAZE

ME – **Greenback**. Maple Lane Farms. **www.tnmaplelanefarms.com** The 8 acres of fully grown corn is a labyrinth of pathways you walk thru past twists and turns and 85 decision points (takes at least one hour). Also food, hayrides, entertainment, and a pumpkin patch. Admission. (September-October)

MYERS PUMPKIN PATCH & CORNFIELD MAZE

NE – **Bulls Gap**. 3415 Gap Creek Road (I-81 exit 23 towards Greeneville). **www.myerspumpkinpatch.com** Kids' games and crafts, hay rides, and a 24-acre corn maze. (Daily, September-October)

FENDER'S MAZE

NE – **Jonesborough**. **www.fendersmaze.com**. 254 Highway 107. Farm animals, corn box, corn cannon, corn tunnel, cow train, hay jump, hayride, pumpkin patch, slides and trikes. Admission. (long weekends Sept-October)

September / October *(cont.)*

SHULTZ FARM FOODS

SE – **Athens**. 245 County Road 603, Hwy 30 to CR 750, left on CR 603. (423) 745-4723. Educational farm tour, hayrides, sample products sold offering everything from assorted veggies to pumpkins and apples. Admission for tours. (Daily, September-October)

THE RIVER MAZE

SE – **Benton (Ocoee)**, Highway 64. **www.therivermaze.com**. Farm animals, corn cannon, cow train, mini-maze, hayrides, pumpkin patch, slides and goatwalk. Admission. (weekends September-October)

ROCK CITY'S ENCHANTED MAIZE MAZE

SE – **Chattanooga**. Blowing Springs Farm (at the foot of Lookout Mountain), (706) 820-2431. **www.seerockcity.com**. Cornfield maze, hay rides, kiddie hay maze, hay pyramid, pumpkin patch, fun barn, food. Checkpoints along the trail post questions that (if answered correctly) will steer you in the right direction to find the way through the maze. Admission. (Sept-October)

MASON'S CORN MAZE

SE – **Athens**. CR 361. (423) 746-9859. Sponsored by Mayfield Dairy, the maze is full of turns, dead ends and choices. Answer dairy questions correctly at the checkpoints to complete the maze the fastest. Admission. (September-October)

MID-SOUTH MAZE AT AGRICENTER INTERNATIONAL

W – **Memphis**, www.agricenter.org. 7777 Walnut Grove Rd. Phone: . **www. cornfieldmaze.com**. Hayrides, pumpkin patch, corn cannon. Admission. (mid-September thru October, mostly Thursday-Sunday)

OCTOBER

OLD SPENCER MILL DAYS

M – **Burns**. Old Spencer Mill (30 miles west off I-40 exit 182). (615) 412-5169 or **www.oldspencermill.com**. Tours of the grist mill plus living history demos of crafts such as basket weaving, using farm tools, tending to farm animals, children interpreters, horse and wagon rides and lots of ground meal foods and dulcimer music. (Last weekend in October)

FALL PILGRIMAGE & OKTOBERFEST

M – **Clarksville**. Historic Collinsville and downtown. **www. historiccollinsville.com**. Battle of Riggins Hill re-enactments, Pioneer Activities: weaving, candlemaking, blacksmithing, spinning, soapmaking, ropemaking, broommaking, woodcarving, rughooking and singing. Open house in historic homes with costumed tour guides and concessions. Special Children's Day, hayrides, face painting and games. Look for the Chicken Dance and polka music and food at the Oktoberfest activity sites. Admission. (First weekend in October)

FALL FEST

M – **Nashville**. Nashville Farmer's Market. (615) 880-2001. Hear bluegrass music as the kids have fun with carnival games, seasonal craft projects, and decorate their own pumpkin for a competition. Free admission. (Second Saturday in October)

MUSIC & MOLASSES FESTIVAL

M – **Nashville**. TN Agricultural Museum. **http://tnagmuseum.org**. (615) 837-5197. See molasses making done the old-fashioned way. Cooking and tasting at the sorghum mill. Children's activities, crafts, carriage rides, outdoor kettle cooking, grist mill, clogging, and bluegrass music. Admission & hours vary, call for details. (Third weekend in October)

NAIA POW-WOW

M – **Nashville**. Long Hunter State Park. **www.naiatn.org/powwow**. A gathering of Native Americans from throughout the U.S. and Canada. Storytelling, competitive dancing, traditional food from various tribes, demonstrations, and fine art displays. Admission. (Third long wkend in Oct)

GERMANTOWN STREET FESTIVAL

M – **Nashville**. **www.HistoricGermantown.org**. (615) 256-2729. Hear live German music, see polka dancing, and enjoy the authentic German food and beverages. Free admission. (Second Saturday in October)

October *(cont.)*

SOUTHERN FESTIVAL OF BOOKS

M – Nashville. War Memorial Plaza. **www.facebook.com/SoFestofBooks**.. Meet authors from around the country. Readings, children's authors and activities, discussions, book signings and sales. Free admission. (Second long weekend in October)

TENNESSEE HISTORY FESTIVAL

M – Nashville, Bicentennial Capitol Mall State Park.. **http://www.tn.gov/environment/parks/Bicentennial/** Living history participants from the period of the Woodland Indians and Hernando DeSoto thru the modern wars. Tennessee legends like Andrew Jackson, Davy Crockett, Sam Davis, Abraham Lincoln and Sergeant Alvin C York. Spectators will witness live demos of tomahawk throwing techniques, firing a blacksmith's forge, loading a rifle or gas-powered machine guns. (second weekend in October)

HERITAGE DAYS

M – Smyrna. Sam Davis Home. (888) 750-9524 **www.samdavishome.org**. A living history celebration with activities such as spinning, weaving, quilting, and blacksmithing. (First weekend in October)

BATTLE OF BOYD'S CREEK

ME – Sevierville. Sevier County Fairgrounds. (888) SEVIERVILLE. Annual reenactment of the Revolutionary War Battle involving Native American, Tennessee and US history. FREE admission. (Last weekend in October)

MUSEUM OF APPALACHIA TENNESSEE FALL HOMECOMING

ME – Norris. Museum of Appalachia. **www.museumofappalachia.com**. The event is a celebration of the culture and heritage of the Appalachian pioneer, mountain and rural life. Four stages of music, demos of early pioneer activities include cane grinding with a mule-powered mill, molasses boiling, saw milling, sheep herding, soap making and rail splitting. 100s of craftspeople make and sell their wares plus smell the kettles of sassafras tea, cider & other country food cooked over fires in iron kettles. (Second long wkend in Oct)

FALL COLOR TRAIN

ME – Oak Ridge. Secret City Scenic Excursion Train. (865) 241-2140. Scenic Fall Color tours by train. 2-3 times daily. (Last three weekends in October)

APPLE FESTIVAL

NE – Erwin. Downtown. **www.unicoicounty.org/apple-festival** . Hundreds of vendors line the streets offering handmade crafts and delicious homemade apple products/treats. (First long weekend in October)

NATIONAL STORYTELLING FESTIVAL

NE – Jonesborough. International Storytelling Center, 116 W. Main Street & Festival tents. **www.storytellingcenter.net**. (423) 753-2171 or (800) 952-8392. Celebrate the power of storytelling during the showcase of the world's stories, storytellers, and storytelling traditions in the most dynamic event dedicated to the oral tradition. Admission $25-$80 per day, ~$100.00 weekend. (First long weekend in October)

SPIRIT OF THE HARVEST

NE – Piney Flats, Rocky Mount Museum. **www.rockymountmuseum. com** Join the Cobb family and their friends as they celebrate the harvest. Blacksmiths will be in the blacksmith shop, watch as volunteers and staff make soap, apple butter and apple cider on the historic site. Storytelling, music, and other activities will take place throughout the day. Admission. (mid-October weekend)

AUTUMN STEAM EXCURSIONS

SE – Chattanooga. Tennessee Valley Railroad Museum. **www.tvrail. com**. Ride behind an authentic steam locomotive on scenic trips through Chattanooga and North Georgia. Some of the interesting points along the way include: Chattanooga /Chickamauga National Military Park, Missionary Ridge, and small towns of Chickamauga, Trion, Summerville, Rock Spring, and Lafayette. Eat lunch in the train's dining car. Call for rates and departure times. (October – early November, some weekdays, most weekends)

October *(cont.)*

FALL COLOR CRUISE & FOLK FESTIVAL

SE – Chattanooga. Ross' Landing & Southern Belle Riverboat. (423) 892-0223. See the grand canyon at its height of fall color by boat, car, or bus. Sample genuine southern cuisine and enjoy traditional, country, and gospel music folk festival. (October)

KETNER'S MILL COUNTRY FAIR

SE – Chattanooga. **www.ketnersmill.org** Children's activities, living history, and fine crafts. (October)

FALL FOLKLORE JAMBOREE

W – Milan. West Tennessee Agricultural Museum, #3 Ledbetter Gate Road. **http://milan.tennessee.edu/FFJ/**   Local folks exhibiting trades and entertainment. The Ag Museum presents a dioramic view of early settler life with displays of equipment and materials. (Third Saturday in October)

DAVY CROCKETT DAYS

W – Rutherford City Hall & historic Crockett log cabin. **www.davycrockettcabin.org**. Full week of celebration includes contests, parade, country music and a visit inside a replica of Davy's log cabin (when he lived in the area). (First week in October)

NOVEMBER

COMMEMORATION OF 11TH PRESIDENT, JAMES K. POLK BIRTHDATE

M – Columbia. (931) 388-2354. **www.polkhome.org**. Honor the 11th President by visiting his historic home on his birthday. FREE. (Nov 2).

NOVEMBER / DECEMBER

CHRISTMAS ON THE CUMBERLAND

M – Clarksville. Riverwalk. See over 3 million lights transform Clarksville's Riverwalk into a holiday festival of sights and sounds. In-ground speakers feature the "sounds of the season" during your walking tour. Free admission. (Last weekend in November – January 1st)

TRINITY CHRISTMAS CITY

M – Hendersonville. Trinity Music City USA. **www.tbn.org**. Tour by car and by foot, the more than one million lights, Virtual Reality Theatre, recording studios, home and gardens. FREE. (Daily, November-January)

A COUNTRY CHRISTMAS

M – Nashville. Opryland Resort. **www.gaylordhotels.com**. A Christmas Spectacular (often featuring the Radio City Rockettes), Enchanted Holiday Dinner, and Fantasy in Ice (theatre full of life-size sculptures in ice). Admission. (mid-November thru Christmas)

CHRISTMAS AT BELMONT

M – Nashville. Belmont Mansion. **www.belmontmansion.com**. A Victorian land of garland, fruit, flowers and tussie-mussies while on tour of the mansion. Admission. (Thanksgiving weekend thru New Years Eve)

NOW THAT'S COUNTRY CHRISTMAS

M – Nashville. General Jackson Showboat. **www.gaylordhotels.com**. Festive cruises begin with a lunch followed by a fun-filled holiday show. Cruise departs at Noon and returns at 2:00pm. Admission. (mid-November thru Christmas)

CHRISTMAS AT THE HERMITAGE

M – Nashville. The Hermitage, Home of President Andrew Jackson. **www. thehermitage.com**. Special holiday exhibits at the mansion feature early traditions and decorations of the 1800s. Café and gift shop open, also with holiday theme. Admission. (mid-November thru weekend after New Years)

FESTIVAL OF THE HOLIDAYS

M – Nashville. Cheekwood Botanical Garden & Museum of Art. **www. cheekwood.org**. Showcase of multi-cultural traditions of Christmas, Hanukah, and Kwanzaa. (Thanksgiving weekend thru New Years Eve)

November / December *(cont.)*

CIVIL WAR CHRISTMAS

M – Smyrna. Sam Davis Home. (615) 459-2341 or (888) 750-9524. Learn about Christmas traditions before the Civil War. Admission. (Thanksgiving weekend thru New Years Eve)

HORSE DRAWN CAROLING AND MOONLIGHT TOURS

ME – Clinton, River Ridge Farms on the Clinch River, 220 Mike Miller Lane. **www.riverridgefarmtn.com**. The tours will include hot chocolate and a bon fire. The tours will be cancelled if it is raining or snowing. Admission (age 5+).(last three weekend evenings in December)

SMOKY MOUNTAIN WINTERFEST

ME – Gatlinburg, Pigeon Forge, Sevierville. **www.mypigeonforge.com**. The gateway towns to the Smokies turn into a winter wonderland with over 7 million lights and fantastic displays throughout every town. Special activities include: Festival of Lights Parade, Christmas on Ice, Christus Gardens, Christmas Lighting, New Years Eve fireworks, Hayrides with Santa, Theatre holiday productions, Dollywood Appalachian Christmas, and Trolley Tour of Lights w/ pickup at various trolley depots (weekdays and evenings, 865-453-6444). FREE to drive thru. Individual admission for activities. (First Saturday in November thru past New Years)

DIXIE STAMPEDE, DOLLY PARTON'S CHRISTMAS AT DIXIE

ME – Pigeon Forge. **www.dixiestampede.com** A seasonal twist to a night at the Stampede with a friendly rivalry between the North and South. Specially designed skating platform and holiday music enhance the show. Audience participation games like wreath tossing and reindeer riding. Highlight celebration of the Christmas story of Jesus' birth. Santa makes an appearance in his reindeer drawn sleigh as Dixie's arena is turned into a Southern winter wonderland of fresh fallen snow. Admission. (First weekend in November thru New Years Day)

SPEEDWAY IN LIGHTS

NE – Bristol. Bristol Motor Speedway & Dragway. (423) 764-1161. Admission. (Mid-November thru early January)

For updates & travel games visit: **www.KidsLoveTravel.com**

ROCK CITY'S ENCHANTED GARDEN OF LIGHTS

SE – Chattanooga. Lookout Mountain. **www.seerockcity.com**. An enchanting outdoor walk that features 25 holiday scenes in a garden nocturnal fantasyland with over a quarter of a million lights. Hot chocolate, gingerbread cookies, carolers, Santa. Daytime hours feature the Legends of Christmas. Admission. (Mid-November-early January, nighttime except Christmas Eve)

RUBY RED CHRISTMAS

SE – Chattanooga (Lookout Mountain). **www.rubyfalls.com**. See the majesty of the 145 foot underground falls transformed with enchanting holiday lights and sound effects. (weekends in December)

WINTER DAYS AND LIGHTS

SE – Chattanooga. **www.chattanoogafun.com** Downtown Chattanooga puts on its Christmas best at the Grand Illumination. Festivities include: An Appalachian Christmas, Christmas on the River (parade of floats & marching bands, food at Ross' Landing, and a lighted boat parade with fireworks), Holiday Nightlight Parade, and New Year's Eve Block Party (laser countdown, Big Band music, and fireworks). Southern Belle Riverboat offers A Christmas Carol, Ho Ho Ho Children's Santa and 'Tis the Season Luncheon Cruises. North Pole Limited weekend trains (**www.tvrail.com**). Most land activities FREE, fee for boat and train cruises. (late November-December)

CHRISTMAS AT GRACELAND

W – Memphis. Graceland. **www.elvis.com**. In all its holiday splendor 24 hours a day, 7 days a week on GracelandCam. In person, visit the estate filled with holiday trees, decorations. Outside on the front lawn Elvis always had a large Santa, sleigh and reindeer. Plus, the lawn also displays a life-size Nativity scene, along with lighted aluminum trees and a winding driveway outlined in hundreds of blue lights. Admission. (Thanksgiving weekend thru Elvis' birthday in early January)

ZOO LIGHTS

W – Memphis. Zoo. **www.memphiszoo.org**. Over a million bulbs, animated displays, live reindeer – Dasher and Dancer. Christmas treats, lighted displays and breakfast with Santa. Admission. (Thanksgiving to end of December)

DECEMBER

CHRISTMAS OPEN HOUSE

M – **Castalian Springs**, Sumner County Museum and Historic Homes. **www.srlab.net/bledsoe/events.html**. Staggered viewing times to include: Rose Mont, Trousdale Place and the Sumner County Museum. (first weekend in December)

CANDLELIGHT TOURS

M – **Clarksville**, Historic Collinsville. **www.historiccollinsville.com**.. Enjoy caroling in the village while you experience the peacefulness of the spirit of Christmas of the past. Reservations required. (December evenings – call for details)

AN 1860 CHRISTMAS

M – **Dover**. Fort Donelson National Park, Dover Hotel (Surrender House). Members of the History Guild portray a pre-civil war family trying to enjoy the holiday season. FREE. (Second weekend in December)

CANDLELIGHT TOUR OF HOMES

M – **Franklin**. Historic Main Street. **www.historicfranklin.com**. Admission. A historic Christmas right out of a Charles Dickens's classic. Living character tours of homes with craftsmen demonstrating 19th century arts, Victorian costumes, and strolling minstrels. (first weekend in December).

YULEFEST

M – **Goodlettsville**. Historic Mansker's Station Frontier Life Center. (615) 859-3678. Experience Christmas during the Colonial Days of the 1770s. Docents in period dress re-enact the customs of the time period. Evening programs have candle lanterns illuminated everywhere. Refreshments are offered and horse-drawn wagon rides carry visitors between the sites. Traditional carols, period music and dancing. Admission daytime, FREE Saturday. (First weekend in December)

FESTIVAL OF LIGHTS

M – **Lebanon**, Ward Agricultural Center. Driving tour that includes hundreds of thousands of lights, animation, lighted scenes. Look for the Grinch in Fiddlers Grove Jail, Jesus in the manger or the post office box to drop a letter to Santa. Over 40 village houses are lit. **www.wilsoncountytn.com/ ag_center.htm**. Admission. (Thursday-Sunday evenings in December)

December *(cont.)*

CHILDREN'S CHRISTMAS SHOW

M – Nashville, Chaffin's Barn Dinner Theatre. **www.dinnertheatre.com**. For the 6-10 year old age group. It's always a fun-filled time for the kids with Santa and his elves trying to get Christmas "off-the-ground" so to speak! The shows are presented as 'brown bag' matinees, and usually last about 40-45 minutes. Admission. (December shows with details on website)

NATIVITY EXHIBIT

M – Nashville. The Upper Room Chapel and Museum. (615) 340-7207. Annual Nativity scenes (more than 100) representative of many styles and cultures. Admission. (December and January)

PLANTATION CHRISTMAS

M – Nashville. Traveler's Rest Plantation & Museum. **www. travellersrestplantation.org**. Experience an 1830s Christmas with costumed docents and Candlelight tours. Enjoy some hot wassail, learn the true story of Twelfth Night and hear about special holiday guests from the past. Occasional kids activities include dancing the Virginia Reel or make a holiday craft. Admission. (December)

SANTA EXCURSIONS

M – Nashville to Watertown. Tennessee Central Railway. **www.tcry.org**. Ride the train with Santa for "Christmas in the Country". Live entertainment and a joyous holiday feeling with a visit to the Santa Post Office Train. Departures at 8:00am & 3:00pm. Adm. (Second & third Saturdays in December)

CHRISTMAS & HOLIDAY CRUISES

ME – Knoxville. Star of Knoxville Boat Cruise. **www.tnriverboat.com**. Lunch With Santa, Caroling Cruise with Santa, Christmas & Holiday Cruises Nightly Admission. (December 1 - December 23)

December *(cont.)*

POLAR BEAR EXPRESS

ME – **Knoxville**. Volunteer Landing at the Waterfront. **www. threeriversrambler.com**. All aboard the Three Rivers Rambler Passenger Train. Admission. (Second weekend in December)

CHRISTMAS IN OLD APPALACHIA

ME – **Norris**. Museum of Appalachia. **www.museumofappalachia.com** The Christmas tree in the schoolhouse is adorned with traditional paper chains, the Daniel Boone cabin's tree bears strings of popcorn and balls of cotton. Mark Twain's cabin features sweet gum and sycamore balls. Musicians, carol singing and stockings hung by the fire. Admission. (First weekend thru New Years Eve in December)

HOLIDAY HOMECOMING

ME - Norris Dam State Park. Celebrate the Holidays by strolling through the decorated cabins at Norris Dam State Park. The cabins will be decorated in different themes that depict a different Tennessee Holiday homecoming. The planned themes consist of a Coal Miners' Cabin, Christmas Bakery, Soldier's Cabin, CCC Memorial Cabin and many more. Christmas Caroling and craft making will also be occurring throughout the cabin area. There will be old time music in the Tea Room where Santa will also be available for taking wish list and pictures. For more information, contact the park at (865) 426-7461. (second Saturday in December)

SANTA TRAIN

ME – **Oak Ridge**. Secret City Scenic Excursion Train. (865) 241-2140. Santa himself rides along on the train ride past historic WWII secret sites. 2-3 tours offered each day. (first & second weekend in December)

CHRISTMAS AT CARTER MANSION AND THE FORT

NE – **Elizabethton**. Sycamore Shoals State Historic Area. (423) 543-5808. **www.thewataugans.org**. Decorated for Christmas in the style of the late 1700s. Costumed interpreters, candlelight tours, refreshments and music. Living history demos of the 18th century in the backwoods of Colonial

America. Admission. (first & second long weekend in December)

1818 CANDLELIGHT CHRISTMAS PARTY

NE – Kingsport. Netherland Inn. **www.netherlandinn.com**. 1818 Christmas Party. Decorations and fiddle/dulcimer/violin music. Admission. (Second long weekend in December)

COUNTRY CHRISTMAS

NE – Kingsport, Exchange Place. **www.exchangeplace.info**. Includes Christmas-related crafts, seasonal and 1850s traditional crafts demonstrated and home-baked goods made and sold. Admission. (First weekend in December)

CANDLE LIGHT CHRISTMAS TOURS

NE – Piney Flats, Rocky Mount Museum. Join the Cobb family as they celebrate Christmas in the 18th Century. Admission. Reservations are recommended. (first two weekends in December)

CHATTANOOGA CHOO CHOO'S VICTORIAN HOLIDAY PACKAGES & POLAR EXPRESS TRAINS

SE – Chattanooga. (423) 266-5000. See the historic Chattanooga Choo Choo Hotel in full dress for the holiday season. Victorian Nights is a selection of four inclusive holiday packages that include one or more nights' accommodations and discount tickets to attractions. Polar Express steam train rides feature hot chocolate and cookies, storytelling, Santa, and lots of holiday cheer to bring on the spirit of the season. (December)

CHRISTMAS CAROL & HO HO HO SANTA CRUISE

SE – Chattanooga. **www.chattanoogariverboat.com** . Either dinner cruises with live band, DJ, Santa, magic show & singing crew or shorter (1½ hour), cruises with Santa, a magic show and characters. (December)

HOLIDAY LIGHTS

SE – Chattanooga. **http://zoo.chattanooga.org**. The most beautiful place to be in winter. The zoo draped in lights with entertainment everywhere. Admission. (Mid-December for one week)

December *(cont.)*

CHRISTMAS AT FORT LOUDOUN

SE – **Vonore**, Fort Loudoun Historic Park. **www.state.tn.us/environment/ parks/loudoun/events.htm**. Ft. Loudoun celebrates an 18th Century Christmas with decorations, period carols sung and games played. Evening highlight of candlelight tour of the fort (weather pending) and concluded with a night firing of the cannon. Admission. (First full weekend in December)

ENCHANTED FOREST FESTIVAL OF TREES

W – **Memphis**. Pink Palace Museum. **www.theenchantedforest.org**. Designed and decorated trees displayed along with kids activities and a holiday laser show at the Planetarium. Kwanzaa Festival after Christmas. Admission. (Month-long in December)

LIBERTY BOWL

W – **Memphis**, Liberty Bowl Memorial Stadium. **www.libertybowl.org**. College football game where the champion of the Conference USA plays the champion from the Mountain West Conference. Parade on Beale Street on December 30th. Admission. (Late December)

NEW YEAR'S EVE

NEW YEAR'S EVE AT NOON

SE – **Chattanooga**, Creative Discovery Museum. (423) 756-2738. Kids can make party hats at Creation Station all day long and enjoy our "Cool Wonders" exhibit and science demonstrations. As our "New Year's Eve at Noon" countdown with Father Time culminates promptly at (what else) Noon, everyone can toast the New Year with apple juice and a kazoo rendition of "Auld Lang Syne." Admission. (New Year's Eve from 11:00am-4:00pm – Toast at NOON!)

Master Index

Activity Index

HISTORY *(cont.)*

MUSEUMS

OUTDOOR EXPLORING

OUTDOOR EXPLORING *(cont.)*

TOURS